INTRODUCTION
to the
LEGAL SYSTEM
of the
EUROPEAN UNION

Philip Raworth
Professor of Law
Faculty of Business
University of Alberta
Barrister and Solicitor

Chapter 2 DL
Regulations Directives Decisions
Pg 20

OCEANA PUBLICATIONS, INC.
Dobbs Ferry, New York

Information contained in this work has been obtained by Oceana Publications from sources believed to be reliable. However, neither the Publisher nor its authors guarantee the accuracy or completeness of any information published herein, and neither Oceana nor its authors shall be responsible for any errors, omissions or damages arising from the use of this information. This work is published with the understanding that Oceana and its authors are supplying information, but are not attempting to render legal or other professional services. If such services are required, the assistance of an appropriate professional should be sought.

You may order this or any other Oceana publications by visiting Oceana's website at http://www.oceanalaw.com

Library of Congress Cataloging-in-Publication Data

Raworth, Philip Marc, 1943-
    Introduction to the legal system of the European Union / by Philip Raworth.
        p. cm.
    Includes bibliographical references.
    ISBN 0-379-21412-1 (cloth : alk. paper)—ISBN 0-379-21413-X (pbk. : alk. paper)
        1. Law—European Union countries. I. Title.
    KJE947 .R39 2001
    341.242'2—dc21

                                                                2001032336

Manufactured in the United States of America on acid-free paper.

to Marie-Gabrielle, Emilie, François, Kristin, James and
Pierre-Alexandre as well as the other members of a
rapidly increasing tribe.

Table of Contents

Note on the Author ix

CHAPTER 1: THE EVOLUTION OF THE EUROPEAN UNION 1

I.1 1945-1957: The Early Years (Treaty of Paris). 1

I.2 1958-1987: The European Communities (Treaties of Rome) 3

I.3 1987-1993: Completion and Renewal (The Single European Act) 8

I.4 1993-2000: The European Union (Treaties of Maastricht and Amsterdam) . 11

    I.4.1 Treaty on European Union (Treaty of Maastricht). 11

    I.4.2 The Treaty of Amsterdam 16

CHAPTER II: THE STRUCTURE OF THE EUROPEAN UNION 21

II.1 Nomenclature 21

II.2 The Legal Base of the European Union 22

II.3 The Components of the European Union 23

    II.3.1 The Concept of the Three Pillars 23

    II.3.2 The European Community Treaty 26

        II.3.2.a The Process of Economic Integration 26

        II.3.2.b The Levels of Economic Integration 28

        II.3.2.c The European Community Treaty 29

        II.3.2.d The Common Market 29

        II.3.2.e Economic and Monetary Union (EMU) 30

        II.3.2.f The External Competence of the European Community . . . 33

        II.3.2.g Union Citizenship 35

        II.3.2.h Fundamental Rights 38

        II.3.2.i Institutional Provisions 38

    II.3.3 The Treaty on European Union. 38

        II.3.3.a The Common Foreign and Security Policy 38

        II.3.3.b Police and Judicial Cooperation in Criminal Matters 41

        II.3.3.c The External Competence of the European Union 42

        II.3.3.d Fundamental Rights 42

        II.3.3.e Accession to the European Union. 42

        II.3.3.f The Amendment of the Treaties. 43

        II.3.3.g Institutional Provisions 46

    II.3.4 Other Acts 46

    II.3.5 Geographical Scope of the European Union 47

    II.3.6 Linguistic Régime of the European Union 47

Note on the Author

Philip Raworth first studied modern languages and linguistics at the University of Manchester in England. For several years, he taught in these areas at universities in England, Austria and Canada. In 1974, he entered law school at the University of Alberta in Canada and was admitted to the Bar of the Province of Alberta in 1978. The same year, he received the prestigious Duff-Rinfret Scholarship from the Canadian federal government in order to complete his LL.M.

Since 1979, Professor Raworth has taught law at the Universities of Ottawa and Alberta and, occasionally, in Mexico. He has also practiced law, both in Canada and Europe, in the area of European Union and international commercial law. Professor Raworth speaks fluent English, German, French and Spanish and has a working knowledge of Italian and Portuguese. He now divides his time between his university duties in Canada and legal research in the south of France.

Professor Raworth is the author of numerous articles and books on the European Union and international commercial law. Two books have already been published by Oceana, *The Law of the WTO* (1995) and *Foreign Trade Law of the European Union* (1995). He has been editor of the *European Union Law Guide* since its inception in 1994. He is also editor of Oceana's looseleaf publication, *International Regulation of Trade in Services*.

CHAPTER 1

THE EVOLUTION OF THE EUROPEAN UNION

I.1 1945-1957: The Early Years (Treaty of Paris)

It has been claimed that Adolf Hitler was the catalyst for present European integration.[1] Certainly, it is true that the destruction wrought by Hitler's legions convinced many Europeans that political union in Europe was the only way to avoid another internecine war. Another motive for European integration was fear of Soviet expansionism after the coup d'état in Czechoslovakia in 1948, the Berlin blockade shortly thereafter and the explosion of the first Soviet atomic bomb in 1949.

The key to the process of European integration was, as Sir Winston Churchill pointed out in his famous Zürich speech of September 19, 1946, reconciliation and partnership between France and Germany. His clairvoyance did not, however, extend to his own country. For Churchill, the United Kingdom[2] was a world power rather than just another European state. The British broadly shared this view, and as a result both the Labor and Conservative post-war governments passed up the chance to take the lead in the construction of Europe. The United Kingdom did participate in the founding of the Council of Europe in 1949, but its insistence that the Council remain a traditional intergovernmental organization meant that it did not satisfy those working for European integration.[3]

---

1   R.L. Leonard, *Guide to the European Community* (5th ed., 1997), at page 3.

2   Although it has been around a long time, this country has never settled on a definitive name. It is called variously Britain (England and Wales), Great Britain (England, Wales and Scotland) and the United Kingdom (England, Wales, Scotland and Northern Ireland). I tend to call it either Great Britain or the United Kingdom . The French simplify matters by referring to it quite simply as "L'Angleterre," which seems to me as an Englishman a very satisfactory way of resolving the confusion! However, out of deference to my Celtic readers, I have not adopted that nomenclature in this book.

3   A traditional intergovernmental organization is run by an organ composed of government representatives, whose decisions are either non-binding or have to be taken by unanimity. Unless the member states of the organization provide otherwise, these decisions have to be implemented by national legislation in order to have effect at the national level—*see* also *infra* in Section II.3.1.

1

It was Great Britain's traditional rival, France, that filled the void left by this imperial disinterest. The foremost protagonist of European integration in these years was Jean Monnet, a friend of Churchill's and the man who had devised the proposal for Anglo-French union in 1940 as France faced defeat. It was under his and Churchill's inspiration that the French foreign minister, Robert Schumann, proposed on May 9, 1950 that the Western European countries place their coal and steel industries under joint, supranational control. Apart from the pragmatic need to secure the reorganization of these industries in Europe, Schumann was motivated by two paramount ideals: to take the first step towards an eventual European federation, and to render war between France and Germany impossible.

Schumann's proposal was eagerly accepted by Germany, Italy and the Benelux countries. The United Kingdom declined to participate. The Treaty of Paris inaugurating the European Coal and Steel Community (ECSC) was signed on April 18, 1951,[4] and the new Community entered into operation on July 25, 1952 with Monnet as its first President. The preamble to the Treaty reflects the two political ideals behind its creation. The third recital refers to building Europe "through practical achievements" while the fifth talks of overcoming "age-old rivalries."

The ECSC Treaty provides for the control of the coal and steel industries of the six signatory states by a High Authority, which is given the necessary powers to carry out its mandate. This represented a significant step along the road of European integration. For the first time, a group of European countries that included the continent's two major powers were pooling part of their sovereignty and transferring it to a body that was independent of the governments of the Member States and which could, on occasion, issue decisions that were applicable in the Member States without the need for national implementation.[5] In addition, an independent court was set up to interpret and enforce the Treaty, and even the traditionally intergovernmental Council of Ministers was given the form of a Community institution that on occasion could act by majority vote. A parliamentary assembly was created to supervise the exercise of the powers conferred by the Treaty on the High Authority and the Council. The ECSC is not a traditional intergovernmental organization; it is supranational.

One must not, however, exaggerate the significance of the ECSC Treaty. It is a purely economic arrangement that covers only two, albeit vital, sectors of the economy. Moreover, the supranational nature of the Community is firmly circumscribed by the detailed provisions of the Treaty, which is what the French call a

---

4   Treaty establishing the European Coal and Steel Community, 261 U.N.T.S. 140. References to articles in this Treaty are indicated by (ESCS).

5   This is the principle of direct applicability, which is discussed *infra* in Section IV.2.6.

traité-loi.[6] The ECSC certainly did not satisfy Monnet. At his urging and again as a result of a speech by Churchill, the French government through its defense minister, René Pleven, proposed a European Defense Community, to which was annexed a European Political Community. This proposal was rejected by the French National Assembly on August 30, 1954 by an unlikely alliance of Gaullists and Communists. The former feared a loss of French sovereignty, the latter wanted nothing to do with an arrangement that permitted Germany a military role. This debacle showed that there was no quick road to a European federation. It would have to come, as Schumann had already understood, through the back door by way of economic integration. This is what is generally called the "functionalist" approach to federalism.[7]

The next logical step after this setback was to extend economic integration to the whole economy. It was left to the Benelux countries to make the proposal, which was discussed at a meeting of the six ECSC states in Messina, Italy at the beginning of June 1955. The Belgian foreign minister, Paul-Henri Spaak, was charged with examining the feasibility of the idea. His report in favor of a general common market accompanied by a separate sectoral arrangement for the atomic industry was presented to the leaders of the six ECSC states on April 21, 1956. By February 1957, the Treaties setting up the European Economic Community (EEC) and the European Atomic Energy Community (EAEC or Euratom) were complete. They were signed in Rome on March 25, 1957 and entered into effect on January 1, 1958.[8] Once again, the United Kingdom stood loftily aside and set up a rival trade grouping, the European Free Trade Association (EFTA), in January 1960.[9]

I.2 1958-1987: The European Communities (Treaties of Rome)

The two new Communities were at their outset markedly less supranational than the ECSC. The center of power shifted from the Commission, which is the equivalent of the High Authority of the ECSC, to the Council of Ministers where the Member States were represented. Important decisions were to be taken by unanimity. On the other hand, the Treaties of Rome are framework treaties (*traités-cadre*) that give more freedom of action to the Community institutions

---

6   This does not mean that the two other Community Treaties do not contain legally-binding or detailed provisions—*see* the discussion *infra* in Section II.2.

7   *See* D. Freestone and J.S. Davidson, *The Institutional Framework of the European Communities* (1988), at pages 4-5.

8   Treaty establishing the European Economic Community, 298 U.N.T.S. 11; Treaty establishing the European Atomic Energy Community, 298 U.N.T.S. 167. The name of the EEC was changed by Article 8(1) of the Treaty on European Union to "European Community" (EC). References to articles in these Treaties are indicated, respectively, by (ECT) and (EAEC).

9   EFTA originally comprised Austria, Denmark, Great Britain, Norway, Portugal, Sweden and Switzerland. Iceland and Liechtenstein joined later. Austria, Denmark, Great Britain, Portugal and Sweden have since joined the European Union.

than the ECSC Treaty, and the independent Commission has in many cases the right to initiate this action.[10] A convention that entered into force at the same time as the two Treaties provided for the two new Communities to use the Court of Justice and Assembly of the ECSC.[11] Moreover, there is reference in the preamble of the EEC Treaty to a determination "to lay the foundations of an ever closer union among the peoples of Europe," which clearly indicates a continuing commitment to functional federalism. Political integration was on hold but not abandoned, and it would gather momentum as the EEC became more supranational.

In any case, the more intergovernmental nature of European integration was not immediately apparent. Under its first President, Walter Hallstein, the EEC Commission played much the same role as the High Authority and aspired to a position of equality with the Council. This incipient supranationalism would have been strengthened by the extension of qualified majority voting in the Council that was scheduled for January 1966. President de Gaulle, however, was determined to prevent this. For six months from July 1, 1965, France paralyzed the working of the Communities by refusing to attend meetings of the Council. De Gaulle's aims were the subordination of the Commission to the Council, the maintenance of unanimity as the basis for important Council decisions and no increase in the powers of the European Parliament. It is a measure of France's pre-eminence at the time that he succeeded in all three objectives.

This French pre-eminence was also apparent in the fate of the first two British attempts to join the Communities. Disillusioned very quickly with EFTA, the British made their first application in 1961. After months of difficult but promising negotiations, President de Gaulle unceremoniously dismissed the British application at a press conference on January 14, 1963. Eight days later, he signed the Franco-German Treaty of Friendship, thereby serving notice that henceforth the destiny of Europe would be decided by France and Germany with the United Kingdom consigned to the sidelines. In November 1967, De Gaulle unilaterally vetoed the second British application.[12]

De Gaulle's firm suppression of supranational aspirations within the Communities and his refusal to countenance their enlargement precluded any significant further integration. In fact, by the time he left office in the spring of 1969, the Communities were at an impasse. Nonetheless, the first ten years of their existence had been a clear economic success. Intra-Community trade had increased on average by 28.4% a year, and tariffs and quotas between the Member States

---

10   The initiatory right of the Commission is discussed *infral* in Section V.1.2.

11   A single Assembly, Court of Justice and Economic and Social Committee were set up by the Convention on Certain Institutions Common to the European Communities (1957). The Convention was replaced by Article 9 of the Treaty of Amsterdam.

12   On the issue of Britain's attempts to join the Communities, *see The United Kingdom and the European Communities* (Cmnd, 4715/1971).

had been abolished on July 1, 1968, eighteen months ahead of schedule. By the end of the 1960's, the EEC was among the world's leading traders. On the political side, however, no progress was discernible towards creating more democratic and supranational institutions. At most, the structures of the three Communities were fused,[13] albeit with each Community retaining its own character and jurisdiction. This continuing separateness, however, did not really matter as the EC came to dominate the other two Communities and in any case the ECSC is scheduled to be wound up in 2002. This is why, in this book, I deal exclusively with the EEC, which was formally renamed the "European Community" (EC) in 1992.[14] Henceforth when reference is made to the "Community," the EC is meant although many points are also valid for the other two Communities.

The replacement of de Gaulle by Georges Pompidou in 1969 and the election of Willy Brandt as German Chancellor the same year transformed the political scene. At the Hague summit that December, the leaders of the six Community states took a number of far-reaching decisions that re-launched the process of European integration. They commissioned the Davignon Report, which resulted in 1971 in the start of political cooperation between the Member States in foreign affairs; they agreed to grant the Community its own resources;[15] and they started the process towards Economic and Monetary Union (EMU). Brandt also prevailed upon Pompidou to lift the French veto on British membership of the Community. Negotiations were opened with the United Kingdom and two of its EFTA partners, Denmark and Ireland, and the three states joined the Community on January 1, 1973. The momentum was kept up by the Paris summit of 1974, where it was decided to institutionalize the meetings of the leaders of the Member States as the European Council. The summit also commissioned the Tindemans Report, which supported EMU and argued for a common foreign policy and a strengthening of the Community institutions. Agreement was finally reached on direct elections to the European Parliament, which resulted in the 1976 Act.[16]

These promising developments proved a false dawn. The rise in oil prices as a result of the Yom Kippur War in 1973 triggered a recession that undermined the Community's plans for EMU. In February 1974, the pro-European Edward Heath

---

13   The two Commissions of the EEC and the EAEC and the High Authority of the ESCS as well as the three Councils were merged in 1965 into a single Commission and Council by the Treaty establishing a Single Council and a Single Commission of the European Communities (OJ L152/67), the so-called Merger Treaty. The Merger Treaty was replaced by Article 9 of the Treaty of Amsterdam.

14   Article G(A)(1) of the original Treaty on European Union.

15   Council Decision 70/243 on the replacement of financial contributions from Member States by the Communities' own resources. This matter is now regulated by Council Decision 00/597 (OJ L253/00). Article 2 of this Decision defines own resources as agricultural levies, customs duties, a percentage of the valued added tax levied by Member States and a percentage of the gross national product of Member States.

16   Act concerning the Election of Representatives of the European Parliament by Direct Universal Suffrage, OJ L278/76.

was replaced as British leader by the equivocal Harold Wilson, who promptly demanded a re-negotiation of Great Britain's terms of entry into the Community. Although the issue was eventually resolved and membership of the Community ratified by the British people in a referendum, the damage was done. Great Britain's partners resented her presumption, and the squabbling engendered a skeptical attitude among the British people towards European integration that has persisted ever since.

The Community also suffered at this time from lack of direction as the founding Treaties contained no clear blueprint for the stage beyond the establishment of a customs union, which had been achieved in 1968. It did not help that the Presidents of the Commission who succeeded Monnet and Hallstein lacked their stature and, apart from Roy Jenkins, who pioneered the European Monetary System (EMS), they achieved very little. As the seventies turned into the eighties, the Community was perceived as suffering from what was called "Eurosclerosis": the common market was unfinished, EMU was but a distant dream, there was no progress in sight on reforming the Community institutions and political cooperation had failed to bring the Member States closer to a common foreign policy. The only harbingers of brighter days to come were the first direct election of the European Parliament in June 1979 and the inauguration of the EMS on March 13, 1979.

The election of an uncompromising nationalist, Margaret Thatcher, as British Prime Minister on May 3, 1979 hardly promised any positive change in the gloomy state of European integration. The dispute over Great Britain's contribution to the Community flared up again, and for five years the Thatcher government haggled aggressively and noisily with its partners. There were also enlargement problems. Greece joined the Community on January 1, 1981, and for the first time the Community had to absorb a country that was much poorer than the others. This costly experience, together with France's desire to protect its agricultural industry, encumbered the negotiations with Spain and Portugal. The Community also lost a member, when Greenland, having obtained home rule from Denmark, left on February 1, 1985. This created a potentially dangerous precedent.

Yet there were also more positive signs. The Report of the Three Wise Men in 1979 re-affirmed Tindemans' proposal in favor of bringing political cooperation in foreign affairs within the Community structure and reforming the Community institutions. The 1982 Genscher-Colombo Plan and the new draft treaty for Europe adopted by the European Parliament on February 14, 1984 gave further impetus to the cause of European union, to which the heads of state or government[17] of the Member States solemnly committed themselves on June 19, 1983

---

17 This clumsy terminology was necessitated originally by the fact that France is represented by both its President and Prime Minister. Since 1995, the Finnish President has also attended. Sometimes the formulation used is "heads of state *and* government" but this gives the erroneous impression that every Member State is represented by its head of state, which is not the case.

at the European Council meeting in Stuttgart.[18] At the same time, dissatisfaction with the imperfections of the unfinished common market were growing, and the Community was much embarrassed by the dramatic protests of truckers over the failure to abolish or even simplify intra-Community border formalities. Newspaper photographs of long lines of trucks waiting to cross the Community's internal frontiers finally pushed the European Council, meeting in Copenhagen in December 1982, to acknowledge the need for radical action.

Once again, it was a change in the French Presidency that unblocked the impasse. President Mitterand was elected in the spring of 1981, but the first years of his presidency were taken up with domestic policy. Then, at the European Council meeting in Fontainebleau in June 1984, he used France's presidency of the Community to clear up the major outstanding issues blocking progress in Europe. A solution was found at last to the British financial contribution to the Community, the way was cleared for Spain and Portugal to join the Community on January 1, 1986 and the completion of the internal market[19] was made an absolute priority.

Fontainebleau also set up the Dooge committee to consider the future of the Community, and shortly thereafter Mitterand secured the appointment of his finance minister, Jacques Delors, as the new President of the Commission.[20] Delors took office on January 6, 1985 and, like Monnet and Hallstein before him, proved a formidable proponent of European integration. He lost no time in preparing—with the assistance of the senior British Commissioner, Lord Cockfield—a detailed blueprint for the completion of the internal market by the end of 1992.[21] This process entailed realizing fully the freedom of movement of persons, services, goods and capital throughout the Community, in other words achieving at last a functional internal market.

---

18 EC Bulletin, 6-1983, pt. 24. It is a mystery to me how Mrs (now Lady) Thatcher was persuaded to sign this declaration. Perhaps she was still under the euphoria of the previous day's celebration of Wellington's victory over Napoleon at Waterloo on June 18, 1815!

19 The internal market is defined by Article 14(2) of the EC Treaty as "an area without internal frontiers in which the free movement of goods, persons, services and capital is ensured. . . ." The common market comprises this internal market together with a number of common policies or activities and harmonization of laws.

20 Delors was a surprise choice as the obvious French candidate was the foreign minister, Claude Cheyson. There is no support in Lady Thatcher's memoirs for the rumor that it was her opposition to Cheyson that cleared the way for the appointment of Delors. However, it is clear that Cheyson's handling of the British contribution issue at Fontainebleau irritated Thatcher, and she also seems to have considered him a dilettante. Delors, whose firm remedial action had rescued France from the crisis caused by the left-wing economic policies of Mitterand's first socialist government, would certainly have appeared preferable to the "Iron Lady." This approval soon dissipated in the face of Delors' "grandiose ambitions and bureaucratic leanings," which Thatcher opposed vehemently until her forced resignation from office in November 1990. See M. Thatcher, The Downing Street Years (1993) at pages 542-543 and 547.

21 This was the White Paper entitled Completing the Internal Market (COM (85) 310 final).

An obvious corollary to Delors' ambitious plan was institutional reform. In June 1985, the Milan meeting of the European Council accepted Delors' blueprint and, on the basis of the Dooge Report, convoked an intergovernmental conference to consider the necessary institutional reforms and the scope of the Community's jurisdiction. The nature of political cooperation was also placed on the agenda. Great Britain, Denmark and Greece voted against the proposal to hold a conference but acquiesced in its convocation.

The intergovernmental conference started its work on September 9, 1985. Some Member States wanted any agreement on political cooperation to form a separate text in order to emphasize its distinct non-Community status. Ultimately, a French compromise was accepted whereby a single act would embrace both the revisions of the treaties and, as a separate intergovernmental accord, the provisions on European cooperation in the sphere of foreign policy. This document, appropriately called the Single European Act (SEA), was signed by the twelve Member States, which now included Spain and Portugal, in February 1986.[22] It entered into force on July 1, 1987.

I.3 1987-1993: Completion and Renewal (The Single European Act)

As expected, the SEA made the completion of the internal market by December 31, 1992 a legal requirement.[23] It also gave legal recognition to the EMS[24] and confirmed the Community's hitherto implicit jurisdiction over health and safety, consumer protection, the environment, research and development and regional policy.[25] However, the SEA did not add any new areas to the Community's jurisdiction.

The SEA institutionalized political cooperation in foreign affairs, which was brought within the ambit if not the jurisdiction of the Community.[26] Henceforth, a member of the Commission would meet with the foreign ministers of the Member States, and the Commission as a body would be "fully associated with the proceedings of political cooperation." The views of the European Parliament now also had to be taken into consideration. A permanent political secretariat was set up with its base in Brussels. Finally, the SEA recognized the controversial practice of discussing foreign affairs in regular Council meetings but nevertheless insisted that this be done "within the framework of Political Cooperation."

---

22   OJ L 169/87. References to articles in this Treaty are indicated by (SEA).

23   Article 13 (SEA), now Article 14(1) (ECT).

24   Article 20(1) (SEA).

25   Articles 21-25 (SEA); now Articles 137, 153 and 168-176 (ECT).

26   Article 30 (SEA). This Article takes the form of an intergovernmental agreement between "High Contracting Parties."

On the institutional front, the major reform introduced by the SEA was the Co-operation Procedure, which gives the European Parliament the right to a second reading of a proposed act, at which time it can adopt additional amendments or even reject the Council's text.[27] This procedure was intended primarily for matters concerning the completion of the internal market. The introduction of the Cooperation Procedure increased the use of majority voting in the Council. In addition, the SEA replaced unanimity by a qualified majority in certain other cases.[28] These changes rendered the Council more of a Community institution because it is not obliged in the case of qualified majority voting to accommodate all Member States and so can act independently of *individual* states.

The SEA also reinforced the supranational character of the Community's institutional structure in other ways. It recognized the change of name from "Assembly" to "European Parliament"[29] and made both the accession of new member states and the conclusion of association agreements with third countries subject to its assent.[30] Finally, it formalized the role of the European Council and gave it a Community dimension by confirming the practice of including the President of the Commission among its members.[31] This body remains, however, essentially intergovernmental, and its increasing importance with each new treaty serves as a counterbalance to the growing supranationalism of the European Union. Federalists may lament this fact, but it is probably the price to pay for progress along the road of European integration.[32]

The SEA was much criticized at its inception,[33] but this criticism proved largely unfounded. Its apparently timid institutional reforms were surprisingly effective. The Cooperation Procedure increased significantly the number of parliamentary amendments adopted by the Council.[34] The one time Parliament used its veto power, the Council did not override it.[35] Perhaps even more important was the fact that the success of the Cooperation Procedure and the responsible use by Parliament of its new powers made possible more radical reform of the Community's decision-making procedures.

---

27 Article 7 (SEA); now Article 252 (ECT).

28 *E.g.* Article 28 (ECT) on the fixing of customs duties, which was amended by Article 16(1) (SEA).

29 *See* Article 6 (SEA). Henceforth, for the sake of brevity, I shall sometimes refer to the European Parliament simply as "Parliament." I hope this does not unduly shock any eurosceptic readers.

30 Articles 8 and 9 (SEA): now Articles 49 (Treaty on European Union); 300(3) and 310 (ECT).

31 Article 2 (SEA); now Article 4 (Treaty on European Union).

32 *See* the discussion on the European Council *infra* in Section III.3.1.

33 *See* T.C. Hartley, *Foundations of Community Law* (1988 edition), at pages 33-34.

34 In Point L of its Resolution on the Cooperation Procedure of January 20, 1993 (OJ C42/93), Parliament calculated that, to the end of September 1992, more than a quarter of its second round amendments had been accepted by the Council.

35 In October 1988, Parliament rejected a proposed directive on the protection of workers exposed to benzene at work.

Likewise, the SEA's provisions on political cooperation and economic and mone-tary policy also had significant repercussions despite their modest scope. The clear reference to a European foreign policy and the obligation placed on Mem-ber States to work towards common positions that were to constitute "a point of reference" for individual national policies, together with the new involve-ment of the Commission and Parliament, paved the way for the introduction of a common foreign policy. The SEA's provision on the EMS clearly anticipated fur-ther developments in the economic and monetary area. In both policy areas, the SEA provided for the convocation of an intergovernmental conference to con-tinue the process.[36]

Despite strong British opposition, events moved quickly after the entry into force of the SEA. At the European Council meeting in Hanover in June 1988, a committee was set up under Delors to study how to achieve EMU. It proposed a three-stage program, which was accepted over British objections at the Madrid European Council meeting in June 1989.[37] It was decided to start the first stage on July 1 1990. An intergovernmental conference was convoked to consider the necessary institutional changes. A second conference was agreed at Dublin by the European Council in June 1990 to consider changes to the foreign policy provisions of the SEA. Later the same year, a timetable for the remaining two stages on the way to EMU was set at a special meeting of the European Council in Rome. Mrs. Thatcher opposed all these development with much vim and vowed to fight any major revision of the Treaties and EMU in particular. How-ever, a month later on November 28 1990, she was constrained by her own Con-servative Party to resign. Her successor, John Major, adopted a more conciliatory approach.

The intergovernmental conferences started in December 1990 and continued for a year. The results were discussed by the European Council in December 1991. British opposition to EMU and the new provisions on social policy were resolved by allowing Great Britain to opt out of both.[38] Denmark was also al-lowed to opt out of the third stage of EMU. The Treaty on European Union (TEU) was signed on February 7, 1992 at Maastricht in the Netherlands.[39]

---

36   Articles 20 and 30(12) (SEA).

37   On the issue of EMU, see the introduction to Section XI of the *European Union Law Guide* by Philip Raworth, published by Oceana Publications Inc.

38   Great Britain entered the first and second stages of EMU. It is the third stage with its intro-duction of a common currency, the euro, that it has opted out of—see Protocol on Certain Provisions relating to the United Kingdom of Great Britain and Northern Ireland, which is at-tached to the EC Treaty. As regards social policy, it is not really a question of an opt-out. In-stead, the eleven other Member States signed an agreement between themselves on social policy to which Great Britain did not subscribe—see Agreement on Social Policy concluded between the Member States of the European Community with the Exception of the United Kingdom of Great Britain and Northern Ireland.

39   [1992] 1 C.M.L.R. 573. References to articles in this Treaty are indicated by (TEU). The Treaty is popularly known as the Maastricht Treaty.

The TEU was designed to come into effect on January 1, 1993. However, on June 2, 1992, Danish voters rejected the Treaty in a national referendum, while opposition to it in the British House of Commons made uncertain its approval in that country. At its Edinburgh meeting in December 1992, the European Council set about making the TEU more palatable to Danish voters and British parliamentarians. It was successful and during 1993 the TEU was duly approved in a second Danish referendum and by the British House of Commons. It entered into effect on November 1, 1993. Around the same time, a far-reaching agreement extending the internal market to Iceland, Norway and Liechtenstein was signed on May 2, 1992 and entered into effect on January 1, 1994. This arrangement is called the European Economic Area.[40]

I.4 1993-2000: The European Union (Treaties of Maastricht and Amsterdam)

I.4.1 Treaty on European Union (Treaty of Maastricht)

The TEU represents a significant step forward on the road to European integration by establishing a European Union. The European Union does not replace the three European Communities. Instead they become one of the pillars upon which the European Union is based.[41] The other two pillars are the common foreign and security policy (CFSP) and cooperation in justice and home affairs (CJHA). This is a cumbersome arrangement, but it reflects the determination of some Member States to make a clear distinction between the Communities and the other two pillars of the Union. It should not, however, obscure the fact that the Communities are, according to the TEU, as much a part of the European Union as the CFSP and CJHA.

The CFSP is a considerable improvement over the foreign policy cooperation in the SEA. Foreign policy becomes a Union matter and, although the Member States retain control over their foreign and security policy in the absence of a common position, they are obliged to conform to this position once the Council has defined it.[42] There is also provision for joint action by the Union, which commits the Member States.[43] The TEU envisages using the Western European Union (WEU) in the future as a vehicle for formulating and implementing a common

---

40   Agreement on the European Economic Area, OJ L1/94. The Agreement originally included all the remaining EFTA states, but the Swiss rejected it in a national referendum.

41   Article 1 (TEU). For a criticism of this concept, *see* the discussion *infra* in Section II.3.1.

42   Article J.2(2) of the original TEU; now Article 15 (TEU).

43   Article J.4(4) of the original TEU; now Article 14(3) (TEU).

defense policy for the Union.[44] CJHA introduces whole new areas of activity for the Union: asylum and immigration policy, combating drug addiction and fraud, judicial cooperation in civil and criminal matters, customs cooperation and police cooperation in the fight against international crime.[45]

The TEU expands the EC to include Union citizenship.[46] All nationals of Member States are citizens of the Union. As it is up to the Member States to determine who are to be considered their nationals, Union citizenship becomes an incidence of national citizenship. It is not, however, an empty shell as it entails a number of important rights.[47]

The first stage of EMU predates the TEU as it started on July 1, 1990, but it is the TEU that defines EMU and sets out in detail how it is to be accomplished and operated.[48] It provides for two further stages. The final stage of EMU started on January 1, 1999 with, among other things, the launching of the single currency, the euro, which will replace national currencies on January 1, 2002. The TEU also sets up the European System of Central Banks (ESCB), of which the European Central Bank (ECB) is a part. The fact that the provisions on EMU are located in the EC Treaty further reinforces the already overriding importance of the EC among the three European Communities.

As well as extending the EC's jurisdiction over economic and monetary policy, the TEU brings other areas within the sphere of the Community, namely visas for non-EU nationals, culture, civil protection, tourism, trans-European networks and overseas development.[49] However, not all these areas are by any means exclusive Community matters. The TEU also strengthens the Community's role in social policy, albeit by a special agreement attached to the Treaty in order to accommodate the British refusal to accept the new provisions.[50] It confirms and

---

44   Article J.4(1) of the original TEU; now Article 17(3) (TEU). The idea of using the WEU for this purpose never made much sense. Not all Member States belong to the WEU, which is in any case more or less moribund. Nevertheless, the idea was preserved and even expanded by the Treaty of Amsterdam, only to be rejected completely by the Treaty of Nice. The latter transfers the progressive framing of a common defense policy to the Union itself and removes all references in the TEU to the WEU. I mention this here in order to obviate the necessity to discuss in this book the complicated relationship that was envisioned between the European Union and the WEU.

45   Article K.1 of the original TEU.

46   Article G(C) of the original TEU; now Articles 17-22 (ECT).

47   These rights are discussed *infra* in Section II.3.2.g.

48   Article G(D)(25) of the original TEU; now Articles 98-124 (ECT). This part of the EC Treaty is in fact more like a *traité-loi*.

49   Articles G(B)(3) and G(D)(23), (37),(38) of the original TEU; now Articles 3, 62, 151, 154 and 177-181 (ECT).

50   Agreement on Social Policy concluded between the Member States of the European Community with the exception of the United Kingdom of Great Britain and Northern Ireland, which is attached to the EC Treaty.

clarifies the EC's jurisdiction in industrial policy, education, energy, public health and consumer protection.[51] Significantly, and despite intensive lobbying by the Commission, the TEU does not give the EC an autonomous taxing power but leaves intact the provision that measures involving the levy of taxes at the European level must be ratified by all Member States.[52] In one way, the TEU even reduces the role of the EC by formalizing three principles that limit its activity: attribution of powers, proportionality and subsidiarity.[53] Subsidiarity applies also to matters coming within the scope of the TEU.[54]

The TEU incorporates the jurisprudence of the Court of Justice recognizing as general principles of Community law the fundamental rights flowing from the 1950 European Convention and the common constitutional traditions of the Member States.[55] The Union must respect these rights.

The institutional reforms of the TEU affect mainly the European Parliament and substantially increase its powers. In the first place, the TEU introduces the Co-Decision Procedure, which is similar to the Cooperation Procedure except for the vital difference that the Council can no longer disregard Parliament's amendments or veto on the second reading.[56] The new procedure finally allows Parliament to share legislative power with the Council although it originally had two significant drawbacks. Under the TEU it applied only to a limited number of matters, and the Council retained a right under certain circumstance to re-affirm its original text, which Parliament could only veto by mustering an absolute number of its members to vote against the text on a third reading.

The second major institutional reform concerns the manner of appointing the Commission. Prior to the TEU, the rules provided for the Member States to appoint the Commission without any involvement of the Community institutions. In practice, Member States did consult with Parliament on their choice for President of the Commission and the new Commission would seek a parliamentary vote of support. The TEU formalizes this arrangement and requires in addition that Member States nominate the other Commissioners in consultation with the presidential nominee.[57] Ironically, the Commission that was appointed under these new, more democratic rules was also the first in the EC's history to be forced to resign.

---

51   Articles G(C)(3) and G(D)(33),(36),(38) of the original TEU; now Articles 3, 149, 151, 152, 153 and 157 (ECT).

52   Article 269 (ECT).

53   Article G(B)(5) of the original TEU; now Article 5 (ECT) These principles are discussed *infra* in Section IV.1.3.

54   Article 2 (TEU).

55   Article F of the original TEU; now Article 6 (TEU).

56   Article G(E)(61) of the original TEU; now Article 251 (ECT).

57   Article G(E)(48); now Article 214 (ECT).

The TEU gives Parliament the right to request the Commission to submit proposals for any act that Parliament feels is necessary to implement the Community Treaties.[58] However, Parliament must act by a majority of its members when making the request and has no recourse if the Commission does not submit a proposal. More significant for Parliament is the fact that the TEU also gives it a veto over the enactment of measures on free movement within the Union, changes to the Statute of the ESCB, the organization of the Structural Funds[59] and the uniform voting procedure for elections to the European Parliament.[60]

Finally, the TEU strengthens the enforcement provisions within the Community by providing for fines against Member States that do not comply with a judgment of the Court of Justice requiring them to fulfill their obligations under Community law.[61]

In contrast to the wrangling that ensued after the SEA, events moved relatively smoothly after the entry into force of the TEU. This was due in large measure to the fact that the euroskeptical British and Danes had already negotiated their opt-outs at Maastricht. The advent of a more Europe-friendly government in London also helped.

On January 1, 1994 the second stage of EMU came into effect in accordance with the TEU. In the spring of that year, negotiations were completed for the accession of Austria, Finland, Norway and Sweden to the European Union, although the Norwegians later voted in a national referendum against membership of the Union. On March 26, 1995 the Schengen Agreement abolishing intra-Union border checks came into effect. It now applies to all Member States except the United Kingdom and Ireland.

In early June 1995, a reflection group was set up to prepare for the 1996 intergovernmental conference to revise parts of the TEU. This group found that, despite some positive developments, a number of shortcomings in the TEU were becoming apparent. The cumbersome and illogical three-pillared structure was particularly criticized, as was the lackluster performance of the CFSP and CJHA. The concept of a single institutional framework had not been realized. Even within the EC, there was a need to render the complex decision-making procedures more efficient and democratic. There was widespread disappointment with the TEU's lack of attention to citizen's rights and employment. Finally, in view of the reticence of certain Member States, such as Denmark and the United

---

58   Article G(E)(41) of the original TEU; now Article 192 (ECT).

59   These comprise the European Agricultural Guidance and Guarantee Fund, Guidance Section, the European Social Fund and the European Regional Development Fund.

60   Articles G(C), G(D)(25), G(D)(38) and G(E)(40) of the original TEU; now Articles 18 (but now replaced by the new Co-Decision Procedure), 107(5), 161 and 190(4) (ECT).

61   Article G(E)(51) of the original TEU; now Article 228(2) (ECT).

Kingdom, to pursue greater integration, the more federalist-minded states wished to have the possibility of advancing more quickly on their own.

The reflection group presented its views to the Madrid meeting of the European Council in December 1995. The start of the intergovernmental conference was set for March 29, 1996 and it was to concentrate on five major themes:

- employment and citizens' rights;
- freedom and security of movement within the European Union;
- a stronger and more unified voice for the European Union in foreign affairs;
- making the institutional structure more efficient, democratic and transparent;
- achieving greater flexibility in the future development of the European Union.

The negotiations ended in June 1997 and the new treaty was signed at Amsterdam on October 20, 1977.[62] This time, the ratifications proceeded without incident, and the new Treaty came into effect on May 1, 1999.

Even before the Treaty of Amsterdam came into effect, the third stage of EMU, comprising the launch of the euro and the transfer of monetary policy to the Community, was successfully completed by the deadline of January 1, 1999. This achievement was not self-evident as the conditions for Member States wishing to enter the third and final stage of EMU were rigorous. However, by a combination of determination and sleight of hand, all the Member States except Greece managed to qualify. Denmark, the United Kingdom and Sweden chose to remain outside. Greece entered the third stage on January 1, 2001.

One final dramatic event was to occur before the Treaty of Amsterdam entered into force. For some time, a number of members of the European Parliament had accused the Commission of sloppy management and tolerating various corrupt practices by some of its members. Eventually, it commissioned a report which was published on March 15, 1999 under the title *Report on Allegations regarding Fraud, Mismanagement and Nepotism within the European Commission*. It was a devastating indictment. Faced with the certainty of a parliamentary vote of censure, the Commission resigned *en masse* the following day. On March 25, 1999, the Member States meeting within the European Council nominated the former Italian Prime Minister, Romano Prodi, as their candidate to replace Jacques Santer as President of the Commission. On May 1, 1999, the Treaty of Amsterdam came into effect and on May 5, 1999 Prodi was approved as President under the Treaty's new provisions.

---

62   OJ C340/97. References to articles in this Treaty are indicated by (TA).

I.4.2 The Treaty of Amsterdam

The Treaty of Amsterdam does not represent such a dramatic step forward in the process of European integration as the TEU. Rather, it operates more to correct some of the insufficiencies of the earlier treaty and to take a number of reforms a little further. It does not touch the provisions on EMU at all. Nevertheless, its revisions are far from mere window-dressing and certainly contribute to the slow but inevitable development of the European Union into some type of federation.

The Treaty of Amsterdam was followed in December 2000 by the Treaty of Nice, which was the product of a particularly acrimonious European Council meeting in the French city of that name.[63] The changes introduced by the Treaty of Nice are not yet in effect, and they have already been rejected by the Irish people in a national referendum. Thus, I have thought it wiser to base this book on the form of the European Union as established by the Treaty of Amsterdam.[64]

The Treaty of Amsterdam strengthens the provisions on fundamental rights and gives the Court of Justice more say in their enforcement. It also gives the Council explicit authority to combat discrimination on the basis of sex, race, religion, disability, age and sexual orientation[65] and extends the protection of individuals with respect to their personal data to Union institutions and bodies.[66] The Treaty enhances Union citizenship by giving its citizens more opportunity for obtaining information from Union institutions.

The Treaty expands the jurisdiction of the EC quite significantly by transferring to it from the third pillar (CHJA) responsibility for external border controls, asylum, immigration, treatment of non-EU nationals and judicial cooperation in civil matters.[67] There are also new provisions with respect to certain matters that were deemed of particular concern to citizens. There is a new title in the EC Treaty on employment that gives the Community responsibility for developing a coordinated strategy in this area,[68] and the Treaty places specific obligations on the Community to integrate human health, consumer and environmental protection requirements into its policies and activities.[69] With the change of government in the United Kingdom, it was also possible to incorporate the Social Agreement attached to the TEU into the main body of EC

---

63 For once, the British were not the spoilers of the party. The main disputes were between France and Germany and between the smaller and larger Member States. The Treaty of Nice was formally signed on February 26, 2001.

64 Some important changes brought about by the Treaty of Nice are footnoted.

65 Article 2(7) (TA); now Article 13 (ECT).

66 Article 2(54) (TA); now Article 286(1) (ECT).

67 Article 2(15) (TA); now Articles 61-69 (ECT).

68 Article 2(19) (TA); now Articles 125-130 (ECT).

69 Article 2(4),(26),(27) (TA); now Articles 6, 152(1) and 153(2) (ECT).

Treaty.[70] One disappointing feature of the Treaty of Amsterdam is its failure to expand the Community's jurisdiction over international commercial relations to services and intellectual property rights. It contains instead a very weak compromise that provides for the Council to bestow such jurisdiction at some time in the future.[71]

The Treaty also revises the two other pillars making up the European Union. The provisions on CHJA in the TEU suffered from lack of focus and paucity of measures to achieve the stated goals. Amsterdam transfers a number of areas to the EC and focuses clearly on what remains, namely police and judicial cooperation in criminal matters (PJC). There are also some important innovations in the decision-making process.[72] The Commission acquires a joint right of initiative with the Member States,[73] which assures a Community input and perhaps also a greater sense of urgency in adopting the necessary measures. The change also gives more validity to the principle of a single institutional structure for the Union's activities that was introduced by the TEU. There is a greater and more flexible array of measures at the Council's disposal, including a new power to approximate the laws and regulations of the Member States. In some cases, qualified majority voting replaces unanimity.

The CFSP as designed by the TEU was not a success. There was a lack of consistency and long-term planning and an inability to react quickly to situations. The Treaty of Amsterdam makes important changes in the way in which the CFSP is conducted and even in its substance. The most apparent innovation is the appointment of the Secretary-General of the Council as High Representative for the CFSP.[74] This position is supported by a policy planning and early warning unit.[75] These arrangements are intended to ensure that the European Union acts more conspicuously and with greater consistency and timeliness in its foreign policy decisions. At the same time, the Treaty provides for the European Council to decide on common strategies in order to give the CFSP more coherence and long-term effect.[76] Implementation of common strategies can now be done by the Council acting by a qualified majority, albeit subject to the right of Member States to prevent this where important and stated reasons of national policy are at stake.[77] The Treaty of Amsterdam also widens the scope of the CFSP by

---

70   Article 2(22) (TA); now Articles 136-143 (ECT).

71   Article 2(20)(TA), now Article 133(5) (ECT).

72   Article 1(11) (TA); now Article 34 (TEU).

73   It had such a right under the TEU with respect to those aspects of CHJA that are transferred by the Treaty of Amsterdam to the EC.

74   Article 1(10) (TA); now Article 26 (TEU).

75   Declaration No. 6 to the TA.

76   Article 1(10) (TA); now Article 13(2) (TEU).

77   Article 1(10) (TA); now Article 23(2) (TEU).

including in it humanitarian and rescue operations, peace-keeping and other tasks of combat forces in crisis management.[78] These activities are to be done through the WEU.[79]

In the area of security and defense, the Treaty of Amsterdam amended the TEU to provide for the *progressive* framing of a common defense policy.[80] At the meeting of the European Council in Helsinki in December 1999, it was decided to launch a common European security and defense policy (CESDP) by setting up an interim Political and Security Committee and a Military Body.[81] A year later at the European Council meeting in Nice, it was decided to make the CESDP operational on the basis of the TEU without awaiting the ratification of the Treaty of Nice.[82] The interim committees were made permanent and expanded.[83] The speed with which the European Union is moving to equip itself with a military arm has caused some concern in the United States, which fears a dilution of NATO.[84]

On the institutional level, the Treaty makes important changes in the direction of greater democracy in the European Union. The Co-Decision Procedure is reformed by removing from the Council its right to adopt an act unilaterally.[85] From now on, all acts requires the agreement of both Parliament and the Council, which puts the former for the first time on an equal footing with the Council. The Treaty also extends substantially the scope of the Co-Decision Procedure, which, except in the area of EMU, replaces the Cooperation Procedure. The manner of appointing the President of the Commission is democratized.[86] Now Parliament has to approve the nominee of the Member States for President before they proceed to choose the other Commissioners *in common accord* with the presidential nominee. Qualified majority voting in the Council is extended, and the Council is required, when acting in a legislative capacity, to

---

78   Article 1(10) (TA); now Article 17(2) (TEU).

79   Article 1(10) (TA); now Article 17(1) (TEU). But *see* note 44.

80   Article 1(10) (TA); now Article 17(1) (TEU).

81   *See* Council Decision 00/143 setting up the Interim Political and Security Committee (OJ L49/00); Council Decision 00/144 setting up the Interim Military Body (OJ L49/00).

82   Declaration on the European security and defense policy.

83   *See* Council Decision 01/78 setting up the Political and Security Committee (OJ L27/01); Council Decision 01/79 setting up the Military Committee of the European Union (OJ L27/01); Council Decision 01/80 on the establishment of the Military Staff of the European Union (OJ L27/01).

84   These fears seem exaggerated. Most NATO countries in the European Union remain firmly committed to the alliance as the events of September 11, 2001 have shown. This is particularly the case of the United Kingdom and Germany, which, together with France, are the most important military powers in the European Union.

85   Article 2(44) (TA); now Article 251 (ECT).

86   Article 2(40) (TA); now Article 214(2) (ECT).

make public the results of votes and explanations of votes as well as statements in the minutes.[87]

Finally, the Treaty of Amsterdam provides a mechanism for Member States that wish to proceed more quickly than others along the path of European integration.[88] The rules are strict so as to reduce the danger of a multi-speed Europe (or Europe à la carte for those of a gastronomical inclination), but nonetheless the possibility now exists for the more federalist Member States to cooperate within the framework of the Treaties. The first such arrangement of closer cooperation, which is formally authorized by the Treaty of Amsterdam,[89] is the Schengen system of the removal of border formalities. It embraces all the Member States except the United Kingdom and Ireland. Denmark applies it in part.

---

87   Article 2(39) (TA); now Article 207(3) (ECT).

88   Articles 1(12) and 2(5) (TA); now Articles 43-45 (TEU) and 11 (ECT).

89   Protocol integrating the Schengen *acquis* into the framework on the European Union, which is annexed to the TEU and the ECT.

CHAPTER II

THE STRUCTURE OF THE EUROPEAN UNION

II.1 Nomenclature

Let us start this discussion of the European Union with the topic of nomenclature, which is not the Europeans' strong suit. There are many names by which the Union is and has been known and much confusion as to what they mean.

After the creation of the European Economic Community (EEC) and the European Atomic Energy Community (EAEC) in 1958 as additions to the European Coal and Steel Community (ECSC), which had existed since 1952, the official name used to designate the ensemble was the *European Communities*. As this term was rather a mouthful, the Communities became popularly known as the *Common Market*, which they were not yet, or the *EEC*, which was only one of the component Communities. As the EEC came to dominate the other two Communities, the popular name became the *European Community* or just simply the *Community*. This was not altogether a felicitous usage as it was never clear how many Communities were meant when the term was used. The change of name of the EEC to the "European Community" (EC) in 1993 by the Treaty on European Union (TEU),[1] while it rightfully recognized the primacy of the EEC, did not solve the problem as the term continued to be used to designate all three Communities.

In fact, the TEU compounded the problem by introducing a new term, the *European Union*. As with *Community*, this term is susceptible of two meanings. It can designate the whole, that is to say, the three European Communities as well as the additional matters covered by the TEU, or it can be used in a specific sense to designate exclusively the matters coming within the TEU, in particular the common foreign and security policy (CFSP) and police and judicial cooperation in criminal matters (PJC). This confusion is reflected in the name of the institutions. The Council styles itself the Council of the *European Union* while the Commission, for example, continues to be called the Commission of the *European Communities*.

---

1   [1992] 1 C.M.L.R. 573.

I believe that the activities of the European Union constitute an integral whole, and that the three Communities are as much a part of the Union as those matters coming within the purview of the TEU.[2] Thus I use the term *European Union (EU)* or *Union*, wherever possible, in the broad sense as designating the whole. In particular, I use this term when referring to any institution or body even if it is officially designated as an institution of the European Communities.[3] I use the term *Community* only when it is indispensable in order to make clear that I am referring exclusively to matters coming within the EC Treaty.

II.2 The Legal Base of the European Union

The European Union is based on the following treaties and acts:

a) The ECSC,[4] EAEC[5] and EC[6] Treaties, as amended by the First and Second Budgetary Treaties (1970,[7] 1975[8]), the Treaty amending the Protocol on the Statute of the European Investment Bank (1975)[9], the Single European Act (1986) (SEA),[10] the TEU (1992) and the Treaty of Amsterdam (1997);[11]

b) The Act concerning the Election of the Representatives of the European Parliament by Direct Universal Suffrage (1976),[12] as amended by Article 5 of the Treaty of Amsterdam;

c) The TEU, as amended by the Treaty of Amsterdam;

d) Article 9 of the Treaty of Amsterdam.

Also important for the structure and functioning of the European Union are the various accession treaties, the rules of procedure and other acts dealing with the Union institutions and bodies and the various financial acts, such as the

---

2   This point is discussed in more detail *infra* in Section II.3.1.
3   *See* the discussion *infra* in Section II.3.2.i.
4   261 U.N.T.S. 140.
5   298 U.N.T.S. 167.
6   298 U.N.T.S. 11.
7   Treaty amending Certain Budgetary Provisions of the Treaties establishing the European Communities, OJ L2/71.
8   Treaty amending Certain Financial Provisions of the Treaties establishing the European Communities, OJ L359/77. This Treaty was signed in 1975 but did not come into force until June 1, 1977.
9   OJ L91/78. This Treaty only affects the EC Treaty.
10   OJ L169/87.
11   OJ C340/97.
12   OJ L278/76.

Financial Regulation of December 21, 1977[13] and Decision 00/597 on the Communities' own resources.[14] However, the basic instruments are those listed earlier.

The EC Treaty is the predominant Community treaty as it embraces practically the whole economy. The EAEC Treaty deals only with the atomic energy sector and, as the Court of Justice has pointed out,[15] is little else than another sectoral common policy like agriculture and transport. Indeed, the EC Treaty applies to atomic energy to the extent that it is not expressly regulated by the EAEC Treaty. The ECSC Treaty is more substantial and has its own procedures and character. However, it is due to expire at midnight on July 24, 2002. It too only deals with one sector of common policy, the coal and steel industry, and plans are already underway to incorporate the sector into the EC. The TEU, however, add important areas to the jurisdiction of the European Union.

For these reasons, this book deals exclusively with the EC Treaty and the TEU. Both are said to be *traités-cadre* because they set out a framework that gives the various institutions considerable freedom to translate the objectives of the two Treaties into concrete actions and legislation. However, one must be careful when comparing these two Treaties with the ECSC Treaty, which constrains the Union institutions by detailed provisions and is often called a *traité-loi*. There is certainly a difference, but the provisions of the EC Treaty and the TEU also have the force of law and contain in part provisions that are as detailed and constraining as those of the ECSC Treaty. Most provisions of the two Treaties are directly applicable and, in some cases, also have direct effect.[16]

The provisions of the EC Treaty and the TEU can be divided into four main categories: scope of the Union, structure of the Union, enabling provisions and matters that are regulated directly by the Treaties.[17] The first three categories set out the basic structure of the European Union, and the question has been frequently posed as to the nature of these provisions. This issue is taken up in Chapter VII.

II.3 The Components of the European Union

II.3.1 The Concept of the Three Pillars

According to Article 1 of the TEU, the European Union is founded on the European Communities, the CFSP and PJC. This formulation has given rise to the con-

---

13   OJ L356/77.

14   OJ L253/00.

15   *Ruling 1/78*, [1978] ECR 2151 at 2172.

16   These two concepts are discussed throughout Section IV.3.2.

17   The Treaty provisions are analyzed in detail *infra* in Section IV.2.6.

cept of three pillars holding up the edifice of the European Union. This is unfortunate as the concept has little to recommend it.

In the first place, the pillars are by no means equal in importance. The CFSP may involve a very sensitive and important area of national policy, particularly now that it is being extended to defense, but nevertheless it is dwarfed by the scope of the European Community. PJC is a relatively minor aspect of the Union's activities. Thus, if indeed the European Union is borne by these three pillars, it threatens to emulate the leaning tower of Pisa.

What is more important, however, is that the concept of the three pillars creates an artificial and misleading dichotomy between Union matters (the CFSP and PJC) and Community matters. It obscures the fact that the Community is just as much part of the European Union as the CFSP and PJC and exaggerates the different nature of the latter two activities. It is true that some Member States insisted on establishing the CFSP and PJC outside the Community because of its increasingly supranational procedures and because they felt that an intergovernmental approach was more appropriate for matters that touch so nearly upon national sovereignty. However, in reality the procedures for running the CFSP and PJC, while they may have a more intergovernmental flavor, are not so distinct from those used in the Community.

By intergovernmental procedures, we mean that the governments of the Member States have a preponderant influence on decision-making through the European Council, the Council acting by unanimity and through direct involvement of the Member States. Within the CFSP, this is only partially true. As far as the Member States are concerned, their direct involvement is limited to the right, which they share with the Commission, to ask questions of the Council and submit proposals to it.[18] The European Council, it is true, defines the principles and general guidelines of the CFSP and decides on common strategies.[19] However, it has the same defining role in all aspects of the Union's activities,[20] including those of the Community, while its decisions on common strategies are taken on a recommendation of the Council.[21] As for the Council, it does not always act by unanimity. The implementation of common strategies, including the adoption of joint actions and common positions, as well as decisions implementing joint actions and common positions are decided by a qualified majority.[22] However, there is provision for a Member State to block a decision by qualified majority voting for important and stated reasons of national policy.

---

18   Article 22(1) (TEU).

19   Article 13(1),(2) (TEU).

20   Article 4(1) (TEU).

21   Article 13(2) (TEU).

22   Article 23(2) (TEU). This provision does not apply to decisions having military or defense implications.

Other Union institutions that originated in the EC Treaty also play a role in the CFSP. The Commission has the right to be fully associated with the conduct of the CFSP.[23] Specifically, it may submit proposals for joint actions at the request of the Council[24] and, together with the Member States, ask questions of the Council and submit proposals to it.[25] The Presidency of the Council must consult the European Parliament on the main aspects and basic choices of the CFSP and keep it regularly informed.[26] Parliament may ask questions of the Council and must hold an annual debate on progress in implementing the CFSP.[27] The Court of Justice, on the other hand, has no role to play in the CFSP, but this is not particularly unusual. Foreign policy in most states is not subject to judicial control.

PJC has the same muted intergovernmental flavor as the CFSP. The European Council has no special role to play. The Commission must be fully associated and has a right to initiate action by the Council.[28] The European Parliament must be consulted by the Council on a number of occasions and be kept regularly informed by the Presidency of the Council and the Commission.[29] It may ask questions of the Council and make recommendations to it.[30] It must hold an annual debate on progress in the area of PJC.[31] Even the Court of Justice has some jurisdiction in this area.[32] On the other hand, the Council normally acts by unanimity in PJC and the Commission shares its right of initiative with the Member States.[33]

I believe that we should turn the concept of the three pillars on its head and see the European Union as the edifice that bears the Communities, the CFSP and PJC rather than the other way round. It is the structure that integrates all the various activities and brings them under one roof. It is unfortunate that the TEU does not confer legal personality on the Union, which would clarify this relationship. However, it makes it clear in other ways. For example, the TEU lists all the activities of the Union in Article 2 without distinguishing between those that take place within the Communities on the one hand and the CFSP and PJC on the other. Indeed, the TEU fuses the two completely when it recognizes

---

23   Articles 18(4) and 27 (TEU).
24   Article 14(4) (TEU).
25   Article 22(1) (TEU).
26   Article 21 (TEU).
27   *Ibid.*
28   Articles 34(2) and 36(2) (TEU).
29   Article 39(1)(2) (TEU).
30   Article 39(3) (TEU).
31   *Ibid.*
32   Article 35 (TEU).
33   Article 34(2) (TEU).

fundamental rights as *Community* law that must be respected by the *Union*.[34] Likewise, it places the provisions on *Union* citizenship in the EC Treaty.[35] The TEU establishes a single institutional structure for the European Union,[36] which underlines the argument made above that the procedures by which the CFSP and PJC are carried out do not differ in their essential nature from those used by the Community. It also expressly provides for the European Parliament, the Council, the Commission, the Court of Justice and the Court of Auditors to exercise their powers in areas within the TEU, albeit only to the extent permitted by its provisions.[37]

The activities of the European Union thus constitute an integral whole. They are all Union activities, no matter under which auspices they take place and according to which procedures. At the same time, the Union is based primarily on two separate treaties, the ECT and the TEU. The first deals primarily with economic integration, the second with political integration. As they set out different aspects of the Union, we shall discuss them separately without, however, losing sight of their essential unity as the foundation stones of the European Union.

II.3.2 The European Community Treaty

II.3.2.a The Process of Economic Integration

The ultimate aim of economic integration is to fuse two or more national economies into one, in which goods, services, persons and capital circulate freely and major economic policies are decided in common. It uses three means to achieve this: removal of restrictions and discrimination, approximation and/or mutual recognition and policy harmonization.

Economic integration requires the elimination of restrictions and discrimination that prevent or impede the free movement between the integrating countries of goods, services, persons and capital. The removal of restrictions is relatively straightforward, but discrimination is more complex. There are in fact two types of discrimination. The first, which is called discrimination in law, involves national measures that openly discriminate against foreigners by prescribing less favorable treatment for them or more favorable treatment for nationals. Discrimination in fact comprises national measures that apply equally to foreigners and nationals but which nonetheless put the latter at a disadvantage. An example would be the requirement of prior residency as a prerequisite for engaging in a certain activity. There is no legal discrimination here as long as foreigners are able to reside in the state in question; nevertheless, they are much less likely

---

34   Article 6(2) (TEU).

35   They are now found in Articles 17 to 22 (ECT).

36   Article 3 (TEU). *See* the discussion *infra* in Section III.1.

37   Article 5 (TEU).

to have done so than domestic nationals with the result that the requirement discriminates against them in fact.

A wide application of national treatment that includes the removal of *all* national measures that disadvantage foreigners would largely secure free movement. However, national treatment does not usually apply to national measures that are based on justifiable grounds of public policy, even if these measures discriminate in fact. Two paramount examples are industrial standards and qualifications. There are two ways to overcome these obstacles. The first is by approximating the various national laws or regulations; the second is through mutual recognition. In the case of qualifications, both may be used; a country recognizes qualifications acquired in another integrating country but on the basis of an approximation of the laws and regulations stipulating the training required to obtain them. Approximation is also used to attenuate differences in national laws that can distort the conditions of competition in the integrating area. Taxation, corporations and intellectual property are prime areas for such approximation.

The removal of restrictions and discrimination together with the approximation of laws and/or mutual recognition is often referred to as negative integration.[38] This is not an entirely felicitous nomenclature, but it is used in order to contrast the removal of obstacles to integration with active steps to further integration of the participating countries. These steps involve policy harmonization, which can have varying degrees of intensity. At its most intense, it means replacing national policies with a common policy. Less radical is where an area policy complements or supplements national policies. The least intense form is the coordination of national policies. Policy harmonization is called positive integration.[39] It has two functions.

One function of policy harmonization is to correct distortions that would otherwise arise if integrating countries were left to pursue purely national policies. Anti-trust policy, for example, can set out common rules that prevent individual countries from abusing state aids or public companies in order to favor local production. The other common distortion in integrating areas is caused by discrepancies between the countries in their commercial relations with third countries. If one country imports inputs from a third country more cheaply than another, this may affect the price of a finished product to the detriment of the latter. This problem can be dealt with by rules of origin, which limit or prohibit third-country inputs in goods that benefit from free movement, or it can be removed by instituting a common commercial policy towards third countries. We can call this type of positive integration "corrective policy harmonization." It is

---

38 *See, e.g.* J. Pinder, "Positive Integration and Negative Integration" in G.R. Denton, ed., *Economic Integration in Europe*, (1969); P.J.G. Kapteyn and P. Verloren van Themaat, *Introduction to the Law of the European Communities* (3rd edition by L.W.Gormley, 1998) at pages 941-942.

39 *Ibid.*

a necessary adjunct to negative integration as it ensures that the benefits intended to accrue from free movement are not frustrated. It varies greatly in the degree to which it is pursued. Some integration areas require only an alignment of national policies to the extent necessary to remove the distortion; other aspire to common policies.

Policy harmonization can also be pursued as an end in itself in order to deepen the integration of the economies of the participating countries, attain common social and economic goals or solve common problems. Sectoral policies in such areas as agriculture, transport or energy go beyond free movement and establish a common policy that fuses the national markets in these areas. A common social policy can be used to improve working and living standards throughout the integrating area on the basis of equal values and levels. A common environmental policy can deal more effectively with an issue that transcends national boundaries. We call this type of positive integration "integrating harmonization." A radical form of integrating harmonization is economic and monetary union.

Sometimes, the two types of policy harmonization overlap. For example, harmonization of consumer protection can both secure a higher level of protection and also correct any distortions that could flow from discrepancies in national policies. The same is true of regional, environmental and social policy.

Despite the clear distinction between negative and positive integration, they too overlap. The approximation of laws may well require a harmonization of the policy on which the laws are based. The area of taxation is a prime example. Conversely, it will often be necessary to approximate laws in order to achieve policy harmonization. Anti-trust policy actually straddles the line between the two types of integration. It can be used not only to correct possible distortions but also to remove barriers to free movement that are caused by restrictive business practices, abuse of dominant position or monopolies.

II.3.2.b The Levels of Economic Integration

The classic view is that there are four levels of economic integration.[40] The lowest level is a free trade area, which provides for the free movement of goods and services and a minimal amount of policy harmonization. Distortions caused by different trade regimes are dealt with by rules of origin. The next level is the customs union, which supplements the free trade area with a common external tariff, thus obviating the need for rules of origin. Then comes the common market, which is an area in which there is free movement of goods, services, persons and capital together with a significant degree of policy harmonization. Finally, there is economic and monetary union, which can exist on its own or together with a common market. In such a union, policy harmonization comprises economic and monetary policy and a common currency.

---

40   *See* B. Balassa, *The Theory of Economic Integration* (1973).

II.3.2.c The European Community Treaty

Nomenclature, as we have noted, is not the Europeans' strong suit. Apart from the confusion over the terms "Union" and "Community," the EC Treaty plays havoc with the classic terminology outlined above. In Article 3, it talks of establishing a common market and of implementing common policies. Yet, common policies are part of a common market. Later, the Treaty invents a new term, "internal market," which is defined as "an area without internal frontiers in which the free movement of goods, persons, services and capital is ensured."[41] One might be forgiven for asking what the difference is between the internal market and the common market, particularly when the latter apparently does not include policy harmonization. The situation is not improved by the additional concept of union citizenship, which has nothing to do with economic integration and belongs more logically in the TEU. In view of this confusion, it is easier to make sense of the EC Treaty by dealing separately with its component parts. These consist of a common market, an economic and monetary union that does not include all Member States and European Union citizenship.

II.3.2.d The Common Market

The EC Treaty contains a classic common market made up of an area of free movement of goods, services, persons and capital (the so-called "internal market") and a substantial amount of policy harmonization. The internal market is achieved by the elimination of restrictions and both types of discrimination, approximation of laws and mutual recognition and corrective policy harmonization in the form of common anti-trust and foreign trade policies. The anti-trust policy also serves to eliminate certain types of restrictions. The relationship between mutual recognition and approximation is interesting. Until 1985, the EC used approximation in its attempt to achieve an internal market. This proved extremely time-consuming and difficult with the result that progress was very slow. In 1985, the EC changed its policy and began to rely on mutual recognition, particularly in the area of industrial standards. This change made it possible to complete in large measure the internal market by the deadline of December 31, 1992.[42] Union law that flows from the internal market measures covers the following areas: anti-trust law, foreign trade, banking, insurance, securities, public procurement, commerce, telecommunications, broadcasting, energy, industrial norms, taxation, corporations and intellectual property.

The common market set up by the EC Treaty also includes considerable integrative policy harmonization that goes beyond mere economics and aims at creating a common European home.[43] There is, for example, a common policy for

---

41   Article 14(2) (ECT).

42   Article 14(1) (ECT).

43   *See* the discussion on the types of Union jurisdiction *infra* in Section IV.1.4.

agriculture and fisheries that creates a single market in these areas. There is also a common transport policy with respect to international transport, cabotage (the right of non-resident carriers to operate in another Member State), safety and anti-trust rules. The two sectoral treaties, the ECSC and EAEC Treaties, set up common policies for coal, steel and nuclear energy. In many other areas, there are Community policies that exist parallel to national policies and both complement and supplement them. Thus, we have Community policies involving social matters, regional development, the environment, consumer protection, industry and public health. In some areas, such as education, culture and employment, policy harmonization is restricted to coordinating national policies. However, many areas where there are now Community policies started out as areas of coordination, and in some instances this process may repeat itself.[44] All this policy harmonization spawns corresponding areas of Union law.

II.3.2.e Economic and Monetary Union (EMU)

EMU is a radical example of integrative policy harmonization that brings the main levers of the Member States' economies under common control. The ensuing harmonization of economic and monetary policy and introduction of a common currency complement the common market. Although EMU is not essential to the existence of the common market, it makes doing business in it much easier by eliminating exchange-rate risks and reducing the danger of macro-economic disturbances. By introducing complete transparency in price comparisons between participating Member States, it should also benefit consumers.

The first stage of EMU started on July 1, 1990 and aimed at a greater convergence of the Member States' economies and an increase in cooperation between their central banks. Member States were also obliged to consider their exchange-rate policies as a matter of common concern.

The second stage of EMU started on January 1, 1994,[45] and it established the following program:

a) the Member States had to ensure a lasting convergence of their economic policies;[46]

b) the European Monetary Institute (EMI) was established to prepare for the third stage of EMU;[47]

---

44   *See* the discussion *infra* in Section IV.1.4.c.
45   Article 116(1) (ECT).
46   Article 116(2)(a) (ECT).
47   Article 117(1),(2),(3)(7) (ECT).

c) the Member States had to enact legislation to ensure compliance with the Treaty prohibitions on exchange controls, overdraft facilities for public bodies with their central banks and privileged access to financial institutions;[48]

d) the Member States had to take steps to ensure the independence of their central banks;[49]

e) the Member States had to continue to regard their exchange-rate policies as a matter of common concern;[50]

f) any Member State that had not already done so had to abolish restrictions on the free movement of capital by December 31, 1995.[51]

The EC Treaty set out only two obligations with respect to the convergence of economic policies in the second stage. These were price stability and budgetary discipline.[52] The first remained very general,[53] but budgetary discipline specifically required that the annual deficit not exceed three percent of GDP and the accumulated national debt not surpass sixty percent of GDP.[54] The Treaty did not take a coercive approach towards this convergence. Member States had to coordinate their economic policies on the basis of broad guidelines recommended to them by the Council.[55] There was provision for multilateral surveillance of national policies but not for any sanctions if the guidelines were breached.[56] Member States also had to endeavor to avoid excessive deficits.[57] Here too, there was provision for monitoring national performances, but no sanctions.[58] A third mechanism for the convergence of economic policies was

---

48 Article 116(2)(a). This obligation does not extend to the British Government's "ways and means facility" as long as the United Kingdom does not move to the third stage of EMU—*see* Article 11 of the Protocol on certain provisions relating to the United Kingdom, which is attached to the EC Treaty.

49 Articles 109 and 116(5) (ECT). This obligation does not apply to the United Kingdom unless it decides to enter the third stage of EMU—*see* Article of the UK Protocol.

50 Article 124(1) (ECT).

51 Article 73(e) (ECT), which was repealed by the Treaty of Amsterdam.

52 Articles 2 and 116(2)(a) (ECT).

53 Article 2 (ECT) refers to "non-inflationary growth" while Article 116(2)(a) talks only of "price stability." It is thus somewhat exaggerated to talk of "a common policy of price stability" during the second stage of EMU—*see* D.R. Dunnett, "Legal and Institutional Issues Affecting Economic and Monetary Union" in D. O'Keeffe & P.M. Twomey, eds., *Legal Issues of the Maastricht Treaty* (1994) at page 136.

54 Articles 104(2) and 121(1) (ECT); 1 of the Protocol on the excessive deficit procedure, which is attached to the EC Treaty.

55 Article 99(2) (ECT).

56 Article 99((3),(4) (ECT).

57 Article 116(4) (ECT).

58 Article 104(6),(7) (ECT).

the continuing obligation for Member States to treat their exchange-rate policies as a matter of common interest.[59]

The third stage of EMU started on January 1, 1999. It comprises a single currency and a common monetary policy that transfers to the Community control
over the money supply, interest rates, foreign exchange transactions and official
foreign reserves of the participating Member States.[60] The European System of
Central Banks (ESCB), comprising the national central banks of the participating
Member States and the ECB, is responsible for conducting the Community's
monetary policy.[61] In doing so, its main objective must be price stability.[62]

The third stage does not introduce a common economic policy. Instead, it continues the regime of the second stage, whereby Member States coordinate their
economic policies on the basis of guidelines set by the Council. This lack of a
common policy must be seen in the present context, wherein most of the instruments of economic policy are still in the hands of national governments. However, it is surprising that there is no provision for sanctions where the guidelines
are breached. An exception is budgetary matters. In the third stage, the rules on
excessive deficits are made binding. Member States are now *obliged* to avoid
such deficits, and if they fail in this obligation, the Council may require them to
take specific measures to reduce their deficit or face sanctions that can include
fines.[63] These provisions take into account the fact that there is no pooling of
external liabilities in the European monetary union, and that the ECB is not a
lender of last resort. Neither the Community nor other Member States are liable
for the debts of a Member State.[64]

[handwritten margin note: 3% annual / 6% accumulated]

The most visible aspect of the third stage is the single currency, which is called
the "euro." As from January 1, 1999 the euro exists as a currency in its own right
and the conversion rates of the Member States participating in the third stage
were fixed irrevocably against it.[65] However, euro banknotes and coins do not
become legal tender until January 1, 2002, and in the meantime national currency is used. Paperless transactions are, however, already possible in euros.
Checks can be written in euros and bank transfers effected in that currency.
Between January 1, 2002 and June 30, 2002, both national and euro money will
be legal tender. As from July 1, 2002, the national currencies of the participating
Member States will cease to exist and national banknotes and coins will be
withdrawn from circulation. The ECB has the exclusive right to authorize the

---

59   Article 124(1) (ECT).
60   Articles 4(2) and 105(2) (ECT).
61   The ECB replaces the EMI in the third stage.
62   Article 105(1) (ECT).
63   Article 104(9),(11) (ECT).
64   Article 103(1) (ECT).
65   Articles 118 and 123(4) (ECT).

issue of euro banknotes by the ECB and the national central banks.[66] Member States may issue euro coins subject to approval by the ECB of the volume of the issue.[67]

Member States must meet the following four criteria in order to enter the third stage of EMU:

a) their annual deficit must not exceed three percent of GDP and their accumulated national debt must not surpass sixty percent of GDP.[68] However, the annual deficit may exceed three percent if it has declined substantially and reached a level near three percent. The accumulated public debt may exceed sixty percent if it is diminishing and approaching sixty percent at a satisfactory pace;

b) their average rate of inflation for the preceding year must not have exceeded by more than one and one-half percent that of the three Member States with the lowest inflation;[69]

c) they must have participated for the preceding two years in the exchange-rate mechanism of the European Monetary System without any abnormal fluctuations or devaluation in the value of their currency against the currency of any other Member State;[70]

d) their average nominal long-term interest rates for the preceding year must not have exceeded by more than two percent that of the three Member States with the lowest inflation.[71]

Austria, Belgium, Finland, France, Germany, Ireland, Italy, Luxembourg, the Netherlands, Portugal and Spain met these criteria and entered the third stage of EMU on January 1, 1999. Greece met the criteria later and was admitted on January 1, 2001. Denmark, Sweden and the United Kingdom chose not to enter the third stage of EMU although they met the criteria.

II.3.2.f The External Competence of the European Community

Unlike the ECSC and EAEC Treaties,[72] the EC Treaty does not bestow upon the Community a general power to act on the international stage. Instead, it gives

---

66   Article 106(1) (ECT).

67   Article 106(2) (ECT).

68   Articles104(2) and 121(1) (ECT); 1 of the Protocol on the excessive deficit procedure.

69   Articles 121 (1) (ECT); 1 of the Protocol on the convergence criteria, which is attached to the EC Treaty.

70   Articles 121(1) (ECT); 3 of the Protocol on the convergence criteria.

71   Articles 121(1) (ECT); 4 of the Protocol on the convergence criteria.

72   *See* Articles 6 (ECSC); 101 (EAEC).

certain specific powers. The Community may conclude international agreements in the areas of research and development,[73] the environment[74] and development cooperation[75] as well as agreements dealing with freedom of movement within the Member States for workers from the associated countries and territories (OCT).[76] It has exclusive responsibility for the conduct of the Community's external trade relations[77] except for services and intellectual property, where it shares jurisdiction with the Member States.[78] However, the Treaty of Amsterdam has introduced a provision into the EC Treaty enabling the Council to extend the Community's exclusive jurisdiction to these two areas.[79] It has a general and exclusive power to conclude association agreements.[80] Ratification by the Member States is only required for OCT agreements.

The Community has a broad power to make agreements and take positions on monetary matters at the international level.[81] This power is exercised by the Council in cooperation with the ECB and the Commission. No ratification by the Member States is required. It includes setting a common exchange-rate policy with respect to third countries. Member States retain control over foreign exchange working balances and certain other foreign assets,[82] but national operations in foreign exchange must, above a certain limit, be approved by the ECB.[83] Individual Member States also retain the right to negotiate in international bodies and conclude international agreements. However, this right cannot go very far as it must be exercised without prejudice to the Community's broad international competence.

---

73   Article 170 (ECT).

74   Article 174 (ECT).

75   Article 191 (ECT).

76   Article 186 (ECT).

77   Articles 131-143 (ECT).

78   The Court of Justice came to this conclusion in *Opinion 1/94*, [1994] ECR I-5267. As a result, the WTO Agreement was signed jointly by the Communities and the Member States.

79   Article 133(5) (ECT). Article 2(5) of the Treaty of Nice will effect this extension of the Community's external trade powers to the negotiation and conclusion of agreements relating to trade in services and the commercial aspects of intellectual property. The Community's jurisdiction under this Article will not, however, include cultural and audiovisual services, educational services and social and human health services, which continue to fall within the shared competence of the Community and the Member States. The Treaty of Nice also provides for the Council to extend the Community's jurisdiction to all aspects of intellectual property.

80   Article 310 (ECT).

81   Article 111 (ECT).

82   Article 105(3) (ECT).

83   Article 31 of the Statute of the European System of Central Banks and the European Central Bank, which is attached to the EC Treaty as a protocol.

The Community also shares with the Member States the power to foster cooperation with third countries and international organizations in the areas of education,[84] vocational training,[85] culture[86] and public health.[87] The Community maintains relations with international organizations such as the United Nations, the Council of Europe and the Organization for Economic Cooperation and Development (OECD).[88]

The Community's external competence under the EC Treaty is thus not negligible, but it is the Court of Justice that has given it a general power to act internationally. In a string of cases, the Court determined that, wherever the Community has power to act in particular areas internally, it enjoys a corollary authority on the international level "even in the absence of an express provision in that connection."[89] This effectively extends the Community's international competence to the whole field of the EC Treaty, as the Court has confirmed.[90] The general international power is exclusive to the Community; once it acts on the international stage in relation to a Treaty area, the jurisdiction of the Member States ceases and no national ratifications are needed.[91] However, in a later decision, the Court backtracked somewhat by declaring that the Community's jurisdiction is exclusive only where the area in question has been completely harmonized internally or if the attainment of Community objectives absolutely requires that the Community's external power be exclusive.[92] As a result, where the Community is not exercising a specific international power, its international agreements often take a "mixed" form with both the Community and the Member States acting as signatories. "Mixed" agreements are always necessary where an agreement requires expenditures by the Member States.

II.3.2.g Union Citizenship

The EC Treaty creates a common citizenship of the European Union.[93] This sounds very impressive, but Union citizenship is by no means a true federal citizenship. This is not because it exists alongside national citizenship,[94] which is

---

84   Article 149(3) (ECT).

85   Article 150(3) (ECT).

86   Article 151(3) (ECT).

87   Article 152(3) (ECT).

88   Articles 302-304 (ECT).

89   *See Opinion 1/76*, [1977] ECR 741 at 741.

90   *See Officier van Justitie v. Kramer*, 3,4 and 6/76. [1976] ECR 1279 at 1279.

91   *See Commission v. Council*, 22/70, [1971] ECR 263 at 273.

92   *Opinion 1/94*, [1994] ECR I-5267.

93   The fact that the provisions are nonetheless placed in the EC Treaty underlines the artificiality of the distinction between the terms "Union" and "Community." *See* the discussion *supra* in Section II.3.1.

94   Article 17(1) (ECT) says that it shall "complement and not replace national citizenship."

common in federations,[95] but because it is an incidence of national citizenship rather than the converse. Nationals of Member States have an automatic right to Union citizenship, whereas federal citizenship is bestowed by the center and gives the right to regional citizenship once any local residency requirements have been met.[96]

This difference has two significant consequences. Firstly, it means that the Member States rather than the Union regulate the acquisition and loss of Union citizenship as they have complete control over who holds their citizenship. A declaration appended to the TEU states categorically that "the question whether an individual possesses the nationality of a Member State shall be settled solely by reference to the national law of the Member State concerned."[97] Furthermore, no Member State may deny Union citizenship and the rights that go with it to a person who holds the citizenship of another Member State according to that State's law even if its own law would not recognize such citizenship under the circumstances.[98]

The second, and more important, consequence of the subordinate nature of Union citizenship is that the rights attached to it are enumerated and expressly accorded by the Treaty; they do not flow automatically from the citizenship itself as in the case of national citizenship. As such they are limited in scope and, in some cases, subject to curtailment. As a result, Union citizenship does not place nationals from other Member States on an equal footing with local nationals.

However, one must not dismiss Union citizenship as an empty shell for the rights attached to it by the EC Treaty are far from negligible despite their shortcomings. The seven rights of Union citizens are the following:

a) The right to move and reside freely within the territory of the Member States, subject to certain limitations and conditions.[99] It is not clear to what extent this right goes beyond the mobility rights established by Articles 39 to 55 of the EC Treaty and the secondary legislation enacted pursuant to them.[100] For example, is it still possible for Member States to subject the right of residence for nationals from other Member States to the requirement

---

95   *See e.g.* Article 74(8) of the German Constitution and the 14th Amendment, section 1 of the United States Constitution.

96   *See* 14th Amendment, section 1 of the United States Constitution, which provides that "all persons born or naturalized in the United States . . . are citizens of the United States and of the State wherein they reside." *See* also Articles 4 and 5 of the Belgian Constitution. *See* also C. Closa, "The Concept of Citizenship in the Treaty on European Union," (1992) 29 *Common Market Law Review* 1137 at 1140-41.

97   *See* also *Micheletti et al v. Delegación del Gobierno de Cantabria,* C-369/90, [1992] ECR 1-4239 at 4262.

98   *Ibid* at 4262.

99   Article 18 (ECT).

100   *See* P. Mengozzi, *European Community Law* (2nd ed., 1999) at page 240.

that they possess adequate health coverage and the means to support themselves?

b) The right to vote and stand as a candidate in municipal and European elections in the Member State in which they reside even if it is not their own.[101] There is still, however, no right to participate in the national political life of another Member State, which has been called "the defining and primordial element of citizenship."[102] Accession to posts in the public service or occupations involving the exercise of official authority is still not allowed.

c) The right to protection in a non-EU country by the diplomatic authorities of another Member States, on the same conditions as its own nationals, in the absence of diplomatic representation in that country by their own Member State.[103] The modalities for this protection have been set down by a Decision of the Member States.[104]

d) The right to write to certain institutions or bodies of the Union in one of the Union's official languages and to receive a reply in the same language.[105]

e) The right, which they share with anyone residing in a Member State, to petition the European Parliament on a matter within the Community's jurisdiction that affects them directly.[106] Although this is Union citizenship, the right to petition Parliament is restricted to Community matters.

f) The right, which they share with anyone residing in a Member State, to complain to the Ombudsman about misadministration by a body or institution set up by the EC Treaty with the exception of the Courts acting in a judicial capacity.[107] Where the Ombudsman finds the complaint justified, the matter is referred to the body or institution concerned for its comments. After three months at the latest, the Ombudsman sends a report to the institution or body and to the European Parliament. At the request of a quarter of its Members, Parliament may set up a temporary Committee of Inquiry to investigate the matter.[108]

g) The right, which they share with anyone residing in a Member State, to access documents of the Council, Commission and Parliament subject to princi-

---

101 Article 19 (ECT).

102 Closa (fn. 96), at 1139.

103 Article 20 (ECT).

104 Decision of the Representatives of the Governments of the Member States meeting within the Council regarding protection for citizens of the European Union by diplomatic and consular representation (OJ L314/95).

105 Article 21 (ECT). A declaration appended to the Treaty of Nice calls upon the institutions to reply within a reasonable period.

106 Articles 21 and 194 (ECT).

107 Articles 21 and 195(1) (ECT).

108 Article 193 (ECT).

ples and limits on grounds of public or private interest.[109] This right is related to (d) as both emanate from a desire to make the workings of the Union more transparent.

II.3.2.h Fundamental Rights

Fundamental rights are covered primarily by the TEU. However, the EC Treaty does contain some provisions on this subject. These are discussed in Section VI.6.

II.3.2.i Institutional Provisions

It is the EC Treaty that creates the following institutions and bodies: the Council, Commission, European Parliament, European System of Central Banks, European Central Bank, European Investment Bank, Court of Justice, Court of Auditors, Economic and Social Committee, Committee of Regions, Committee of Permanent Representatives, Economic and Financial Committee, Employment Committee and Transport Committee. For this reason, these institutions and bodies are called *Community* bodies as opposed the European Council, which is a *Union* body set up by the TEU.

However, as with all distinctions between what is "Union" and what is "Community," the difference is artificial and misleading. While it is true that some of the bodies created by the EC Treaty only operate within its confines, others are expressly co-opted by the TEU to exercise their powers with respect to matters involving that Treaty.[110] These are the Council, Commission, European Parliament, Court of Justice and Court of Auditors. At the same time, the European Council establishes the general political guidelines for all the activities of the European Union, including those that fall within the scope of the EC Treaty. It also true to say that, as the European Community is part of the European Union, any institution or body it creates belongs to the Union. It is therefore quite silly to continue to make this distinction and the time has surely come to attribute all institutions and bodies operating within the European Union, under whatever Treaty, to the Union. This, at any rate, seems to be the preference of the Council, which changed its name in 1993 to the "Council of the European Union."[111]

II.3.3 The Treaty on European Union

II.3.3.a The Common Foreign and Security Policy

The CFSP has undergone a significant change in scope since the Helsinki meeting of the European Council in December 1999, when it was decided to develop

---

109   This right is listed separately in Article 255 (ECT).

110   Article 5 (TEU).

111   Council Decision 93/591 concerning the name to be given to the Council following the entry into force of the Treaty on European Union (OJ L281/93).

the security aspect of the common policy. It now comprises two separate aspects: a common foreign policy and a common European security and defense policy (CESDP). The CESDP at present incorporates the so-called Petersburg tasks, namely humanitarian and rescue tasks, peacekeeping and crisis management, but it may eventually be expanded to the overall defense of the European Union. To accommodate the change, the Political Committee set up by the TEU has to all intents and purposes been replaced by the Political and Security Committee (PSC), whose mandate covers both aspects of the CFSP.[112]

At the Nice meeting of the European Council in December 2000, it was decided to make the new CESDP operational without waiting for the Treaty of Nice to enter into force.[113] Originally, it was intended to use the Western European Union (WEU) to handle the military aspects of the CFSP, but this idea has been dropped. Once ratified, the Treaty of Nice will remove all reference to the WEU from the TEU. Instead, military matters will be handled for the European Union by the new Military Committee and the Military Staff of the European Union.[114]

Once again the nomenclature chosen by the Europeans is not a model of clarity, for we have now two common policies, but one—the CESDP—is an aspect of the other—the CFSP. The justification for this is that the CESDP is based on the provisions in the TEU on the CFSP and is governed by the same procedures. For the sake of simplicity, we shall therefore refer from now on only to the CFSP, but both aspects are meant.

The CFSP covers all areas of foreign and security policy, including now some defense elements, and has the following objectives:[115]

– to safeguard the common values, fundamental interests, independence and integrity of the Union;

– to strengthen the security of the Union;

– to preserve peace and strengthen international security;

– to promote international cooperation;

– to develop and consolidate democracy, the rule of law and fundamental rights.

The European Council defines the principles and guidelines of the CFSP, which is realized by means of common strategies, joint actions and common

---

112 *See* Council Decision 01/78 setting up the Political and Security Committee (OJ L27/01).

113 Declaration on the European security and defense policy, attached to the Treaty of Nice.

114 *See* Council Decision 01/79 setting up the Military Committee of the European Union (OJ L27/01) and Council Decision 01/80 setting up the Military Staff of the European Union (OJ L27/01).

115 Article 11(1) (TEU).

positions.[116] Joint actions and common positions may be adopted in isolation or as a means of implementing a common strategy. A joint action addresses a specific situation where operational action by the European Union is deemed necessary, while common positions define the approach of the Union to a particular matter.[117] Where a joint action or a common position provides for economic sanctions against a third country, the necessary action is taken under the EC Treaty.[118]

Common strategies are decided by the European Council acting on a recommendation of the Council.[119] Joint actions and common positions and measures to implement them are adopted by the Council.[120] The Council is assisted by the PSC, the High Representative for the CFSP and the policy planning and early warning unit, which together form an embryonic foreign ministry.[121] The European Parliament, the Member States and the Commission can all ask questions of the Council and make recommendations or proposals to it.[122] Beyond this, the Member States have no direct role in the conduct of the CFSP, although they are obliged to inform and consult one another within the Council.[123] On the other hand, the Commission must be fully associated with the work carried on within the CFSP,[124] and the Council, through the Presidency, must consult the European Parliament on the main aspects and basic choices of the CFSP.[125] Parliament must also be kept regularly informed by both the Presidency and the Commission. The Court of Justice has no jurisdiction within the area of the CFSP, but this is not unusual. Judicial review of foreign policy is rare even in nation-states.

Externally, the European Union is represented in principle by the Presidency of the Council.[126] In practice, this means the foreign minister or head of government[127] of the Member State holding the rotating presidency of the Council. However, there is also the High Representative for the CFSP, who, in addition to assisting generally in the formulation and implementation of the CFSP, also

---

116   Articles 12 and 13 (TEU).

117   Articles 14(1) and 15 (TEU).

118   Articles 60(1) and 301 (ECT).

119   Article 13(2),(3) (TEU).

120   Articles 14 and 15 (TEU).

121   *See* Articles 25 and 26 (TEU) and the Declaration on the establishment of a policy planning and early warning unit, appended to the Treaty of Amsterdam.

122   Articles 21 and 22(1) (TEU).

123   Article 16 (TEU).

124   Article 27 (TEU).

125   Article 21 (TEU).

126   Article 18(1) (TEU).

127   In the case of France, it includes the President, who shares responsibility for foreign affairs with the Prime Minister.

conducts political dialogue with third countries at the request of the Presidency.[128] This office, which is held by the Secretary-General of the Council, resembles that of a European Union foreign minister. At the same time, a member of the Commission also has responsibility for foreign affairs. The relationship between the Commissioner and the High Representative is unclear and causes some friction. It also serves to confuse third countries.

II.3.3.b Police and Judicial Cooperation in Criminal Matters

Originally this Title of the TEU was extremely diffuse, but the Treaty of Amsterdam transferred a number of areas to the EC Treaty, namely asylum, external border controls, immigration and other matters involving third-country nationals, judicial cooperation in civil matters and customs cooperation.[129] What remains has been brought into clearer focus under the rubric of police and judicial cooperation in criminal matters (PJC).

The stated objective of PJC is to provide citizens of the European Union with a high level of safety within an area of freedom, security and justice.[130] This is to be achieved by preventing and combating crime, including terrorism, trafficking in persons and offences against children, illicit drug and arms trafficking, corruption and fraud. The means that are put at the Union's disposal are closer cooperation between the police, customs and judicial authorities of the Member States and, somewhat surprisingly, the approximation of their criminal laws where this is necessary. The maintenance of law and order and the safeguarding of internal security remain the exclusive responsibility of the individual Member States.[131]

Apart from the European Council's general authority to define Union policy, it is left to the Council to enact the measures necessary to achieve the goals of PJC. It does this by adopting common positions and framework decisions for the approximation of national laws and regulations as well as other decisions and by drawing up conventions for adoption by the Member States.[132] It acts on the initiative of the Member States or the Commission, which gives them both a more direct role in PJC than they enjoy in the CFSP. The Member States are also obliged to inform and consult one another within the Council with a view to coordinating their actions.[133] The Council is assisted by a Coordinating Committee and must obtain the opinion of Parliament in certain cases.[134] Parliament may

---

128 Article 26 (TEU).
129 Titles IV and X (ECT).
130 Article 29 (TEU).
131 Article 33 (TEU).
132 Article 34(2) (TEU).
133 Article 34(1) (TEU).
134 Articles 36 and 39(2) (TEU).

ask questions of the Council and make recommendations to it.[135] The Presidency and the Commission, which must be fully associated with the work carried on in PJC, are obliged to keep Parliament regularly informed.[136] The Court of Justice has jurisdiction to rule on the legality, validity and interpretation of the Council's framework decisions and decisions as well as the validity and interpretation of the measures implementing conventions.[137] It also has the power to rule on the interpretation and application of these conventions. However, there are limitations on this jurisdiction, which are discussed later in Section VI.4.2.a.

II.3.3.c The External Competence of the European Union

The international competence of the European Union is a moot point. As it is not expressly given legal personality, it is widely assumed that the Union cannot enter into international agreements.[138] However, the wording of the Treaty casts doubt on this view while not entirely contradicting it. Article 24 of the TEU gives the Council the right to authorize the Presidency, assisted by the Commission, to negotiate agreements with third countries or international organizations within the field of the CFSP. The Council also has the power to conclude them. These powers are extended to PJC by Article 38. This would seem to imply that the Union does indeed have the legal standing to enter into international agreements. On the other hand, in contrast to international agreements concluded by the EC, these agreements are not binding on Member States in which ratification is required until this has taken place. The issue needs clarifying.

II.3.3.d Fundamental Rights

These are discussed in Section VI.6.

II.3.3.e Accession to the European Union

The essential unity of the European Union is well illustrated by the uniform procedures for accession to the Union. These uniform provisions replace the separate provisions in the three original Community Treaties.[139]

Accession is open to any European state that respects the fundamental rights set out in Article 6 of the TEU.[140] The first requirement excludes the Union's trans-Mediterranean neighbors in North Africa and the Middle East. Turkey,

---

135 Article 39(3) (TEU).

136 Article 36(2) and 39(2) (TEU).

137 Article 35 (TEU).

138 *See* Kapteyn and Verloren van Themaat (fn. 38) at page 1254. For a more nuanced approach, *see* Mengozzi (fn. 100) at pages 34-35.

139 Articles 236 and 237 (EEC Treaty); 96 and 98 (ECSC Treaty); 204 and 205 (EAEC Treaty).

140 Article 49 (TEU).

which has a toehold on the European continent, is eligible for accession, but it has so far not satisfied the second requirement of respect for human rights. An intriguing question is the status of Russia, whose territory spans the European and Asian continents. As the European Union can hardly admit only that part of Russia that lies west of the Urals, does this mean that Russia is disqualified altogether? This would certainly be the most convenient solution as the presence of the Russian colossus within the Union would pose enormous problems.

A state that wishes to join the European Union addresses its application to the Council. There then ensues a long and laborious process that is not set out in the TEU. The Commission studies the issue and draws up reports for the European Council. Once political agreement among the existing Member States is reached at the European Council level, negotiations start and are led by the Commission. Finally, the Council approves the accession after consulting the Commission and obtaining the assent of the European Parliament acting by an absolute majority. An Accession Treaty is then concluded collectively by the Member States with the acceding state,[141] which must be ratified by all Member States in accordance with their constitutional requirements as it normally contains adjustments to the Treaties. In most cases, there is a considerable lapse of time between the application for accession and accession. Hungary and Poland, for example, applied for accession in 1994 and are not likely to become members of the Union before 2002-4. Turkey's application dates back to the 1960's and it is still not a member.

At present the following states have applied for membership of the European Union: Bulgaria, Cyprus, Czech Republic, Estonia, Hungary, Latvia, Lithuania, Malta, Poland, Romania, Slovakia, Slovenia and Turkey. The first new entrants are expected to be Cyprus, Czech Republic, Estonia, Hungary, Poland and Slovenia. The others will follow later, although there are still doubts about Turkey's respect for fundamental rights.

II.3.3.f The Amendment of the Treaties

The uniform procedure set out in the TEU for the revision of the Treaties on which the Union is founded accords to the Member States and the Commission an equal right to initiate the process.[142] Either may submit proposals for amendments to the Council, which, after consulting Parliament and, where the initiative comes from a Member State, the Commission, decides whether or not to favor the calling of a conference of representatives of the governments of the Member States. The ECB must be consulted if an amendment concerns the monetary area. If the Council is favorable, the Presidency convenes the intergovern-

---

141 Article 49 (TEU) does not specifically direct the Member States to act by common accord, but it would not be necessary to ratify these agreements if they were concluded by the Member States acting individually according their own constitutional processes.

142 Article 48 (TEU).

mental conference (IGC). Amendments are agreed by the Member States acting collectively and then have to be approved individually by all Member States in accordance with their respective constitutional arrangements. They enter into force after they have been so ratified.

There are two main points to be made with respect to this amendment process. Firstly, it is noteworthy that, apart from the Commission's right of initiative, the Community institutions have no formal role in the IGC. The Commission participates in the IGC and submissions are taken from the other bodies of the Union, but this is not required by the TEU. It is essentially an intergovernmental process. What particularly irks Parliament is that amendments to the Treaties do not require its assent.

The second point is related to the first. It is in the final analysis the Member States acting individually according to their own constitutional processes that amend the Treaties. This is how international treaties are normally amended, and it suggests that the Union Treaties are no different than other international agreements with respect to their amendment. In this case, the normal rule of international law should apply, under which a later treaty may amend an earlier treaty without the need to follow the amendment procedure set out in the latter. All that is required is the unanimous agreement of the signatory states.

The Court of Justice has rejected this approach to the amendment process. As far as the Court is concerned, the legal order of the Union is autonomous and beyond national control.[143] It would contravene this principle to permit the Member States to amend the Union Treaties merely by agreeing among themselves on a new treaty. Thus the Court has held that the Treaties can only be amended by the procedure set out therein,[144] which now means the uniform procedure set out in the TEU. This in turn raises the issue of the character of the Union Treaties. The fact that they can be amended only by using the procedure which they provide suggests that they are constitutional documents rather than international treaties. This issue is discussed later in Section VII.2.4.a.

In addition to the general amendment procedure, the Treaties also bestow upon the Member States acting collectively, the European Council and the Council an executive power to amend the Treaties in specific instances by a simpler and quicker process. The scheme for these amendments is as follows:

a) amendment decided by the Member States acting collectively:

    – adjustments to the Treaties in Accession Treaties with new Member States;[145]

---

143   *See* the discussion *infra* in Section IV.6.

144   *Defrenne v. SABENA*, 43/75, [1976] ECR 455 at 478.

145   Article 49 (TEU).

b) amendments decided by the European Council;

- expand the CFSP to include a common defense policy;[146]
- integrate the WEU into the European Union.[147]

c) amendments decided by the Council;

- transfer areas in PJC to Title IV of the EC Treaty and establish the voting procedures that will apply;[148]
- provisions to strengthen or add to Union citizenship rights;[149]
- extend free movement of services to third-country nationals;[150]
- extend transport rules to sea and air transport;[151]
- provisions to replace the Protocol on implementation of the excessive deficit procedure;[152]
- amend certain Articles of the ESCB Statute;[153]
- give the EU jurisdiction over international agreements on services and intellectual property;[154]
- provision for election of the European Parliament by direct universal suffrage;[155]
- make changes to the Statute of the Court of Justice to accommodate the Court of First Instance;[156]
- amend provisions of Title III of the Statute of the Court of Justice.[157]

Where these administrative amendments change the main text of the Treaties, they must be ratified by the Member States acting individually even where they are agreed by the same states acting collectively.[158] Amendments involving an

---

146 Article 17(1) (TEU).
147 Article 17(1) (TEU).
148 Article 42 (TEU).
149 Article 22 (ECT).
150 Article 49 (ECT).
151 Article 80 (ECT).
152 Article 104(14) (ECT).
153 Article 107(5) (ECT).
154 Article 133(5) (ECT).
155 Article 190(4) (ECT.
156 Article 225(2) (ECT).
157 Article 245 (ECT).
158 This is necessary in the case of Articles 17(1), 42 and 49 (TEU); 22 and 190(4) (ECT).

extension of Union jurisdiction within an area already covered by the Treaties do not require ratification,[159] nor do amendments to the Protocol on excessive deficits and the Statutes of the ESCB/ECB and the Court of Justice.[160] The provision for the direct election of Parliament and the amendment of the ESCB Statute require Parliament's assent.

II.3.3.g Institutional Provisions

The TEU provides the legal basis for the European Council[161] although this body was originally institutionalized by the Single European Act. The European Council also acts within the domain of the EC Treaty by setting the general guidelines for the Union's activities and, more specifically, the guidelines for economic policy.[162] It provides annual conclusions on employment in the EC.[163] The TEU also sets up the High Representative for the CFSP[164] and the Political Committee.[165] The latter has now been largely supplanted by the Political and Security Committee that the Council has created.[166] The TEU establishes the Coordinating Committee for PJC,[167] which helps prepare the work of the Council in this area. There has been some tension between this committee and the Committee of Permanent Representatives, which is generally in charge of preparing the work of the Council.

II.3.4 Other Acts

There are two other Acts that contribute to establishing the structure of the European Union. The Act concerning the election of the representatives of the European Parliament supplements the rules in the EC Treaty on the European Parliament. Article 9 of the Treaty of Amsterdam replaces the provisions of the 1957 Convention[168] and the Merger Treaty[169] with respect to the exercise of the powers of the European Parliament, the Council, the Commission, the Court of Justice and the Court of Auditors by single institutions.

---

159   Article 49, 80 and 133(5) (ECT).

160   Articles 104(14), 107(5), 225(2) and 245 (ECT).

161   Article 4 (TEU).

162   Article 99(2) (ECT).

163   Article 128(1) (ECT).

164   Articles 18 and 26 (TEU).

165   Article 25 (TEU).

166   Council Decision 01/78 setting up the Political and Security Committee (OJ L27/01).

167   Article 36(1) (TEU).

168   Convention on Certain Institutions Common to the European Communities, which was annexed to the ECSC, EEC and EAEC Treaties in 1957.

169   Treaty establishing a Single Council and a Single Commission of the European Communities, OJ L152/67.

II.3.5 Geographical Scope of the European Union

The TEU is strangely silent on this matter, and we are left to assume that the geographical scope of the Community as set out in the EC Treaty[170] applies to the Union as a whole.[171] However, Union law does not apply equally to all parts.

Union law applies in full to the European territory of all Member States,[172] albeit with some exceptions. It does not apply to the Faroe Islands (Denmark) or the Channel Islands and the Isle of Man (UK). Nor does it apply to the Sovereign Base Areas retained by the United Kingdom in Cyprus or, since the adoption of the Constitution of 1993, Andorra (Spain and France). It applies in principle to Gibraltar (UK), although significant parts of Union law, such as the common agricultural policy and the common customs tariff, do not apply. Upon its absorption into the Federal Republic of Germany on October 3, 1990, the former German Democratic Republic became part of the European Union, or the Community as it then was. Upon Finland's accession, Åland became part of the European Union.

Certain foreign territories of Member States belong fully to the European Union. These are the French overseas departments (Guadeloupe, Martinique, French Guyana, Réunion and St. Pierre and Miquelon), the Azores and Madeira (Portugal) and the Canary Islands, Ceuta and Melilla (Spain). Other foreign territories have an association arrangement with the Union covering commercial policy and investment. These are listed in Annex II to the EC Treaty.

Neither San Marino, Monaco or Vatican City are members of the European Union, although Monaco is part of the customs union.

For those who are fascinated by such trivia, the European Union comprises seven monarchies and eight republics. However, the new adherents will soon drown the Union in a sea of republics. This is not an inviting prospect for your author, who regards the French Revolution as the beginning of the end of European civilization.

II.3.6 Linguistic Régime of the European Union

As the hullabaloo over the entry of the Freedom Party into the Austrian government illustrated, the European Union places enormous emphasis on cultural and ethnic tolerance. If one reads the proceedings of the European Parliament, one can be forgiven for thinking that it has become something of an obsession. Certainly, the Union's linguistic régime testifies more to an obsessive desire to avoid discrimination than any notion of common sense.

---

170   Article 299 (ECT).

171   On this point, *see* Kapteyn and Verloren van Themaat (fn. 38) at page 93.

172   In some cases, of course, a Member State has an opt-out from some parts of Union law. For example, the United Kingdom and Denmark have an opt-out from the third stage of EMU.

The European Union functions in eleven official languages—Danish, Dutch, English, French, Finnish, German, Greek, Italian, Portuguese, Spanish and Swedish. Irish has semi-official status. In order to assure the functioning of the Union in all these languages, fifteen percent of the Commission's posts are required, one third of its budget and sixty percent of the budget of the European Parliament. To obtain an idea of the practical complexity of the problem, aside from its ruinous cost, simultaneous translation involving all official languages requires 110 linguistic combinations.[173]

One does not have to be a xenophobe to realize that the already heavy burden, both financial and administrative, imposed by the present linguistic diversity of the Union will become intolerable once Polish, Czech, Hungarian, Slovak, Slovenian, Estonian, Latvian, Lithuanian, Maltese, Turkish, Romanian and Bulgarian are added to the equation. Compared to the menace that such an influx of languages poses for future integration in Europe, the troublesome British are but an insignificant irritant.

In fact, the European Union, besotted with its own idealism, has already missed the boat and shows no signs of realizing it. As the South African statesman, Jan Smuts, once observed with great shrewdness in connection with the grant of dominion status to the British colonies, freedom once given cannot be taken away. So it is with language rights. If the Union had put its foot down at the time of the entry of Austria, Finland and Sweden, all was not yet lost. Now it is difficult to imagine the Union denying equal linguistic rights to new entrants, let alone rolling back the rights that already exist. Yet, if it does not want to drown in a sea of languages, it will somehow have to find the will to replace idealistic absurdity with common sense. One solution would be to eliminate languages that are not spoken by a certain minimum of people within the Union. If this minimum were set at 20 million, it would eliminate all languages but English, French, German, Italian and Spanish. Among the languages of the new adherents, only Polish would qualify.

II.3.7 Financial Arrangements in the European Union

The financial arrangements of the Union are complex, but here we are concerned only with the basic framework and the budget process.[174]

The budget is referred to in the Treaties as the Community budget, which is a misnomer as it includes almost all items of expenditure incurred by the Union, including those under the CFSP and PJC.[175] The expenses that are not included

---

173 Albeit in more measured tones, this problem is also invoked by Kapteyn and Verloren van Themaat (fn. 38) at page 107.

174 An excellent discussion of the finances of the Union is found in Kapteyn and Verloren van Themaat (fn. 38) at pages 344-389.

175 Article 268 (ECT).

are military and defense expenditures,[176] certain operational expenditures under the CFSP and PJC,[177] and expenditures involving the European Development Fund and the European Investment Bank. The Member States are responsible for expenditures under the CFSP and PJC that are not charged to the Union budget[178] as well as for most environmental measures.[179] Expenditure arising from closer cooperation is borne by the participating Member States unless the Council decides otherwise by unanimity.[180] The expenditures in the budget are usually authorized for one financial year, which runs from January 1 to December 31.[181] The structure of the budget is set down in the Financial Regulation of December 21, 1977, as amended.[182]

The revenue of the Union is provided by its own resources. This system was introduced in 1970 and assures the Union a certain financial independence. The matter is now regulated by Council Decision 00/597.[183] Article 2 of this Decision defines own resources as agricultural levies, customs duties, a percentage of the valued added tax levied by Member States and a percentage of the gross national product of Member States. The United Kingdom benefits from a reduction in its contributions to compensate for the disproportionately high amount that it would otherwise have to pay to the Union's budget.[184] The cost of this compensation is borne by the other Member States. However, Austria, Germany, the Netherlands and Sweden pay only one fourth of their normal share as they are also net contributors to the Union budget.[185]

The Union budget must be in balance and financed entirely by the Union's own resources.[186] Any proposal from the Commission to adopt, modify or implement a Union act must be accompanied by an assurance that the proposal can be financed within the limits of the Union's own resources.[187]

The introduction of the own resources system was accompanied by the First Budgetary Treaty (1970), which strengthened the role of the European Parliament in the budgetary process. Parliament's powers were further increased by the Second Budgetary Treaty (1975). The latter Treaty also introduced the dis-

---

176 Article 28(3) (TEU).
177 Articles 28(3) and 41(3) (TEU).
178 Articles 28(3) and 41(3) (TEU).
179 Article 175(4) (ECT).
180 Article 44(2) (TEU).
181 Articles 271 and 272(1) (ECT).
182 OJ L356/77.
183 OJ L253/00.
184 Council Decision 00/597, Article 4.
185 *Ibid,* Article 5(1).
186 Articles 268 and 269 (ECT).
187 Article 270 (ECT).

tinction between compulsory expenditure and non-compulsory expenditure. Compulsory expenditure is defined as "such expenditure as the budgetary authority is obliged to enter in the budget by virtue of a legal undertaking entered into under the Treaties or acts adopted by virtue of said Treaties".[188] All other expenditure is non-compulsory. Examples of compulsory expenditures are the common agricultural policy, expenditure resulting from international agreements, contributions to international organizations, wages, damages, the monetary reserve and the loan guarantee reserve.[189] Examples of non-compulsory expenditures are rural development measures, emergency aid reserve, the pre-accession structural instrument and the PHARE program for applicant countries.

The Commission establishes a preliminary draft budget on the basis of estimates from the various institutions and sends it to the Council no later than September 1.[190] The Council, acting by a qualified majority on the basis of the preliminary budget, adopts the draft budget and forwards it to the European Parliament no later than October 5. The Council can depart from the preliminary budget as long as it consults the Commission and the institutions concerned before doing so. This is the Council's First Reading.

If Parliament approves the draft by a simple majority or does not alter it within forty-five days, the budget is declared adopted by the President of the European Parliament.[191] This is a rare occurrence. Normally, Parliament makes use of its power to *adopt* amendments to the non-compulsory expenditures and *propose* modifications to the compulsory expenditures. In the first case it acts by an absolute majority, in the second by a simple majority. In both cases, it must act within forty-five days and forward its changes to the Council. This is Parliament's First Reading.

If within fifteen days the Council does not modify Parliament's amendments and accepts its modifications, the budget is declared adopted by the President of the European Parliament.[192] Acceptance of Parliament's modifications happens in one of two ways.[193] Modifications that do not increase the total compulsory expenditure of an institution are deemed accepted unless the Council rejects them within fifteen days. Modifications that increase the total compulsory expenditure of an institution must be accepted within fifteen days by the Council; otherwise they are deemed rejected. It is also open to the Council to amend any

---

188   Point 30 of the Interinstitutional Agreement of May 6, 1999 between the European Parliament, the Council and the Commission on budgetary discipline and improvement of the budgetary procedure, OJ C172/99.

189   The examples of compulsory and non-compulsory expenditure are taken from Annex IV to the Interinstitutional Agreement of May 6, 1999.

190   The budget procedure is set out in Articles 272 to 276 (ECT).

191   Article 272(4),(7) (ECT).

192   Article 272(5),(9) (ECT).

193   Article 272(5) (ECT).

of Parliament's modifications. In all these instances, the Council acts by a qualified majority. This is the Council's Second Reading.

Parliament has the last word over non-compulsory expenditures. If its amendments are modified by the Council, it may reject or modify the changes, acting by an absolute majority and three-fifths of the votes cast. On the other hand, if it disagrees with the Council's rejection or amendment of its modifications of compulsory expenditures, Parliament's only recourse it to reject the budget altogether, acting by an absolute majority and two-thirds of the votes cast. Where the budget is so rejected, the Treaty permits one-twelfth of the budget amount for the preceding year to be spent each month until a new budget is agreed.[194] The Council, acting by a qualified majority, may authorize expenditure in excess of this amount, in which case Parliament has thirty days in which to modify these excess expenditures. It acts by an absolute majority and three-fifths of the votes cast. If Parliament fails to reject the budget within fifteen days, it is declared adopted by the President of the European Parliament.[195] This is Parliament's Second Reading.

Article 272(9) of the EC Treaty provides for the Commission to fix a maximum annual rate of increase for non-compulsory expenditures on the basis of certain objective economic indicators. This rate of increase can be increased by agreement between the Council and Parliament. However, these provisions existed prior to the insertion into the EC Treaty of Article 269, requiring the Union budget to be financed wholly from own resources. This new provision made it necessary to establish a stricter budgetary discipline to make sure that the expenditures of the Union remained under the own resources ceiling. Thus the statutory procedure is complemented by the 1999 Interinstitutional Agreement between the European Parliament, the Council and the Commission,[196] which sets out for the years 2000-2006 the maximum amounts that can be spent in various areas each year. This includes both compulsory and non-compulsory expenditures. The three institutions agree to abide by these maximum amounts,[197] which may, however, be altered in the event of unforeseen circumstances as long as the own resources ceiling is not surpassed.[198] The Council and Parliament act on a proposal from the Commission.

The Agreement also sets up a procedure for collaboration between the institutions, consisting of a trialogue between all three and a conciliation procedure between Parliament and the Council.[199] The aim of both types of meeting is to

---

194   Article 273 (ECT).

195   Article 272(6),(7) (ECT).

196   OJ C172/99.

197   Point II of the Interinstitutional Agreement.

198   *Ibid*, Point 19.

199   *Ibid*, Annex III.

secure agreement on the budget between the three institutions, and in particular between Parliament and the Council. The first trialogue takes place before the Commission establishes the preliminary draft budget. A second trialogue occurs before the Council's First Reading. and is followed by conciliation afterwards. A third trialogue takes place before Parliament's First Reading and is followed by a fourth afterwards. The results of the fourth trialogue are discussed at a conciliation meeting held the day before the Council's Second Reading. After the Council's Second Reading, there is provision for continuing discussions on non-compulsory expenditure.

The above budget procedure applies to both expenditures under the EC Treaty and those occasioned by the CFSP and PJC that are charged to the Union budget.[200]

It is the responsibility of the Commission to implement the Union budget[201] and it must submit annual accounts and financial statements with respect to this implementation.[202] Parliament and the Council examine these documents together with the annual report of the Court of Auditors. If they are in order, Parliament, acting on a recommendation of the Council, grants the Commission a discharge on its implementation of the budget.[203]

II.3.8 The Concept of Union Loyalty

Article 10 of the EC Treaty places a general obligation on the Member States to observe three principles of loyalty towards the Community.[204] This general obligation is supplemented by a number of specific obligations on Member States scattered throughout the Treaty. In a way, these additional provisions are not necessary, but they clarify how the general principles apply to particular situations or policies.

The first principle is the duty of Member States to take all appropriate measures, whether general or particular, to ensure fulfillment of the obligations arising out of the Treaty or resulting from action taken by the institutions or bodies of the Community. There are five ways in which Member States fulfill this obligation:

a) They must ensure the effective application of Community law and policies. Specific provisions require them to conduct their economic and employment policies in accordance with Community objectives.[205] They must also comply

---

200   Articles 28(4) and 41(4) (TEU).

201   Article 274 (ECT).

202   Article 275 (ECT).

203   Article 276 (ECT).

204   The following discussion owes much to Kapteyn and Verloren van Themaat (fn. 38) at pages 148-162.

205   Article 98, 126(1) and 159 (ECT).

with judgments of the Court of Justice and see that their national central banks do likewise.[206] This obligation was reinforced by the TEU, which introduced a provision into the EC Treaty that Member States may be fined where they fail to comply with a judgment of the Court.[207] When the implementation of labor policy is entrusted to management and labor, the Member States must ensure that they act in time or implement the directives themselves.[208] Community decisions imposing pecuniary obligations must be enforced by Member States upon verification of the decision.[209] Member States must take the same measures to counter fraud affecting the financial interests of the Union as they take to protect their own financial interests.[210]

b) They must ensure the protection of rights in favor of natural and legal persons that flow from Community law. If they fail in this obligation, Member States may be liable in damages if the breach of Community law is sufficiently serious[211] and there is a direct causal link between the breach and the damage suffered by the injured party.[212]

c) They must act themselves to achieve objectives of the Treaty where Community action is not forthcoming. One way of doing this is to use their right to bring an action before the Court of Justice against other Member States that violate the Treaty or against Community institutions or bodies that fail to act.[213] In *Thieffry*, the Court even held that Member States have an obligation to accord mutual recognition to diplomas from other Member States in the absence of Community legislation on the topic.[214]

d) They must ensure the effective functioning of the Community institutions and bodies. Specific provisions on this point require them to accord the most extensive legal capacity to the Community as well as such privileges and immunities as are necessary for the performance of its tasks.[215]

e) They must act on the international scene in a way that accords with their obligations above. Specifically, the Treaty provides that they are bound by

---

206 Articles 228(1) and 237(d) (ECT).

207 Article 228(2) (ECT).

208 Article 137(4) (ECT).

209 Article 256 (ECT).

210 Article 280(2) (ECT).

211 Failure to implement a directive is generally considered a sufficiently serious breach—*see Dillenköffer et al v. Germany*, C-178/94, [1996] 3 CMLR 469.

212 *Francovich et al v Italy*, 9/90, [1993] 2 CMLR 66. The principle established in this case by the Court of Justice was confirmed and expanded in a series of cases, e.g. *R. v. H.M.Treasury, ex parte British Telecommunications plc*, 392/93, [1986] 2 CMLR 217; *Faccini Dori v. Recreb Srl*, C-91/92, [1994] ECR I-3325; *Dillenköffer*.

213 These actions are brought under Articles 227 and 232 (ECT), respectively.

214 *Thieffry v. Conseil de l'Ordre des Avocats à la Cour de Paris*, 71/76, [1977] ECR 761 at 777.

215 Articles 282 and 291 (ECT).

agreements concluded by the Community.[216] They must also eliminate incompatibilities with Community law in any agreements that they have concluded with third countries.[217]

Leaving aside for the moment the second principle, the third principle is the duty of Member States to abstain from any measure that could jeopardize the attainment of the objectives of the EC Treaty. Here too, we can separate out three aspects of the obligation:

a) Measures that could impede the effectiveness of Community law and policies. A specific example of this is the obligation upon Member States not to maintain in force measures in relation to monopolies that are contrary to Community law, particularly its anti-trust provisions.[218] Member States must also not submit a dispute concerning the EC Treaty to a non-Treaty method of settlement.[219]

b) Measures that could undermine the internal functioning of the institutions or bodies. One measure that could be considered to fall into this category is the decision by the Member States to split up the location of the European Parliament into three sites.[220]

c) Measures that hinder the Community's integration. Thus, if the Community is preparing a common approach to a matter, Member States should not introduce national measures.

The third principle is the obligation on Member States to facilitate the achievement of the Community's tasks. In a way, this obligation is contained within the other two and is redundant. If it means anything, it requires the Member States to act always in good faith towards the Community and its institutions and bodies.

It is noteworthy, and regrettable, that the general obligation of loyalty appears uniquely in the EC Treaty and thus only applies to Community matters. It would be more logical for this obligation to be placed in the TEU and to apply to the European Union as a whole. As it is, the TEU echoes the obligation but solely with respect to the CFSP.[221] It has two parts. The Member States are enjoined to support the Union's common policy actively and unreservedly in a spirit of loyalty and mutual solidarity and to refrain from any action that is contrary to the

---

216   Article 300(7) (ECT).

217   Article 307 (ECT).

218   Article 86(1) (ECT).

219   Article 292 (ECT).

220   Article (a) of the Protocol on the location of the seats of the institutions and of certain bodies and departments of the European Communities and of Europol, which is attached to the TEU and the EC Treaty. *See* the discussion of this ridiculous arrangement *infra* in Section III.3.4.a.

221   Article 11(2) (TEU).

interests of the Union or is likely to impair its effectiveness internationally. Specifically, joint actions commit all Member States.[222] Moreover, even where a Member State abstains from and opposes a decision in the area of the CFSP, it must honor the second part of the loyalty obligation.[223] No similar general obligations exist with respect to PJC. In both areas, however, the Member States must present a common front internationally and inform other Member States of any matter of common interest that arises in international conferences or organizations where not all Member States participate.[224] Member States that sit on the UN Security Council must uphold the positions and interests of the CFSP.[225]

The loyalty principle also applies to closer cooperation as Member States are prohibited from impeding its implementation by participating States.[226]

These loyalty obligations under the EC Treaty and the TEU go beyond the normal international obligation of *pacta sunt servanda*. Essentially, they are a statement of federal loyalty or *Bundestreue* as it is known in German jurisprudence.[227] Unlike the signatories of other international treaties, the Member States cannot take action within their areas of jurisdiction that conflicts with Union law or policies.[228] This federalist concept of Union loyalty also underpins the Court's development of the concept of the autonomy of the Union legal order.[229]

As a final point on this topic, it should be noted that the loyalty principle also applies to the Community. A Community institution or body whose act has been voided or whose failure to act has been established by the Court of Justice must take the necessary measures to comply with the judgment of the Court.[230] The Community must also combat fraud and other illegal activities affecting its financial interests.[231]

---

222 Article 14(3) (TEU).

223 Article 23(1) (TEU).

224 Articles 19 and 37 (TEU).

225 Article 19(2) (TEU). The United Kingdom and France are permanent members of the UN Security Council.

226 Article 43(2) (TEU).

227 *See* P. Hay, *Federalism and Supranational Organizations* (1966) at pages 194-197.

228 *See Commission v. France*, 6 & 11/69, [1969] ECR 523 at 540: "The exercise of reserved powers cannot therefore permit the unilateral adoption of measures prohibited by the Treaty."

229 *See* the discussion of this concept *infra* in Section IV.6.

230 Article 233 (ECT).

231 Article 280(1) (ECT).

II.4 Closer Cooperation[232]

II.4.1 Introduction

The Treaty of Amsterdam introduces the possibility for certain Member States to integrate more deeply than others by establishing closer cooperation between themselves to the exclusion of other, more reluctant Member States. In fact, the Treaty was regularizing and institutionalizing a practice that already existed. In 1985, a number of Member States signed the Schengen Agreement under which they agreed to do away with internal border controls. Eventually, all the Member States except Ireland and the United Kingdom signed up to this Agreement. A second example was the Social Agreement that was signed between all the Member States except the United Kingdom at Maastricht in 1992. The Labor government that was elected in the United Kingdom in 1997, however, accepted the Agreement and it is now incorporated into the EC Treaty.[233]

Closer cooperation is possible for matters coming within the scope of the EC Treaty and for PJC.[234] It is not available in the area of the CFSP.[235] Authorization for closer cooperation in EC matters is given by the Council acting by a qualified majority of sixty-two votes in favor on a proposal from the Commission and after consulting the European Parliament.[236] In the case of PJC, the procedure is slightly different. The Council grants the authorization at the request of the Member States concerned and after receiving the opinion of the Commission.[237] It acts by a qualified majority comprising sixty-two votes in favor cast by at least ten Member States. In both cases, a member of the Council can, as a safeguard to protect important and stated reasons of national policy, oppose the authorization being granted by a qualified majority. It is then up to the Council, acting by a qualified majority, to refer the matter to the European Council for a decision by unanimity. Other Member States have the right to join in closer cooperation at a later date.[238]

II.4.2. Conditions for Authorizing Closer Cooperation

In order to prevent a proliferation of closer cooperation arrangements and the reduction of the Union to a series of concentric circles of varying degrees of in-

---

232 The Treaty of Nice calls this "enhanced cooperation." The different nomenclature changes nothing.

233 Articles 136-145.

234 Articles 40(1) (TEU); 11(1) (ECT)

235 The Treaty of Nice permits enhanced cooperation in the CFSP with respect to the implementation of a joint action or a common position—*see* Article 1(6).

236 Article 11(2) (ECT).

237 Article 40(2) (TEU).

238 Articles 40(2) (TEU); 11(2) (ECT).

tegration, the authorization of closer cooperation is subject to a number of strict conditions. These are found in both the TEU and the EC Treaty.[239]

The TEU sets out general conditions that must be met by all closer cooperation arrangements. Thus, cooperation must:[240]

a) be aimed at furthering the objectives of the Union and at protecting and serving its interests;

b) respect the principles of the Union Treaties and the single institutional framework;

c) be used only as a last resort;

d) concern at least a majority of Member States; 8

e) not affect existing Union law;

f) not adversely affect non-participating Member States;

g) be open for all Member States to participate.

In the case of closer cooperation in the area of PJC, the TEU requires that it meet two additional conditions:[241]

a) it must respect the powers of the European Community and the objectives of PJC;

b) it must have the aim of enabling the Union to develop more rapidly into an area of freedom, security and justice.

For closer cooperation in EC matters, it is the EC Treaty that sets out the additional conditions that must be met. Thus, cooperation in the Community must:[242]

a) not concern areas that fall within the exclusive competence of the Community;

b) not affect Community policies, actions or programs;

c) not concern citizenship of the Union or discriminate between nationals of Member States;

d) remain within the limits of the Community's jurisdiction;

---

239 Under Articles 1(9)-(13) of the Treaty of Nice, the conditions under which enhanced cooperation can take place and the arrangements therefor are brought together in a number of provisions that are located in the TEU. It make only minor substantive changes. One of note is that enhanced cooperation now requires a minimum of eight Member States instead of a majority of them. This makes no difference in the present 15-member Union, but the change ensures greater flexibility as the Union expands its membership.

240 Article 43(1) (TEU). It is interesting that this Article does not maintain the distinction between "Union" and "Community" matters.

241 Article 40(1) (TEU).

242 Article 11(1) (ECT).

e) not constitute discrimination or a restriction of trade between Member States or distort the conditions of competition in the Community.

II.4.3 Procedure in Closer Cooperation

The acts and decisions that are necessary to establish closer cooperation are adopted pursuant to the relevant provisions of the Union Treaties and according to the procedures set out therein.[243] All Member States take part in the deliberations but only the participating Member States may vote. It will be necessary to adapt the number of votes needed for a qualified majority according to the votes represented by the participating Member States. Acts and decisions emanating from closer cooperation are part of formal Union law.[244]

Expenditure resulting from the implementation of closer cooperation, other than the administrative costs of the institutions, is borne by the participating Member States unless the Council, acting unanimously, decides otherwise.[245] Non-participating Member States must not impede the implementation of closer cooperation.[246]

One final point concerns the relationship between opt-outs and closer cooperation. The two are similar in that they both involve an arrangement in which not all Member States participate. For example, the United Kingdom and Ireland do not participate in the Schengen arrangement, which is an example of closer cooperation, and have also obtained an opt-out from Title IV of the EC Treaty,[247] which contains many elements of the Schengen arrangement. Nevertheless, there are major differences between the two concepts. A Member State must request and be accorded an opt-out whereas it can decide freely not to take part in closer cooperation. Opt-outs are granted only exceptionally and rarely involve more than two or three Member States; closer cooperation is also somewhat exceptional but the number of Member States not participating may be as high as seven. Finally, opt-outs are never available for new entrants, but this may not necessarily be the case with closer cooperation arrangements. It should be noted, however, that new entrants will be obliged to accept the Schengen arrangement.[248]

---

243   Article 44(1) (TEU).

244   *See* the discussions *infra* in Sections IV.2.2 and IV.3.1.

245   Article 44(2) (TEU).

246   Article 43(2) (TEU).

247   Articles I and 2 of the Protocol on the position of the United Kingdom and Ireland, which is attached to the TEU and the EC Treaty.

248   Article 8 of the Protocol integrating the Schengen *acquis* into the framework of the European Union, which is attached to the TEU and the EC Treaty.

II.4.4 An Example of Closer Cooperation: the Schengen Arrangement

The Schengen arrangement comprises the 1985 Schengen Agreement, the 1990 Schengen Convention, the Accession Agreements of other Member States joining the arrangement and the acts and decisions of the Executive Committee and its delegate organs.[249] The arrangement aims to abolish internal border controls within the Union and harmonize rules involving non-EU nationals, such as external border controls, visas and asylum. Much though not all of the Schengen arrangement is now incorporated into Title IV of the EC Treaty, but many anticipated measures do not have immediate effect. The arrangement still represents a greater degree of integration than the regular law of the Union.

As the United Kingdom and Ireland are not signatories to the Schengen arrangement, it was decided to continue it under the new provisions of the Union Treaties on closer cooperation.[250] Thus, the arrangement is now based on specific Articles of the Treaties and future acts and decisions will be adopted on the basis of these provisions by Union institutions.[251] Council Decision 99/436 determines the legal basis in the Treaties for each of the provisions that constitute the Schengen arrangement.[252] The Schengen Executive Committee is replaced by the Council,[253] and the Schengen Secretariat is integrated into the General Secretariat of the Council.[254]

---

249 *Ibid*, Annex.

250 *Ibid*, Preamble, 5th and 6th recitals (attached to the Treaty of Amsterdam).

251 *Ibid*, Articles 2(1) and 5(1).

252 OJ L176/99.

253 *Ibid*, Article 2(1).

254 Council Decision 99/307 (OJ L119/99).

CHAPTER III

THE BODIES AND INSTITUTIONS OF THE EUROPEAN UNION

III.1 The Single Institutional Structure of the European Union

Article 3 of the Treaty on European Union (TEU)[1] provides that the European Union is to be served by a single institutional structure. This is necessary to preserve consistency and continuity in the various activities of the Union, particularly between the common foreign and security policy (CFSP) and police and judicial cooperation in criminal matters (PJC) on the one hand and the activities carried on pursuant to the European Community (EC) Treaty[2] on the other. In this way, the essential unity of the Union is maintained.[3]

It has been suggested that the single institutional structure consists exclusively of the European Council,[4] but this is far too narrow a view. Certainly, the European Council has a broad authority to lend impetus to the development of the Union as a whole and to define the general political guidelines for its activities, which is a role that bridges the divide between the TEU and the EC Treaty. However, the institutions that are set up by the EC Treaty also operate within the TEU. They are given the general power to do so by Article 5 of that Treaty. In addition, there are other provisions in the TEU giving them the authority to do specific acts. The Council in particular is very active in the CFSP and PJC. The fact that the role of the other institutions is more limited in the TEU hardly permits us to disregard them altogether. They are definitely part of the single institutional structure of the Union together with the European Council.

---

1   [1992] 1 C.M.L.R. 573.

2   298 U.N.T.S. 11.

3   *See* the discussion *supra* in Section II.3.1.

4   *See* P.J.G. Kapteyn and P. Verloren van Themaat, *Introduction to the Law of the European Communities* (3rd edition by L.W.Gormley, 1998) at pages 49-50.

III.2 Institutions and Bodies

There are five institutions in the European Union: the European Parliament, the Council, the Commission, the Court of Justice and the Court of Auditors.[5] The last-named institution was added to the original four by the TEU. All other organs within the Union are called bodies.

Originally, there was a clear distinction between institutions and bodies of the Union. The former were endowed with the powers of state governance, executive, legislative or judicial. It is by them that the tasks of the Union were to be realized. Bodies, such as the Economic and Social Committee, merely assisted the institutions in carrying out their roles.

Subsequent developments have blurred this distinction. The European Council was created in 1974 and now exercises broad policy-making powers. The European Central Bank (ECB) came into existence on January 1st, 1999 and is responsible for the Union's monetary policy. Neither of these organs is an institution. Furthermore, many of the powers of the institutions are now exercised by bodies. The Administrative Commission on Social Security, for example, exercises the power of the Council and the Commission to apply the rules on social security. The Court of First Instance exercises some of the judicial powers of the Court of Justice. Given these developments, it really no longer makes sense to insist on the distinction. Thus, for the sake of simplicity, I refer to all organs that operate within the Union as bodies except where the institutions alone are concerned. It is, for example, only the institutions that have an untrammeled right to bring an action for failure to act under Article 232 of the EC Treaty[6] or which receive the annual report from the Court of Auditors.[7]

III.3 The Major Bodies of the European Union

III.3.1 The European Council

The European Council grew out of the summit conferences of the leaders of the Member States. It was set up at the Paris Summit in December 1974[8] and was formally recognized as a body of the Community, as it then was, in the SEA. It is now composed of the heads of state or government of the Member States[9] and the President of the Commission.[10] The leaders are assisted by their foreign

---

5   Article 7(1) (ECT).

6   This action is discussed *infra* in Section VI.4.2.b.iv.

7   Article 248(4) (ECT).

8   The then French President, Giscard d'Estaing, announced dramatically at the end of the summit: "Le sommet européen est mort. Vive le conseil européen!"

9   France and Finland are both represented by their President and Prime Minister.

10   Article 4 (TEU).

ministers and a member of the Commission.[11] In all, this makes thirty-two persons. The European Council has to convene twice a year but often meets on other occasions to consider urgent matters. It is chaired by the head of state or government of the Member State that holds the Presidency of the Council. No minutes are taken but the Presidency issues a set of conclusions at the end of the meeting. The European Council acts by consensus.

The European Council is clearly intergovernmental in character, but it did not arise from a desire to impose this type of decision-making on the Community. It arose in response to a need to take far-reaching decisions in order to advance the cause of European integration. The European Council meeting at Milan in June, 1985, for example, gave the impetus for the completion of the internal market, while the Madrid meeting in June 1989 cleared the way for progress towards economic and monetary union (EMU). This role of the European Council is recognized in the TEU, which stipulates that it "shall provide the Union with the necessary impetus for its development."[12]

The other major role of the European Council is to set general policy directions, sometimes even opening up new areas for action by the Union. It has been particularly active in the areas of energy, foreign commercial policy, technological cooperation, regional development and reform of the common agricultural policy. The TEU now formally gives the European Council the right to define the general political guidelines of the Union.[13] The European Council also has a specific role to play in policies involving the CFSP and employment.[14]

The European Council has also come to act as a form of appellate body to which the Council can send matters that it is unable to resolve. One particularly thorny issue that was transmitted to the European Council in this way was the question of the British contribution to the Union's budget, which was settled at the Fontainebleau meeting in June, 1984. This appellate role now appears in the Treaties in the safeguard mechanism, which permits a Member State to have certain matters sent from the Council to the European Council.[15]

The European Council is an overtly political body that fills a void in the Union structure by enabling the leaders of the Member States to implicate themselves directly in the affairs of the Union. This permits difficult problems to be resolved

---

11 The presence of the foreign ministers is due in large part to the fact that, in some Member States, their presence at international meetings is a constitutional obligation.

12 Article 4 (TEU).

13 Article 4 (TEU).

14 Articles 13(1) (TEU); 128(1) (ECT).

15 See Articles 23(2) and 40(2) (TEU); 11(2) (ECT). The safeguard mechanism is discussed *infra* in Section V.2.1.d.iv.

at the highest political level.[16] The European Council does not, however, interfere with the regular decision-making processes of the Union. It has never adopted subordinate acts itself but has left this up to the appropriate Union bodies. This is not strictly necessary as, although the European Council has no authority *qua* European Council to adopt subordinate acts, it could do so *qua* Council of the European Union. The heads of state or government may represent the Member States in the Council and the presence of the two Commission representatives is also in order.[17] The latter may not, however, vote in Council meetings.

The European Council has been quite widely criticized. This criticism is centered on three points. Firstly, the decisions taken by the European Council are often the result of hard bargaining between the leaders and obviously comprise certain trade-offs between the various national interests. As a result, they are sometimes ill-conceived or, at the very least, incoherent, and it is left up to the Union institutions to make sense of them. This criticism is valid as far it goes, but it is perhaps better to have to make sense of a solution to a problem than having no solution at all. A second criticism is that there is no mechanism for following up on the decisions of the European Council so that sometimes they fall by the wayside. This is true, but the fault must be shared by the Union institutions, who could do the follow-up if they wished. Finally, it is said that the European Council has usurped the Commission's role as the initiator of Union action. There is some truth in this assertion, but overall the criticism is invalid. In the first place, the rise of the European Council was due in large part to the inability of the Commission to come up with news ideas to advance European integration.[18] Secondly, the European Council is mainly concerned with policy, where the Commission's initiatory role is in any case much narrower.[19] Thirdly, the European Council includes in its membership the President of the Commission and a Commissioner. In this way, the influence of the Commission is brought to bear directly on the leaders of the Member States.

---

16   D. Rometsch and W. Wessels, "The Commission and the Council of Ministers" in G. Edwards and D. Spence (eds.), *The European Commission* (1994) at page 219 point out pertinently that "[o]nly Heads of Government can take decisions which might combine economic, social, environmental, foreign, budgetary and institutional issues."

17   *See* the discussion *infra* in Section III.3.2.a.

18   G. Edwards and D. Spence, "The Commission in Perspective," in G. Edwards and D. Spence (eds.), *The European Commission* (1994) at page 2 put it this bluntly: "The Commission appeared able only to propose meaningless and unacceptable measures of harmonization."

19   *See* the discussion on the Commission's initiatory role in Section V.1.2.

III.3.2 The Council of the European Union[20]

III.3.2.a The Council

The Council is the major legislative and executive organ of the European Union.[21] It may act in the legislative sphere on the initiative of the Commission and share its power under Co-Decision with the European Parliament, but it is nonetheless a dominant actor. It shares executive power with the Commission, the ECB and Parliament but again it is dominant. The Council's executive power covers such important areas as economic policy, the conclusion of international agreements, the CFSP and PJC. It also shares budgetary authority with Parliament.[22]

The Council is made up of a representative of each Member State.[23] Governments of Member States are free to send whomever they wish as long as it is a minister with the authority to commit them.[24] Sometimes, the Council meets in the composition of heads of state or government, and it is required to do so in some instances.[25] The chair or Presidency of the Council is held by each Member State in turn for a period of six months.[26] The Commission is normally represented at meetings of the Council as is the ECB where the Council is considering a matter that it has initiated, but both can be excluded.[27] They have no vote.

The Council is a single body but the practice is for different sets of ministers to meet in separate configurations within their areas of competence. These configurations are: General Affairs, Agriculture, Economic and Finance Affairs, Environment, Transport and Telecommunications, Employment and Social Policy, Fisheries, Industry and Energy, Justice, Home Affairs and Civil Protection, Internal Market, Consumer Affairs and Tourism, Research, Budget, Culture, Development, Education and Youth Affairs and Health. The most important formation is the General Affairs Council, which supervises the other Councils. It meets, like the Economic and Finance and Agriculture Councils, at least once a month. Other less important Councils, such as that for culture, may meet as little as

---

20 The Council changed its name from the Council of the European Communities to the Council of the European Union by virtue of Council Decision 93/591 (OJ L281/93).

21 *See* the discussions on the Council's competences *infra* in Sections V.1.1.

22 The budgetary procedure is discussed *supra* in Section II.3.7.

23 Article 203 (ECT).

24 *See* Point C of the Annex to the Follow-Up to the Helsinki European Council, OJ C174/00.

25 Articles 7(1) (TEU); 121(4) and 122(2) (ECT). These provisions have to do with a finding of a breach of fundamental rights by a Member State and entry into the third stage of EMU.

26 The order in which the Presidency is held is set out in Council Decision 95/2 (OJ L1/95).

27 Article 5(2) of the Rules of Procedure of the Council, which are contained in Council Decision 00/396 (OJ L149/00), as amended by Council Decision 01/216 (OJ L81/01).

twice a year.[28] The Council in all its configurations meets in Brussels except in the months of April, June and October when it meets in Luxembourg.[29] The Council or the Committee of Permanent Representatives (Coreper)[30] may, in exceptional circumstances, decide to hold a Council meeting elsewhere.

The agenda of Council meetings is divided into "A" and "B" items.[31] "A" items are intended for approval without discussion although members of the Council or the Commission may express an opinion on them and have statements included in the minutes. "A" items must be withdrawn from the agenda at the request of a member of the Council or the Commission or if it appears that further discussion is necessary, unless the Council decides otherwise.[32] They are then referred back to Coreper. "B" items are those on which agreement is unlikely; they are included more in order to elucidate the differences dividing the members of the Council. They are invariably sent back to Coreper for more discussion so that eventually they may end up as an "A" item on the Council's agenda.

The Council is not obliged to vote in its meetings and may adopt its decisions by consensus.[33] Many "A" items and other non-controversial decisions are adopted in this way. Where a formal vote takes place, the matter is decided by a simple majority, a qualified majority or unanimity.[34] The Presidency votes. Urgent matters may be decided by a written vote at the proposal of the Presidency or on the initiative of the Council as a whole.[35] All members must agree and, where the written vote is on a matter that the Commission has brought before the Council, the Commission must agree also.[36] Measures implementing the CFSP may be adopted by another simplified written procedure unless a member of the Council objects to its use.[37] The proposal for a measure is deemed to be

---

28   The formations were newly reconfigured by the Follow-Up to the Helsinki European Council. The result is not entirely felicitous. One might ask why transport and telecommunications or the internal market and consumer affairs are put together while culture, which is a relatively unimportant area of Council activity, has its own formation. The French and Danish governments included statements in the document making just this criticism.

29   Article 1(3) of the Council's RoP. *See* also the Protocol on the location of the seats of the institutions and certain bodies and departments of the European Communities and of Europol, which is annexed to the Treaties.

30   Coreper is discussed *infra* in Section III.3.2.b.

31   Article 3(7) of the Council's RoP.

32   Article 3(8) of the Council's RoP.

33   This is the effect of Article 11 of the Council's RoP.

34   The voting rules for the Council are discussed *infra* in Section V.2.1.

35   Article 12(1) of the Council's RoP.

36   Article 12(2) of the Council's RoP.

37   Article 12(4) of the Council's RoP.

adopted at the end of the period laid down by the Presidency except where a member of the Council objects. A similar procedure exists for decisions to undertake the mandatory consultation of Union bodies.[38]

As a general rule, Council meetings are held in private.[39] However, the Councils for General Affairs and Economic and Financial Affairs are obliged to hold a public policy debate every six months on the work program of the current Presidency of the Council and possibly on the Commission's annual work program as well.[40] The Council or Coreper may decide that the Council should hold at least one other public debate on important new legislative proposals.[41] Public debates may even be held on a case-by-case basis if the Council or Coreper so decide.

The transparency of the Council's work is further increased by the rules on voting and access to documents. Under the EC Treaty, the Council must make public the results of votes and explanations of votes as well as the statements in the minutes of the meeting when it acts in a legislative capacity.[42] In its Rules of Procedure, the Council has extended this obligation to the adoption of common positions under the Co-Decision and Cooperation Procedures and the decisions of Council representatives on the Conciliation Committee.[43] However, in these latter cases, the statements in the minutes do not have to be made public. Other decisions, including some relating to the CFSP and PJC, may also be covered by the obligation if the Council so decides.[44] The Council is also obliged by the EC Treaty to set out the conditions under which the public may have access to its documents, which it has done.[45]

---

38   Article 12(5) of the Council's RoP.

39   Article 5(1) of the Council's RoP.

40   Article 8(1) of the Council's RoP.

41   Article 8(2) of the Council's RoP. Given the lack of distinction that is made between executive and legislative acts of the Union (*see* the discussion *infra* in Section IV.2.1), this provision is probably not restricted to legislative proposals.

42   Article 207(3) (ECT). The Council has defined this as meaning when it adopts rules that are legally binding—Article 7 of its RoP. For a discussion of this definition, see the discussions *infra* in Sections IV.2.1 and VI.1.

43   Article 9(1) of the Council's RoP. These procedures and the Conciliation Committee are discussed *infra* in Section V.3.2.

44   Article 9(3) of the Council's RoP.

45   *See* Council Decisions 93/731 (OJ L340/93), as amended by Council Decisions 96/705 (OJ L325/96) and 00/527 (OJ L212/00), and 01/320 (OJ L111/01); EP/Council Regulation 1049/01 (OJ L145/01).

III.3.2.b The Preparation of Council Meetings

The work of the Council is prepared by Coreper and its dependent groups.[46] Coreper meets in two different formations, one consisting of the Ambassadors of the Member States to the European Union (Coreper II) and the other of the Deputy Permanent Representatives (Coreper I). Although each acts autonomously within the areas that fall within its competence, Coreper II is naturally the senior body. It deals with the more politically sensitive areas, such as external affairs and financial services, leaving to Coreper I those areas where the problems are more technical in nature, such as the internal market and transport. Commission officials participate in meetings of Coreper, which is chaired by the representative of the Member State holding the Presidency of the Council.[47]

All matters that are destined for the attention of the Council are examined first by Coreper except in the case of particularly urgent matters where the Council may decide to deal with them directly.[48] Ideally, the task of Coreper to reach agreement so that the matter may be submitted as an "A" item to the Council. Of course, this is not always possible and so, in practice, there is a dialogue between the Council and Coreper until a solution is found. Where agreement is impossible, the matter is shelved or submitted to a special ad hoc group. In 1989, for instance, the Spanish Presidency set up a group to examine the thorny issue of the removal of tax barriers after all attempts to find a compromise solution had failed. A particular responsibility of Coreper is to ensure that Union acts are consistent with the principles of the attribution of powers, subsidiarity and proportionality.[49]

Coreper is assisted in its task by committees and working parties. There are about 250 of these groups in existence, both standing and ad hoc. They are composed of desk officers from the Permanent Representations and national functionaries. Both act under instructions from their governments. Commission officials normally participate as well. The task of these groups is to undertake the preliminary examination of a dossier on behalf of Coreper with a view to settling the technical details. Coreper then seeks to iron out the political differences between the Member States on the basis of the group's conclusions.

---

46 Articles 207(1) (ECT); 19(1) of the Council's RoP. This committee was regarded with great suspicion at its inception. European enthusiasts from Germany were fond of calling it the *Kommission der ständigen Verräter* (Committee of Permanent Traitors) rather than its correct name in German, *Kommission der ständigen Vertreter*.

47 Article 19(4) of the Council's RoP.

48 Article 19(2) of the Council's RoP.

49 Article 19(1)(a) of the Council's RoP. These principles are discussed *infra* in Section IV.1.3.

Various other bodies are also involved in the preparation of the Council's work. There is the Coordinating Committee (the K4 Committee[50]) for matters coming within PJC,[51] the Political and Security Committee for the CFSP,[52] the Economic and Financial Committee for some financial matters and EMU[53] and the Special Committee for Agriculture for the common agricultural policy. The K4 Committee and the Political and Security Committee are composed exclusively of senior officials from the Member States. The other two contain representatives of the Commission. The exact relationship between these bodies and Coreper has never been clearly established. In view of the Treaty provisions, which stipulate that these bodies operate without prejudice to Article 207 of the EC Treaty setting up Coreper, it might be thought that they are subordinate to Coreper, but this is disputed.[54] In fact, the relationship between them and Coreper is uneasy, particular as concerns the K4 Committee.

III.3.2.c The Presidency

The complex, multi-tiered organization that makes up what is collectively called 'the Council" is under the control of the Presidency of the Council. It is the Presidency's responsibility to organize and coordinate the work of the various Councils, Coreper with its various groups and the other Committees that prepare the work of the Council. Unless the Council decides otherwise, all groups and Committees are chaired by a representative from the Member State holding the Presidency.[55] It is also up to the Presidency to set the number and dates of Council meetings at all levels and to convene them.[56] The dates for meetings are supposed to be set seven months in advance, but in practice they are rarely finalized until just before a Member State commences its Presidency. The Presidency also sets the agenda of Council meetings.[57] Although Member States and the Commission can also request the inclusion of an item on the agenda,[58] they normally leave the Presidency a relatively free hand. This enables the Presidency to determine in which areas the Council will attempt to make progress during its six months.

---

50   So called after the original article of the TEU that set it up.

51   Article 36 (TEU).

52   Article 25 of the TEU sets up a Political Committee to carry out this role. The Political and Security Committee was set up by Council Decision 01/78 (OJ L27/01) as a formation within the Political Committee, but it essentially takes over the latter's role—*see* the discussion *infra* in Section III.4.3.

53   Article 114(2) (ECT).

54   *See* M. Westlake, *The Council of the European Union* (1995) at page 220.

55   Article 19(4) of the Council's RoP.

56   Article 1(1),(2) of the Council's RoP.

57   Article 3(1) of the Council' RoP.

58   Article 3(2) of the Council's RoP.

The Presidency thus plays a pivotal role in the Council's work and direction. An efficient Presidency like that of the first Spanish Presidency in 1989 can do much to ensure that progress is made; a weak Presidency like that of France in 2000 can paralyze the Union. One problem that is always present is the length of the Presidency, which is perhaps too short and discourages long-term planning. There have been various suggestions for reform,[59] such as restricting the Presidency to the larger Member States or combining this solution with regional Presidencies for the smaller states. Another possibility is a permanent executive body, which might be possible in conjunction with a more radical reform of the Council.[60] None of these suggestions have even been seriously taken up.

The Presidency is assisted in its task by a General Secretariat, which administers the Council and provides it with legal, linguistic, administrative and policy support. It is headed by a Secretary-General, but as this position is combined with that of High Representative for the CFSP, the Deputy Secretary-General is responsible for running the General Secretariat.[61] The Secretariat's support services are divided into ten Directorates-General and a Legal Service.

III.3.2.d The Council as a Union Institution

The Council is the body through which the Member States exert their control over the executive and legislative powers of state governance in the European Union. It is nevertheless a Union institution and, as such, subject to the loyalty principle vis-à-vis the Union.[62] Its acts are Union acts, not international agreements between the Member States. This Union status is underlined by the terminology of the Treaties and the Council's Rules of Procedure. They do not refer to the Member States sitting in the Council but to the *members* of the Council. However, it is also true that these members are representatives of the Member States who do the will of their governments.

There are, however, some more concrete factors, apart from terminology, that influence the Council towards a more Union orientation. In the first place, it can act in many instances only on a proposal from the Commission or, occasionally, some other Union body.[63] This is particularly so for legislative acts. Moreover, the Commission can withdraw its proposals if the Council changes them in a way that it considers unacceptable. Secondly, the Council acts under Co-Decision jointly with the European Parliament and needs Parliament's approval under the Cooperation and Assent Procedures. These two factors mean that the Council cannot disregard the views of two institutions that are very

---

59   *See The Economist*, January 11, 1992 at page 48.

60   *See* the discussion *infra* in Section VI.5.3.

61   Article 207(2) (ECT).

62   *See* the discussion *supra* at the end of Section II.3.8.

63   The right of initiative is discussed *infra* in Section V.1.2.

Union-minded. Then, there is the widespread use of majority voting, which means that the Council does not have to satisfy the national interest of every Member State and so come up with a decision that represents the lowest common denominator in terms of Union integration. Finally, there is the impetus of the process of economic integration itself, which has gathered great speed since the completion, more or less, of the internal market and EMU. The development of the Union has thereby acquired a dynamism of its own, and the Council has little choice but to continue further along the same path. Progress on the economic front has also had political repercussions with the adoption of a common European security and defense policy (CESDP).

None of all this means that national interests do not continue to be at the center of the Council's deliberations, but they alone can no longer determine the outcome. To this extent, we may say the Council acts like a Union institution.

III.3.3 The Commission of the European Communities

III.3.3.a The Commission

The Commission has no legislative role but is an important executive organ of the European Union.[64] It is primarily responsible for the adoption of tertiary acts implementing the secondary acts of the Council, adopts the preliminary draft budget, provides technical and statistical support during the budgetary process and implements the budget, negotiates international agreements and ensures the observance and application of Union law. Another crucial aspect of its executive power is the right of initiative,[65] particularly with respect to legislative acts under the EC Treaty. It also plays an important mediating role between the Member States, the Council and the European Parliament.

The Commission is a collegiate body consisting of 20 members, all of whom must be citizens of the European Union.[66] They serve for renewable terms of five years.[67] Each Member State has a right to one Commissioner and, by convention, the larger Member States (France, Germany, Italy, Spain and the United Kingdom) furnish two Commissioners each. Although, as we shall see, the Commissioners are appointed essentially by the Member States, they are obliged to be completely independent in the performance of their duties.[68] Member States undertake to respect this principle, which, as a general rule, they do. Commissioners may not combine their position as members of the Commission with any other activity, lucrative or not. They may not be MEPs. The Commission is

---

64   *See* the discussions *infra* in Sections V.1.1., VI.2.2. and VI.3.
65   This right is discussed *infra* in Section V.1.2.
66   Article 213(1) (ECT).
67   Article 214(1) (ECT).
68   Article 213(2) (ECT).

chaired by its President, who is nominated separately from the other Commissioners. It has the right to elect one or two Vice-Presidents from among its members.[69] The Commission is based mainly in Brussels but some departments are located in Luxembourg.

At present, the manner of appointing the Commission comprises the following steps:

1st stage: The Member States nominate by common accord the person whom they wish to appoint as President of the Commission. No Union body is involved in this decision but, as Parliament must approve the choice, one might have thought that it would be closely consulted. This has not been the case.

2nd stage: The nominee for President must make a statement and present his political program to Parliament.[70] Parliament then approves or rejects the nomination by a simple majority. If the nominee is rejected, the Member States must nominate someone else and the process is repeated.[71] This has never happened.

3rd stage: The Member States now draw up a list of people they wish to appoint as members of the Commission. Member States do not interfere with each other's choices. They are supposed to work in conjunction with the nominee for President, but it is still very much the Member States that make the decisions. At the very most, the nominee has a power of veto.

4th stage: The individual Commissioners appear at public hearings before the parliamentary committee that is appropriate to their portfolio.[72] Then, the Commissioners and their program are presented by the President-elect of the Commission to the whole Parliament.[73] After a debate, Parliament votes by a simple majority whether to elect or reject the Commission.[74] If the Commission is rejected, the Member States and the President-elect must present a new list of names to Parliament and the process is repeated. Parliament cannot reject individual Commissioners, but this accords with national practice in parliamentary countries where the government is approved *in toto* or not at all.[75]

---

69   Article 217 (ECT).

70   Rule 23(1) of the Consolidated version of the Rules of Procedure of the European Parliament (14th ed., OJ L202/99), as amended by OJ L189/00.

71   EP RoP, 33(2).

72   EP RoP, 33(1).

73   EP RoP, 33(3).

74   EP RoP, 33(4).

75   As to whether the European Union can be considered to have a parliamentary system, *see* the discussion *infra* in Section VI.5.3.

Commissioners that no longer fulfill the conditions required for the performance of their duties (e.g. independence, Union citizenship, no other occupation) or who are guilty of serious misconduct may, on the application of the Council or the Commission, be dismissed by the Court of Justice.[76]

The Commission operates under the political guidance of its President.[77] The Commission's Rules of Procedure define this as meaning that its priorities and annual work program must comply with the political guidelines laid down by the President.[78] The EC Treaty is silent on the matter, but, under the previous Rules, the allocation of areas of responsibility or portfolios to the individual Commissioners was done by consensus although the President played a decisive role. It was also subject to lobbying by some Member States. A declaration appended to the Treaty of Amsterdam calls for the President to be given broad discretion in the allocation of portfolios as well as the ability to reshuffle them during a Commission's term of office.[79] The present Rules of Procedure give these powers to the President of the Commission,[80] but the matter is not completely settled. What is clear is that the President has no power to dismiss a Commissioner.[81] It is equally clear that with one vote out of twenty, the President must rely on persuasion if he or she wishes to have proposals adopted by the Commission.

The Commission is under the ultimate control of Parliament, which can force its collective resignation by passing a vote of censure.[82] Parliament must act by an

---

76   Article 216 (ECT).

77   Article 219(ECT).

78   Article 2 of the Commission's Rules of Procedure (OJ L308/00).

79   The present allocation of portfolios is: President Romano Prodi (Italy) (Secretariat General, Legal Service and Press and Communication Service), Vice-President Neil Kinnock (UK) (Personnel and Administration, Inspectorate General, Joint Interpreting and Conference Service and Translation Service), Vice-President Loyola de Palacio (Spain), (Transport, Energy and Relations with Parliament), Michel Barnier (France) (Regional Policy), Frits Bolkenstein (Netherlands) (Internal Market and Taxation and Customs Union), Philippe Busquin (Belgium) (Research and Joint Research Center), David Byrne (Ireland) (Health and Consumer Protection), Anna Diamantopolou (Greece) (Employment and Social Affairs), Franz Fischler (Austria) (Agriculture and Fisheries), Pascal Lamy (France) (Trade), Erki Liikanen (Finland) (Enterprise and Information Society), Mario Monti (Italy) (Competition), Poul Nielson (Denmark) (Development and Humanitarian Aid), Chris Patten (UK) (External Relations), Viviane Reding (Luxembourg) (Citizens' Europe, Education and Culture), Michaele Schreyer (Germany) (Budget, Financial Control and Fraud Prevention), Pedro Solbes Mira (Spain) (Economic and Financial Affairs, Eurostat), Günther Verheugen (Germany) (Enlargement and Relations with Central and Eastern European Countries), Antonio Vitorino (Portugal) (Justice and Home Affairs) and Margot Wallström (Sweden) (Environment).

80   Article 3 of the Commission's RoP.

81   Under Article 2(24) of the proposed Treaty of Nice, the President is given the formal power to allocate and reshuffle portfolios and to dismiss Commissioners with the approval of a majority of the Commission.

82   Article 201 (ECT); EP RoP, 34.

absolute majority and a majority of two-thirds of the votes cast. Because of the serious repercussions it can have, a motion of censure cannot be voted on by Parliament until at least three days after it has been tabled. The vote must be open. A motion of censure has never been passed, but the Santer Commission resigned in March 1999 in the face of a virtual certainty that this would happen.[83]

As a general rule, the Commission meets every Wednesday and on other occasions when this is necessary.[84] The President convenes the meetings and adopts the agenda, although individual Commissioners may add items.[85] As with the Council, the Commission's agenda is divided into "A" points and "B" points. "A" points are intended for quick adoption but any Commissioner may open up a discussion on them. Before proposals may come before the Commission, they must be vetted by the Legal Service department to make sure that they are compatible with the Treaties. This includes verifying that they respect the principles of attribution of powers, subsidiarity and proportionality.[86] The Commission does not meet in public. However, like the Council, it has adopted a decision facilitating public access to its documents.[87]

The Commission normally acts by consensus but a vote may be taken upon the request of a member.[88] Proposals are adopted by an absolute majority of the Commissioners[89] but this is considered to be a collective act of the entire Commission.[90] The President votes. Routine, non-controversial and urgent matters may be decided by a written procedure with the agreement of the Directorate-General[91] from which the proposal emanates and the endorsement of the Legal Service.[92] Under this procedure, the text of the proposal is circulated to all members of the Commission and, if no Commissioner objects within the time limit set for the purpose, the proposal stands adopted. The Commission may also empower one or more Commissioners to adopt routine management and administrative measures on its behalf subject to any restrictions and conditions that it might impose.[93] Powers conferred in this way on Commissioners

---

83 This incident is described *supra* in Section I.4.1.

84 Article 5 of the Commission's RoP.

85 Article 6 of the Commission's RoP.

86 Article 21 of the Commission's RoP. These principles are discussed *infra* in Section IV.1.3.

87 Commission Decision 94/90 (OJ L46/94), as amended by Commission Decision 96/567 (OJ L247/96).

88 Article 8 of the Commission's RoP.

89 *See* the discussion *infra* of voting procedures in the Commission in Section V.2.2.

90 Article 1 of the Commission's RoP.

91 Directorates-General are discussed *infra*.

92 Article 12 of the Commission's Rules of Procedure.

93 Article 13 of the Commission's RoP.

may be sub-delegated to Directors-General and Heads of Service or delegated to them directly by the Commission.[94] Empowerment and delegation must respect the principle of collective responsibility of the Commission.

The Commission is assisted by a Secretariat-General. It comprises six Directorates and is managed by a Secretary-General.[95]

III.3.3.b The Preparation of Commission Meetings

The work of the Commission is prepared in the first instance by what is called "the Services." These consist of 24 Directorates-General for the various fields of the Union's activities[96] and 11 specialized departments, including the important Legal and Translation Services. Each of them is headed by a Commissioner, although many share a Commissioner. For example, the Directorates-General for the Internal Market and Tax and Customs are both headed by Frits Bolkenstein. It is from the Services that all proposals emanate.

Each Commissioner has a cabinet of around six members, one of which must come from a different Member State to the Commissioner. The head of the cabinet is called the chef de cabinet.[97] These cabinets act as a liaison with other Commissioners and with the Directorates-General and specialized services under the control of their Commissioner as well as with members of the Permanent Representation of the Member States.

Every proposal from the Services comes first to the cabinet of the appropriate Commissioner. It is then discussed at a technical level in a meeting of members of the cabinets who have responsibility for the area which the proposal concerns. This is called the Special Chefs Meeting (SCM),[98] and there can be a number of these every week on various proposals. In this way, the requirement under the Rules of Procedure is met that other Directorates-General and the Legal Service must be consulted on a proposal before it comes before the Commission.[99] The SCM is chaired by the member from the President's cabinet. The conclusions of the SCM are laid before the Monday meeting of the chefs de cabinet, which is chaired by the Secretary-General of the Commission. The job of the Chefs de Cabinet Meeting is to achieve consensus on a proposal so that it can be submit-

---

94   Articles 13 and 14 of the Commission's RoP.

95   Article 17 of the Commission's RoP.

96   The Directorates-General used to have Roman numerals to designate them. Now, unfortunately, they are known only by the field that they occupy.

97   This is one of the many French expressions that permeate Union jargon. The practice now is not to italicize them.

98   Interestingly, in view of my earlier comments on the linguistic regime of the European Union, these meetings are conducted in three languages only: English, French and German.

99   Article 21 of the Commission's RoP.

ted to the Wednesday meeting of the Commission as an "A" point. This system of funneling proposals from the Services through the cabinets of the Commissioners has caused some friction between these two levels of bureaucracy.

III.3.3.c The Importance of the Commission

The Commission has been called the motor of European integration,[100] and although at times in its history it has not shown itself up to the task, this is in essence true. It is, according to Jacques Delors, the guarantor of the integration process and a custodian of the Union's interests.[101] This role is contained within the primary responsibility it has under the EC Treaty to ensure that Union law is applied.[102] The independence of its members and the various executive powers it has under the Treaties, in particular the right of initiative in legislative matters, enable it carry out this supranational task. Together with the European Parliament, it constitutes the Union antidote to the national interests that often sway the Council and doubtless influence the European Council as well. At the same time, the Commission is bound by the obligation imposed by Article 6(3) of the TEU to respect the identities of the Member States. As one scholar has put it, an essential part of the Commission's role also consists in reconciling the concerns of the different Member States in a way that serves the Union and isolates no one or group of states.[103] As mediator between the Member States, the Council and Parliament, the Commission has played this role well.

III.3.4 The European Parliament

III.3.4.a The European Parliament

The Assembly, as the European Parliament was originally called, had few powers. It was accorded only a consultative role in some legislative and executive acts of the Council and had the right to pass a vote of censure on the Commission. Its members were seconded from national parliaments and had little credibility. The change of name to *European Parliament* in 1962[104] was the first step in Parliament's campaign to wield more influence within the Union, and the adoption in 1976 of the act providing for the election of Members of the European Parliament (MEPs) by direct universal suffrage[105] gave substance to its claims.

---

100 *See* the discussion in G. Edwards and D. Spence (fn. 18) at pages 15-19.

101 EC Bulletin, 1987.

102 Article 211 (ECT).

103 R Marjolin, *Memoirs 1911-86: Architect of European Unity* (1989) at page 314.

104 This name was not formally recognized until the advent of the Single European Act in 1986.

105 Act concerning the Election of the Representatives of the European Parliament by Direct Universal Suffrage (1976) (OJ L278/76), as amended by Article 5 of the Treaty of Amsterdam.

The European Parliament now shares legislative, budgetary and, in some cases, executive power with the Council while retaining its original consultative powers.[106] Its own executive powers have been extended and are now quite important. In addition to the motion of censure on the Commission,[107] it approves the nomination of the Commission,[108] sets up temporary committees of enquiry,[109] appoints the Ombudsman[110] and grants the Commission a discharge on its implementation of the budget.[111] It may also request the Commission to submit proposals for a Union act.[112] In sum, it has to a relatively large extent attained the stature of a normal legislature.

The European Parliament comprises 626 members who are elected directly in each Member State by universal suffrage. However, there is as yet no uniform electoral procedure. The number of seats that is allotted to each Member State is based roughly on population. The present allotment is as follows:[113]

Germany	99
France	87
Italy	87
United Kingdom	87
Spain	64
Netherlands	31
Belgium	25
Greece	25
Portugal	25
Sweden	22
Austria	21
Denmark	16
Finland	16
Ireland	15
Luxembourg	6

626 > 732

↓

Bulgaria 17

Romania 33

The numbers are more equitable that they used to be, but they are far from perfect. It still takes 830,000 votes to elect one MEP in Germany as opposed to 660,000 for Italy and 70,000 for Luxembourg.

---

106   For discussions of Parliament's various powers, *see infra* in Chapters V and VI.

107   Article 201 (ECT).

108   Article 214(2) (ECT).

109   Article 193 (ECT).

110   Article 195(1) (ECT).

111   Article 276(1) (ECT).

112   Article 192 (ECT).

113   Article 190(2) (ECT).

The European Parliament is elected for a fixed term of five years, which may be extended or curtailed by one month by a decision of the Council.[114] Parliament cannot be dissolved before its term has ended. The first election took place in June 1979 and the subsequent five elections have also been held in June. MEPs must exercise their mandate independently and accept no binding instructions.[115] They are representatives and not delegates and may be re-elected. The office of MEP is incompatible with that of a minister in the government of a Member State, a member of the Commission or a Union court and certain other Union positions.[116] If a MEP accepts any such office, his or her seat becomes vacant. MEPs may be members of their national legislatures.[117]

MEPs may form political parties.[118] These groups cross over national boundaries, a phenomenon that is encouraged by Parliament's Rules of Procedure, which require that a political group must comprises MEPs from more than one Member State.[119] Moreover, the minimum number of MEPs required to form a political group is reduced as more Member States are involved. Twenty-three are needed where the group comprises two Member States, eighteen in the case of three Member States and fourteen in the case of four or more Member States.

The standing of the political groups in the European Parliament as at October 2nd, 2001 is, from right to left, the following:

Union for Europe of the Nations (UEN)	21
European People's Party[120] (EPP)	232
European Liberal, Democrat and Reform Party (ELDR)	52
Party of European Socialists (PSE)	181
Group for a Europe of Democracies and Diversities (EDD)	18
Greens/European Free Alliance (Verts/ALE)	46
Confederal Group of the European United Left/Nordic Green Left (GUE/NGL)	42

---

114 Articles 190(3) (ECT); 3(1) and 10(2) of the Act.

115 EP RoP, 2.

116 The complete list is found in Article 6(1) of the Act.

117 Article 6(1) of the Act.

118 Article 191 (ECT); EP RoP, 29(1).

119 EP RoP, 29(2).

120 This group also includes the former European Democrats, which comprised British and Danish Conservatives. Their fusion was held up for many years because of the euroskepticism of the British Conservative Party under Mrs (now Lady) Thatcher. The fusion took place after John Major took over as British Prime Minister from Mrs Thatcher. They have remained together despite the resurgence of euroskepticism in the party under William Hague's leadership.

The Technical Group of Independent Members (TDI) has 19 members and the remaining 15 MEPs are officially non-attached. One week per month is set aside for meetings of the political groups.

In addition to the political groups, there are parliamentary inter-groups for certain issues. These bodies cut across party lines. Examples are the groups for institutional reform, research and development and the internal market. These groups exert considerable influence in Parliament because of the wide spectrum of opinion that they represent. They meet once a month.

The location of the European Parliament is an example of the victory of political compromise over common sense. The twelve periods of monthly plenary sessions, including the budgetary session, take place in Strasbourg. Additional plenary sessions take place in Brussels, where the committees of Parliament meet. The General Secretariat is based in Luxembourg. These illogical arrangements seriously hamper Parliament's efficiency[121] but they were confirmed by the Member States at Amsterdam.[122]

The work of Parliament is organized by the General Secretariat, which is headed by a Secretary-General. It provides MEPs with the necessary administrative, legal and language services. The Secretariat is divided into eight Directorates-General and a Legal Service. One third of the staff are involved in language services (translation and interpretation).

III.3.4.b The Operation of the European Parliament

The MEPs elect a President and fourteen Vice-Presidents,[123] which together form the Bureau.[124] The President is normally elected by an absolute majority of votes cast (i.e. fifty percent plus one vote), but if a fourth ballot is necessary, the candidate with the most votes is elected. The other major organ of the European Parliament is the Conference of Presidents, which comprises the President of Parliament and the chairpersons of the political groups.[125] The President directs all the activities of Parliament, presiding over plenary sessions and

---

121 *The Economist* (October 14, 1989, p.58) describes the problem, which has since become more acute, thus:

>   Deputies and Eurocrats waste days each month just traveling. Many services have to be performed three times over. The work of the committees is delayed because they cannot meet in the week of plenary sessions. Lorries cart trunks of documents from one city to another, yet still deputies often find they lack the document they need (the library and research departments are in Luxembourg)."

122 Article 1(a) of the Protocol on the location of the seats of the institutions and of certain bodies and departments of the European Communities and of Europol, which is attached to the TEU and the EC Treaty.

123 EP RoP, 14 and 15.

124 EP RoP, 21(1).

125 EP RoP, 23(1).

chairing meetings of the Bureau and the Conference of Presidents.[126] The President also represents Parliament on official occasions and in international relations. The Bureau is the regulatory body that is responsible for Parliament's budget and for administrative, organizational and personnel matters.[127] The Conference of Presidents sets the agenda for plenary sessions, establishes the timetable for Parliament's work and decides upon the terms of reference and size of Parliament's committees.[128]

The work of the plenary sessions of Parliament is in most cases prepared by the parliamentary committees, of which there are seventeen.[129] When Parliament wishes to adopt a resolution, a recommendation to the Council under the CFSP and PJC, a request for a proposal from the Commission, an opinion on a proposed Union act, a common position or an assent to a Union act, the matter is first referred to the appropriate committee.[130] The decision of the plenary session is based on this committee's report. In the case of proposals for Union acts, the matter is referred to the Legal Affairs Committee (CO6) if there is any query about the legal base or problems related to subsidiarity.[131] Other matters, such as the appointment of the Commission, a motion of censure on the Commission or the approval of a joint text under the Co-Decision Procedure[132] come directly before the plenary session.[133] Apart from the procedure for electing its officers, Parliament makes its decisions by a simple majority, an absolute majority or a double majority.[134]

The plenary sessions of Parliament are open to the public. In addition, it has adopted an act giving access to its documents.[135]

---

126 EP RoP, 19.

127 EP RoP, 22.

128 EP RoP, 24.

129 There are committees for foreign affairs, human rights and the CFSP (CO1), budgets (CO2), budgetary control (CO3), citizens' freedoms and rights and PJC (CO4), economic and monetary affairs (CO5), legal affairs and the internal market (CO6), industry, external trade, research and energy (CO7), employment and social affairs (CO8), environment, public health and consumer policy (CO9), agriculture and rural development (C10), fisheries (C11), regional policy, transport and tourism (C12), culture, youth, education, media and sport (C13), development and cooperation (C14), constitutional affairs (C15), women's rights and equal opportunities (C16) and petitions (C17). The terms of reference of these committees can be found in Annex VI of Parliament's Rules of Procedure.

130 EP RoP, 48, 49, 59, 60, 76 and 86.

131 EP RoP, 63. CO6 may also take up the matter on its own initiative.

132 This procedure is discussed *infra* in Section V.3.2.e.

133 EP RoP, 32, 33 and 34.

134 The rules for voting in Parliament are discussed *infra* in Section V.2.3.

135 EP Decision 97/632 (OJ L263/97).

III.3.4.c The Importance of the European Parliament

The European Parliament has been dismissed in the past as an irresponsible talking shop and repository of strange causes. In the early nineties, MEPs wasted time discussing the abolition of monarchy in the Member States, which was not only highly presumptuous but also beyond their jurisdiction. Parliament is still capable of agonizing *ad nauseam* over violations of human rights. Nevertheless, it is the only Union body that can claim democratic legitimacy and the right to speak for the 375 million Europeans that it represents. Moreover, accusations of irresponsibility are longer apposite. The European Parliament plays an influential and thoughtful role in the decision-making process, representing at once the Union interest and the different strains of political opinion throughout the Union. Unlike the Commission, it does not go out of its way to seek compromises with the Council and the Member States. It may accept such compromises in the end but not before giving full expression to its own points of view. Above all, it is the only part of the decision-making machinery in the European Union that acts in public. It is a body whose importance can only increase as the Union moves along the path of political integration.

III.3.5 The Court of Justice

III.3.5.a The Court

The role of the Court of Justice is to ensure that Union law is correctly interpreted and applied.[136] The Court has taken this to mean that it must ensure that Union law is applied effectively and consistently in all fifteen Member States. To achieve this goal, it has expanded the concept of direct applicability of Union law and evolved new concepts of direct effect and supremacy of Union law over national law.[137] The Court also has a plenary and accorded jurisdiction over certain matters.[138] In addition, it acts as an appellate court for the Court of First Instance.[139]

The Court consists of fifteen judges and eight advocates-general appointed by the Member States acting collectively.[140] They serve a term of six years and can be re-appointed. They must be chosen from persons whose independence is beyond doubt and who possess the highest legal qualifications. They must not

---

136 Article 220 (ECT). The exercise of the judicial power in the European Union is discussed *infra* in Section VI.4.

137 These two concepts are discussed *infra* in Sections IV.2.6 and IV.2.7, respectively.

138 These fields of jurisdiction are discussed *infra* in Sections VI.4.2.b.v and VI.4.2.b.vi, respectively.

139 Article 225(1) (ECT).

140 Articles 221, 222 and 223 (ECT).

hold any political or administrative office or engage in any other occupation.[141] The task of the advocates-general is to provide the Court with an impartial and reasoned submission on the cases before it so as to assist it in giving judgment. Judges and advocates-general can only be dismissed by a unanimous decision of the judges and advocates-general together.[142] The judges elect a President of the Court from among their number for a renewable term of three years. The President directs the work of the Court and presides over the full court when it is in session. The Court of Justice is based in Luxembourg.

In 1989, a Court of First Instance (CFI) was attached to the Court of Justice to alleviate its workload. It has jurisdiction over a certain number of matters.[143] It is not an independent court but part of the Court of Justice, to which the decisions of the CFI can be appealed on points of law.[144] It comprises fifteen judges who are appointed for a renewable term of six years by the Member States acting collectively.[145] They must also be independent and possess adequate legal qualifications. They may not hold any political or administrative office or engage in any other occupation.[146] These judges select the President of the CFI.[147] The CFI does not have a separate body of advocates-general; instead their duties are performed, when required, by the judges themselves.[148] Judges of the CFI can be dismissed in the same way as judges of the Court of Justice.[149] The CFI is also located in Luxembourg.

III.3.5.b The Operation of the Court

The Court of Justice sits in plenary session or in chambers of three, five or seven judges.[150] Member States or Union institutions that are party to a proceeding may request the Court to sit in plenary session. A plenary session must comprise at least nine judges.[151] Decisions of the Court are only valid when an uneven number of judges participate in the proceeding. The CFI sits in chambers

---

141 Articles 4 and 8 of the Statute of the Court of Justice, which is attached as a protocol to the EC Treaty and was last amended by Article 6 III 3(c) of the Treaty of Amsterdam.
142 Articles 6 and 8 of the Statute.
143 The CFI was established by Council Decision 88/591 (OJ L241/89), as amended by Council Decisions 93/350 (OJ L144/93) and 99/291 (OJ L114/99). It is discussed *infra* in Section VI.4.1.b.
144 Article 225(1) (ECT).
145 Article 225(3) (ECT); Council Decision 88/591, Article 2(1).
146 Articles 4 and 44 of the Statute.
147 Council Decision 88/591, Article 2(2).
148 Council Decision 88/591, Article 2(3).
149 Article 6 and 44 of the Statute.
150 Article 221 (ECT).
151 Article 15 of the Statute.

of three or four judges but, in certain cases, it sits in plenary session or as a single judge.[152]

The procedure of the Court of Justice comprises a written and oral procedure.[153] The written procedure differs depending on whether it is a direct action or a reference for a preliminary ruling.

Direct actions are brought before the Court by a written application addressed to the registrar.[154] In the case of Member States or Union institutions, an agent may make the application; in the case of other parties, it must be a lawyer who is entitled to practice in a Member State.[155] The application is served on the other parties, who may lodge a defense. The applicant may then submit a reply and the defendant a rejoinder. One month is allowed for each of these submissions. The Member States or Union institutions may intervene in any case before the Court.[156] If no defense is lodged, the Court may give judgment by default.[157] The defendant has one month in which to lodge an objection against this judgment.

In the case of a reference for a preliminary ruling, a national court submits the question to the Court.[158] The request is served on the parties to the national proceedings, the Member States, the Commission and, if it is concerned by the question, the Council. All have two months to submit written observations.

The oral procedure has three stages:

1st stage: The judge-rapporteur and the advocate-general who have been selected for the case give their report to the Court, which decides whether to hold a preliminary enquiry and whether the case should be heard in chambers or plenary session. Once the enquiry, if any, is complete, the President sets the date for the main hearing. The report of the judge-rapporteur summing up the facts and legal aspects of the case is made public.

2nd stage: The case is heard by the Court in open session. Lawyers or agents put the arguments for the parties and may call witnesses and experts.[159] The parties, however, may only address the Court through their representatives. The Court may examine whomever it wishes.

---

152 Council Decision 88/591, Article 2(4).

153 Article 18 of the Statute.

154 Article 19 of the Statute.

155 Article 17 of the Statute.

156 Article 37 of the Statute.

157 Article 38 of the Statute.

158 Article 20 of the Statute. This procedure is discussed *infra* in Section VI.4.2.b.i.

159 Article 29 of the Statute.

3rd stage: Some weeks later, the advocate-general makes his or her submission to the Court. The submission analyzes the facts and legal aspects of the case and proposes a solution for the Court. This ends the oral procedure.

The judges now deliberate in secret on the basis of a draft judgment drawn up by the judge-rapporteur.[160] Once they have reached agreement on the final text, the judgment is given in open court. All judgments are judgments of the whole Court; there is no provision for dissenting opinions. There is no appeal as such against a judgment of the Court, but an application for its revision may be made to the Court on discovery of a decisive fact that was unknown to the Court and the party claiming the revision at the time of the judgment.[161]

Actions before the Court do not automatically have suspensory effect, but the Court may order the act in question to be suspended if the circumstances so require.[162] The Court may also prescribe interim measures.[163] Parties wishing such relief must make a separate application to the Court.[164] The President normally makes the decision but he or she can delegate the task to another judge.[165] Only the person challenging a Union measure may apply to have it suspended, whereas any party to a proceeding may apply for interim measures. In both cases, the Court will only grant relief where it is necessary to avoid "serious and irreparable damage."[166]

The procedure before the CFI is more or less identical to that before the Court of Justice.

III.3.5.c The Importance of the Court of Justice

The Court of Justice has been extremely influential in the process of integration With its generous interpretations of Union law, it has overcome the more narrow confines of the Treaties, while its development of the concepts of direct applicability, direct effect and supremacy has given a secure foundation to this law. It has also established the concept of an autonomous Union legal order, which is the basis upon which the Union may yet develop into statehood.[167] Without the Court of Justice and the nearly nine thousand cases that it has decided, it is unlikely that the European Union would have reached the degree of integration that it enjoys at present.

---

160   Article 32 of the Statute.

161   Article 41 of the Statute.

162   Article 242 (ECT).

163   Article 243 (ECT).

164   Rules 83(3) of the Rules of Procedure of the Court of Justice (OJ C34/01).

165   Article 36 of the Statute.

166   *R. Arbed SA v. Commission*, 20/81, [1981] ECR 721 at 731.

167   This concept is discussed *infra* in Section IV.6.

III.3.6 The Court of Auditors

The Court of Auditors, in the words of the EC Treaty, assists the European Parliament and Council in exercising their powers of control over the implementation of the Union budget.[168] It was created in 1977 by the Second Budgetary Treaty[169] and upgraded to the status of an institution by the TEU. It is located in Luxembourg.

The Court of Auditors comprises fifteen members, who are appointed by a unanimous decision of the Council for a renewable term of six years.[170] They must be qualified auditors and act independently, neither taking nor seeking instruction from anyone.[171] They make not engage in any other activity, whether lucrative or not.[172] They can be dismissed for cause by the Court of Justice.[173] The members of the Court elect a President for a renewable term of three years.[174]

The Court examines the accounts of all revenue and expenditure by the Union bodies unless this is implicitly excluded by a body's constituent document.[175] Its job is to verify that all the Union's revenue has been properly collected and that its expenditures have been incurred in a lawful and responsible manner.[176] It also provides the European Parliament with a statement of assurance as to the reliability of the accounts and the legality of the underlying transactions.[177] The audits are based on records but can be carried out, if necessary, on the ground.[178] Member States and Union bodies must, at the Court's request, forward any pertinent documents or information. When operating on the ground in a Member State, the Court must work in liaison with the appropriate national authorities. When the audits are complete, the Court draws up an annual report, which is forwarded to the Union institutions[179] and published in the *Official Journal* together with the institutions' replies.[180]

---

168 Article 248(4) (ECT).

169 Treaty amending Certain Financial Provisions of the Treaties establishing the European Communities, OJ L359/77.

170 Article 247(1),(3) (ECT).

171 Article 247(2),(4) (ECT).

172 Article 247(5) (ECT).

173 Article 247(7) (ECT).

174 Article 247(3) (ECT).

175 Article 248(1) (ECT).

176 Article 248(2) (ECT).

177 Article 248(1) (ECT).

178 Article 248(3) (ECT).

179 This means the Council, Commission, Parliament and Court of Justice.

180 Article 248(4) (ECT).

The Court is divided into three audit groups containing a number of divisions that deal with specific areas of the Union's activities. There is another group that works on the statement of assurance. These groups do the groundwork that forms the basis for the deliberations of the whole Court. The Court is assisted by a Secretariat that provides administrative, language, personnel, informatics, documentation and budget assistance. The Secretariat is directed by a Secretary-General.

In addition to the annual report, the Court of Auditors may issue special reports on its own initiative and, at the request of another institution, deliver an opinion.[181] It always acts by a majority of its members (i.e. an absolute majority).[182]

III.3.7 The European System of Central Banks (ESCB) and the European Central Bank (ECB)

The primary objective of the ESCB is the maintenance of price stability.[183] Without prejudice to this objective, the ESCB must also support the general economic policies of the Community. It always acts in accordance with the principle of an open market economy with free competition.

The basic tasks of the ESCB are to define and implement the monetary policy of the Union, which includes the conduct of foreign exchange operations, the management of the official foreign reserves of the Member States and the promotion of the smooth operation of payment systems.[184] The ESCB is also supposed to contribute to the smooth conduct of national policies relating to the prudential supervision of credit institutions and the stability of the financial system.[185] The ESCB's jurisdiction over foreign exchange-rate policy is more limited as the Council has authority to conclude formal agreements with third countries and formulate general orientations for the policy.[186] The Council may also adopt, adjust or abandon the central rates of the euro within the exchange-rate system. The ESCB issues euro banknotes while the Member States issue the coins, subject to approval by the ESCB of the volume of the issue.[187]

---

181   Article 248(4) (ECT).

182   *Ibid*.

183   Article 105(1).

184   Article 105(2) (ECT). Per Article 105(3), Member States may hold and manage working balances of foreign exchange.

185   Article 105(5) (ECT).

186   Article 111 (ECT).

187   Article 106 (ECT).

The ESCB is composed of all the national central banks and the ECB.[188] However, the central banks of those Member States that have not entered the third stage of EMU do not participate in the work of the Governing Council or the Executive Board.[189] The ESCB must act with complete independence.[190] To this end, the Member States must ensure that their national central banks are likewise independent.[191] In particular, they must provide that the term of office of the governor of their central bank is no less than five years.[192] The ECB has its seat in Frankfurt.

The national central banks are the sole providers of capital to the ECB.[193] The subscription of capital is based on a key established on the basis of the Member States' respective shares of the aggregate gross domestic product and population of the Union. The capital of the ECB is constituted by the subscriptions of the national central banks of those Member States participating in the third stage of EMU. In addition, these national central banks provide the ECB with foreign reserve assets in proportion to their share of the subscribed capital of the ECB.[194]

The main decision-making bodies of the ECB are the Governing Council and the Executive Board.[195] The Governing Council comprises all the members of the Executive Board and the governors of the national central banks of those Member States that have entered the third stage of EMU.[196] The Executive Board comprises a President, Vice-President and four other members, who are chosen from among persons of recognized standing and professional experience in monetary or banking matters.[197] They are appointed by the Member States acting collectively at the level of heads of state or government. They serve eight years and cannot be re-appointed. The length of the term and the fact that they need not curry favor in order to secure their re-appointment encourage the members of the Executive Board to act independently. They may

---

188 Article 112(1) (ECT). Luxembourg, which is in a monetary union with Belgium, is represented by the *Institut Monétaire Luxembourgeois.*

189 Articles 122(3) (ECT); 43.4 of the Statute of the ESCB and the ECB, which is attached as a protocol to the EC Treaty. The Statute reproduces many of the Treaty provisions and is only cited where this is not the case.

190 Article 108 (ECT).

191 Article 109 (ECT).

192 Article 14.2 of the Statute.

193 Article 48 of the Statute.

194 Article 49 of the Statute.

195 Article 107(3) (ECT).

196 Articles 112(1) (ECT); 43.4 of the Statute.

197 Article 112(2) (ECT).

be dismissed for just cause by the Court of Justice.[198] There is also the General Council of the ECB, which has a less important role.[199] It comprises the President and Vice-President of the ECB and the governors of all the national central banks, including those of Member States with a derogation from the third stage of EMU.[200]

The decision-making authority in the ESCB is the ECB,[201] which determines to what extent the responsibilities of the ESCB will be carried out by the national central banks.[202] Certain tasks are conferred directly on the ECB by the Treaty and the ESCB/ECB Statute. The ECB, for example, has exclusive authority to authorize the issue of euro banknotes and control the money supply,[203] establish general principles for open market and credit operations,[204] ensure the proper operation of clearing systems[205] and manage foreign reserve assets.[206] The Council may confer on the ECB additional tasks concerning the prudential supervision of financial institutions.[207] In addition, it is the ECB that exercises the advisory and initiatory functions of the ESCB.[208] On the other hand, it is the national central banks that carry out, to the extent possible, the collection of statistical information.[209]

The EC Treaty requires the ECB to be consulted by the Council on a number of occasions.[210] The ECB must also be consulted regarding any proposed act of the Union and, to the extent determined by the Council, of the Member States within its field of competence.[211] The ECB can submit opinions on its own initiative and has a limited right to recommend action to the Council.[212]

---

198   Article 11.4 of the Statute.

199   Article 123(3) (ECT).

200   Article 45.2 of the Statute.

201   Article 106(3) (ECT).

202   Article 9.2 of the Statute.

203   Articles 106 (ECT); 20 of the Statute.

204   Article 18.2 of the Statute.

205   Article 22 of the Statute.

206   Article 30.5 of the Statute.

207   Article 105(6) (ECT). This does not include insurance undertakings.

208   *See* Articles 105(4), 107(5),(6) and 111(1) (ECT).

209   Article 5.1 and 2 of the Statute.

210   *E.g.* Articles 104 (14) (replacement of the excessive deficit protocol), 105(6) (conferral of specific tasks on the ECB), 106(2) (harmonization of coins), 107(5) (amending certain provisions of the ESCB/ECB Statute), 107(6) (adoption of provisions pursuant to the ESCB/ECB Statute), 111 (foreign exchange policy), 114(3) (composition of the Economic and Financial Committee) and 123(4) (conversion rates for the euro). All these articles are from the EC Treaty.

211   Article 105(4) (ECT).

212   *See* Articles 107(5),(6) and 111(1) (ECT).

The ECB acts by way of regulations, decisions, recommendations and opinions.[213] Within the limits and under the conditions set by the Council, the ECB is able to impose fines and other penalties upon undertakings that fail to comply with its regulations and decisions.[214]

Within the ECB, it is the Governing Council that formulates the monetary policy of the Union, including decisions on monetary objectives, key interests rates and the supply of reserves in the ESCB.[215] *Inter alia,* it also exercises the advisory and initiatory functions of the ECB,[216] decides on the international representation of the ESCB,[217] sets the terms of employment for the Executive Board,[218] authorizes the issue of banknotes,[219] decides on additional methods of monetary control,[220] authorizes an increase in the capital of the ECB[221] and sets guidelines for national operations concerning foreign reserve assets.[222] The Governing Council acts by a simple majority of votes cast except where the ESCB/ECB Statute provides otherwise.[223] For certain decisions, the votes of the members are weighted according to the share of the subscribed capital held by the Member State's central bank, in which case the votes of the members from the Executive Board are zero.[224]

The Executive Board of the ECB implements monetary policy in accordance with the guidelines and decisions of the Governing Council.[225] In doing so, it gives the necessary instructions to the national central banks. The Executive Board also looks after the day-to-day management of the Union's monetary affairs.[226] It acts by a simple majority of votes cast.[227]

---

213 Article 110 (ECT).
214 Article 110(3) (ECT).
215 Article 12.1 of the Statute.
216 Article 12.4 and 41.2 of the Statute. Article 41.2 only mentions a recommendation under Article 107(5) of the EC Treaty, but it implies that all recommendations emanate from the Governing Council.
217 Article 6.1 of the Statute.
218 Article 11.3 of the Statute.
219 Article 16 of the Statute.
220 Article 20 of the Statute.
221 Article 28.1 of the Statute.
222 Article 31 of the Statute.
223 Article 10.2 of the Statute.
224 Article 10.3 of the Statute.
225 Article 21.1 of the Statute.
226 Article 11.6 of the Statute.
227 Article 11.5 of the Statute.

The General Council exists in order to give Member States with a derogation from the third stage of EMU some role in the activities of the ESCB. It will cease to exist once all Member States have entered the third stage and adopted the single currency.[228] It contributes to the following activities of the ESCB:[229]

- the advisory function;

- the collection of statistical information;

- the preparation of the ECB's quarterly and annual reports and weekly consolidated financial statements;

- the establishment of rules for standardizing the accounting and reporting of operations by the national central banks;

- the adjustment of the key for calculating the share of national central banks in the ECB's subscription;

- laying down the conditions of employment of the ECB's staff; and

- the irrevocable fixing of the exchange rates against the euro of the currencies of Member States with a derogation.

III.3.8 The European Investment Bank (EIB)

The EIB is the European Union's financial institution. It finances projects that contribute towards the balanced and steady development of the Union.[230] In doing so, it works closely with the Structural Funds, in particular the European Regional Development Fund, and other financial instruments established by the Union, such as the Cohesion Fund. The EIB is based in Luxembourg.

The shareholders of the EIB are the Member States, who contribute capital to the Bank according to their gross domestic product and population.[231] Not all this capital is paid up, but the Board of Governors may call on it when required.[232] The EIB is directed and managed by a Board of Governors, a Board of Directors and a Management Committee.[233] The Board of Governors consists of a minister from each Member State.[234] Its major responsibility is to lay down general directives for the credit policy of the Bank.[235] The Board of Directors comprises

---

228   Article 123(3) (ECT).

229   Article 47 of the Statute.

230   Article 267 (ECT).

231   Articles 266 (ECT); 4(1) of the Statute of the EIB, which is attached as a protocol to the EC Treaty.

232   Article 5(1),(3) of the Statute.

233   Article 8 of the Statute.

234   Article 9(1) of the Statute.

235   Article 9(2) of the Statute.

twenty-five directors and thirteen alternates, who are appointed by the Board of Governors for a renewable five-year term.[236] Each Member State is allotted a certain number of directors and alternates. The Board of Directors has sole responsibility for granting loans and guarantees and raising money on the capital markets.[237] It must ensure that the Bank is run properly in accordance with the directives of the Board of Governors. The Management Committee consists of a President and seven Vice-Presidents, who are appointed by the Board of Governors for a renewable six-year term.[238] It looks after the current business of the Bank and prepares the decisions of the Board of Directors.[239]

The EIB finances projects through loans and guarantees. It uses its own capital and money that it raises in the international capital marketplace to do this. It makes loans both to Member States and directly to undertakings. It is active in all sectors of the economy but must concentrate on the following types of projects in the European Union:[240]

– projects for developing less-developed regions;

– major projects for modernizing and converting undertakings, and

– major projects involving more than one Member State.

The EIB also implements the financial provisions of development and aid agreements with third countries.

III.3.9 The European Ombudsman

The Ombudsman is appointed by the European Parliament after each election and holds office during the five-year term of Parliament.[241] He or she may be re-appointed. The Ombudsman must act with complete independence and may not engage in any other activity, whether lucrative or not.[242] He or she may be dismissed for cause by the Court of Justice.[243]

Every resident of the European Union has the right to address a complaint to the Ombudsman concerning maladministration by a body of the European Community.[244] This excludes the European Council, which is set up by the TEU. The

---

236 Article 11(2) of the Statute.
237 Article 11(1) of the Statute.
238 Article 13(1) of the Statute.
239 Article 13(3) of the Statute.
240 Article 267 (ECT).
241 Article 195(2) (ECT).
242 Article 195(3) (ECT).
243 Article 195(2) (ECT).
244 Article 195(1) (ECT).

Court of Justice and the CFI are also excluded with respect to judicial acts. The complaint must be made within two years of the occurrence complained of, and the complainant must first have contacted the body concerned.[245] Interestingly, the complainant need not be directly affected by the maladministration.

Maladministration means that a body has failed to do something, has done it badly or has done something that it ought not to have done. It concerns in particular incidents of unfairness, discrimination, abuse of power, lack or refusal of information and unnecessary delays.

Upon receiving a complaint, and also on his or her own initiative, the Ombudsman conducts inquiries.[246] Where an instance of maladministration is established, the Ombudsman refers the matter to the body concerned, which has three months in which to make its views known. The Ombudsman then forwards a report to Parliament and the body concerned and informs the complainant. The Ombudsman must also submit an annual report to Parliament on the outcome of his or her inquiries.

III.4 Major Consultative and Advisory Committees

III.4.1 The Economic and Social Committee (ECOSOC)

The role of ECOSOC is to provide a non-political input into the Union's decision-making process from European civil society. It has to be consulted by the Council in a number of areas, such as personal mobility, transport, social policy, gender equality, public health, industrial, consumer protection, regional and environmental matters and research and development. It may also deliver opinions on its own initiative.[247]

ECOSOC comprises 222 members drawn from a broad spectrum of economic and social groups, in particular producers, farmers, carriers, workers, dealers, craftsmen, professionals and the general public.[248] They are appointed by the Council for renewable terms of four years on the basis of lists submitted by the Member States.[249] Members of ECOSOC are bound to act independently in the general interest of the Union. The number of members from each Member State is weighted according to population, but, even more so than with the European

---

245 Article 2(4) of Council Decision 94/262 on the regulations and general conditions governing the performance of the Ombudsman's duties (OJ L113/94).
246 Article 195(2) (ECT).
247 Article 262 (ECT).
248 Article 257 (ECT).
249 Articles 258 and 259(1) (ECT).

Parliament, the result is not particularly equitable. The allotment of members is as follows:

France	24
Germany	24
Italy	24
United Kingdom	24
Spain	21
Austria	12
Belgium	12
Greece	12
Netherlands	12
Portugal	12
Sweden	12
Denmark	9
Finland	9
Ireland	9
Luxembourg	6

ECOSOC's opinion is not binding on the Council even where consultation is mandatory. It has purely advisory status.[250] Moreover, the Council may set a time limit for delivery of the opinion, after which time it can act without obtaining it.[251]

ECOSOC adopts its opinions in plenary session on the basis of preparatory work carried out by six specialized Sections,[252] to which all requests for an opinion are first referred.[253] ECOSOC normally makes its decisions by a simple majority of votes cast.[254] The members of the various Sections are appointed by the Committee as a whole.[255] In addition, the members may join a Group.[256] There are three Groups: the Employers' Group, the Workers' Group and the Various Interests Group. These Groups meet separately to prepare their common approach to the

---

250 Article 257 (ECT).

251 Article 262 (ECT).

252 Rule 23(1) of the Rules of Procedure of the Economic and Social Committee (OJ L82/96).

253 ECOSOC RoP, 24 and 25. These Sections are: Agriculture, Rural Development and the Environment (NAT), Economic and Monetary Union and Economic and Social Cohesion (ECO), Employment, Social Affairs and Citizenship (SOC), External Relations (REX), the Single Market, Production and Consumption (INT) and Transport, Energy, Infrastructure and the Information Society (TEN).

254 ECOSOC RoP, 49(2)

255 ECOSOC RoP, 13(3).

256 ECOSOC RoP, 22(1). Those members who do not join a group are referred to "Members without a Group."

work of the Sections and to decide on amendments that they wish to place before the plenary sessions. The President[257] of ECOSOC is elected in turn from among these three Groups.[258] To be elected, a candidate must obtain either three-quarters of the votes on the first ballot or a simple majority of them on subsequent ballots.[259] The President directs the work of the Committee and represents it in its external relations.[260] A President is elected for a term of two years and may not be re-elected for the two years immediately following.[261] ECOSOC is served by a Secretariat-General.

III.4.2 The Committee of Regions (CoR)

The role of CoR is to represent local and regional interests in the Union's decision-making process. It has to be consulted by the Council in a number of areas, such as regional policy, trans-European networks, transport, social and employment policy, culture, education, health and the environment. It may also deliver opinions on its own initiative.[262]

CoR comprises 222 members and the same number of alternates who represent regional and local bodies.[263] They are appointed by the Council for renewable terms of four years on the basis of proposals from the Member States. Members of CoR are bound to act independently in the general interest of the Union. The number of members from each Member State is weighted according to population in exactly the same way as ECOSOC.

The opinion of COR is not binding on the Council even where consultation is mandatory. It has purely advisory status.[264] Moreover, the Council may set a time limit for delivery of the opinion, after which time it can act without obtaining it.[265]

CoR adopts its opinions in plenary session on the basis of preparatory work carried out by eight internal Commissions, to which all requests for an opinion are

---

257 The EC Treaty provides for a chairman (no gender equality here!) in Article 260, but the Rules of Procedure have changed the designation to "President."

258 ECOSOC RoP, 5.

259 ECOSOC RoP, 6(3).

260 ECOSOC RoP, 10(1),(2).

261 ECOSOC RoP, 5.

262 Article 265 (ECT).

263 Article 263 (ECT).

264 Article 263 (ECT).

265 Article 265 (ECT).

first referred.[266] CoR normally makes its decisions by a simple majority of votes cast.[267] The members of the various Sections are appointed by the Committee as a whole.[268] Members of CoR are divided up into national delegations[269] and may also join political groups.[270] There are also interregional groups.[271] The national delegations and political groups are supposed to help in a balanced way the organization of the Committee's work.[272] The President[273] of CoR is elected for a two-year term by the members of the Committee by an absolute majority of votes cast on the first ballot or by the highest number of votes on the second ballot.[274] The President directs the work of the Committee and represents it in its external relations.[275] CoR is served by a Secretariat-General.

III.4.3 The Political and Political and Security Committees

Article 25 of the TEU sets up the Political Committee as the body that is to monitor the international situation and contribute to the CFSP by delivering opinions to the Council at the request of the latter or on its own initiative. It also helps in the preparation of the work of the Council.[276] Council Decision 00/143[277] sets up an interim Political and Security Committee (PSC), which was to meet as a separate formation of the Political Committee when the latter was not in session in order to deal on a day-to-day basis with the CFSP.[278] However, when the PSC was made permanent by Council Decision 01/78,[279] there is provision for it to take

---

266 Rules 13(a), 39 and 44 of the Rules of Procedure of the Committee of Regions (OJ L18/00). These internal Commissions are as follows: regional policy, structural funds and economic and social cohesion (Com. 1), agriculture, rural development and fisheries (Com. 2), trans-European networks, transport and information society (Com. 3), spatial planning, urban issues, energy and the environment (Com. 4), social policy, health, consumer protection, research and tourism (Com. 5), employment, economic policy, single market, industry and small and medium-sized enterprises (Com. 6), education, vocational training, culture, youth and sport (Com. 7) and institutional affairs and fundamental rights (Com. 8).

267 CoR RoP, 22(1).

268 CoR RoP, 44(1).

269 CoR RoP, 8(1).

270 CoR RoP, 9(1).

271 CoR RoP, 10.

272 CoR RoP, 7.

273 The EC Treaty again provides for a chairman in Article 264, but the Rules of Procedure have changed the designation to "President."

274 CoR RoP, 31(2).

275 CoR RoP, 37.

276 *See* the discussion *supra* in Section III.3.2.b.

277 OJ L49/00.

278 Council Decision 00/143, Article 1.

279 OJ L27/01.

over both the advisory and preparatory functions of the Political Committee,[280] which seems consigned to oblivion. It comprises senior officials or ambassadors of the Member States from their Permanent Representation in Brussels.[281]

III.4.4 The European Union Military Committee (EUMC)

The EUMC was set up on a permanent basis by Council Decision 01/79.[282] It comprises the Chiefs of Defense of the Member States,[283] although in most circumstance the Chiefs are replaced by their representatives. The EUMC acts by consensus and provides advice on all military matters.[284] It also directs all military activities of the European Union.

III.4.5 The Economic and Financial Committee (EFC)

The EFC took over from the Monetary Committee at the start of the third stage of EMU.[285] It comprises two members and two alternates from the Commission, the ECB and each Member State.[286] These persons must be selected from experts possessing outstanding competence in the economic and financial field.[287] The two members appointed by the Member States must be senior officials from the civil service and the central bank, respectively.[288] The Committee elects a President for a two-year renewable term from among the members from the national administrations.[289] The EFC is served by a Secretariat.

The EFC must on occasion be consulted by the Council or Commission[290] and may deliver other opinions at the request of these institutions or on its own initiative.[291] In addition, it may be consulted with respect to decisions on the exchange-rate mechanism of the third stage of EMU.[292] The Committee also

---

280 Council Decision 01/78, Annex. The Annex in fact refers to the PSC as "the linchpin of the European security and defense policy (ESDP) and of the common foreign and security policy (CFSP)."

281 Council Decision 01/143, Article 1.

282 OJ L27/01.

283 Council Decision 01/79, Article 1.

284 *Ibid*, Annex, Point 2.

285 Article 114(2) (ECT).

286 Council Decision 98/743 on the detailed provisions concerning the composition of the Economic and Financial Committee (OJ L358/98).

287 *Ibid*, Article 2.

288 *Ibid*, Article 3.

289 Article 5 of Council Decision 99/8 adopting the Statutes of the Economic and Financial Committee (OJ L5/99).

290 Articles 104(3),(4) and 120(3) (ECT).

291 Article 114(2) (ECT).

292 Council Decision 99/8, Article 2.

helps prepare the work of the Council[293] as well as the Council's reviews of the development of the exchange-rate of the euro. It assists with the dialogue between the Council and the ECB. The Committee normally acts by consensus but, where a vote is requested, by a majority of its members.[294] It has purely advisory status.

III.4.6 The Employment Committee

The Employment Committee was created pursuant to Article 130 of the EC Treaty by Council Decision 00/98.[295] It comprises two members and two alternates from the Commission and each Member State.[296] These persons must be chosen from among senior officials or experts possessing outstanding competence in the field of employment and labor market policy. The members of the Committee elect a chairperson for a two-year non-renewable term from among the members appointed by the Member States.[297]

The function of the Committee is to promote coordination between the Member States on employment and labor market policies.[298] It does so *inter alia* by monitoring the employment situation and employment policies in the Member States and formulating opinions at the request of the Council or the Commission or on its own initiative. The Council is bound to seek its views when carrying out an examination of the employment policies of the Member States.[299]

III.4.7 The Transport Committee

An advisory committee consisting of experts designated by the Member States is attached to the Commission.[300] The Commission may consult the Committee on transport matters at its discretion.

III.4.8 Other Committees

Both the Council and the Commission have set up a variety of committees to assist them in an advisory capacity in carrying out their duties. There are hundreds of these secondary committees. Recently, for example, the Council set up the Social Protection Committee.[301] Its mandate is couched in the same terms as

---

293   *See* the discussion *supra* in Section III.3.2.b.

294   Council Decision 99/8, Article 4.

295   OJ L29/00.

296   Council Decision 00/98, Article 2.

297   *Ibid*, Article 3(1).

298   Article 130 (ECT).

299   Article 128(4) (ECT).

300   Article 79 (ECT).

301   Council Decision 00/436 (OJ L172/00).

that of the Employment Committee except that it is concerned with social protection policies.[302] Its structure is identical to that of the Employment Committee. The committees set up by the Commission provide it with advice at its request. They comprise experts from the Member States and/or the Commission and are appointed by the latter. An example is the Scientific Committee for Occupational Exposure Limits to Chemical Agents.[303] There is also a whole array of committees set up by the Council to advise or control the Commission's exercise of its implementing powers under the secondary legislation of the Council. These are discussed later in Section V.3.4.b. The Council also sets up committees to assist the Commission in the negotiation of international agreements.[304]

III.5 Agencies of the European Union

These agencies are not important for an understanding of the legal system of the European Union. However, for the sake of completeness, here is a list of them and where they are based:

Europol and Europol Drugs Unit, located at the Hague, Netherlands

European Agency for Health and Safety at Work, located in Bilbao, Spain

Office for Harmonization in the Internal Market (trade marks, designs and models), located in Alicante, Spain

European Training Foundation, located in Turin, Italy

European Agency for the Evaluation of Medicinal Products, located in London, Great Britain

Office for Veterinary and Plant-Health Inspection and Control, located in Dublin, Ireland

European Monitoring Center for Drugs and Drug Addiction, located in Lisbon, Portugal

European Center for the Development of Vocational Training, located in Thessalonika, Greece

Translation Center for the Bodies of the Union, located in Luxembourg

European Environment Agency, located in Copenhagen, Denmark

Community Plant Variety Office, located in Angers, France

European Foundation for the Improvement of Living and Working Conditions, located in Dublin, Ireland

---

302 *Ibid*, Article 1.

303 Commission Decision 95/320 (OJ L188/95).

304 Articles 133(3) and 300(1) (ECT).

CHAPTER IV

THE LEGAL ORDER OF THE EUROPEAN UNION

IV.1 The Issue of Jurisdiction

IV.1.1 Introduction

In federal states, the division of state power between the federation and the states or provinces takes one of two forms. In some states, federal competences are enumerated and those which are not attributed to the federation are reserved to the provinces or states. This is the case with the United States. In other federations, such as Canada, the competences of the provinces are set out and those not specifically attributed to them are reserved for the federation. In the European Union, which can be considered a federation for the purposes of this discussion, the situation is more opaque. Specific competences are attributed to both the European Union and the Member States, without any precision as to where the reserved powers lie. Thus, the demarcation of jurisdiction between the Union and the Member States is somewhat fluid.

IV.1.2 The Jurisdiction of the European Community

In the original European Community (EC) Treaty,[1] the Community was accorded few specific competences and if its jurisdiction had been based on these powers, its scope for action would have been quite limited. However, it also possessed a general power under Article 235 (now Article 308) to take any measures necessary to attain the objectives of the Treaty. Taking the view that its jurisdiction was based on these objectives, it used this general power to go beyond its few attributed competences into such areas as consumer protection, research and development, the environment, regional policy, public health, industrial policy, education and energy. In addition, acting pursuant to its broad power to harmonize national laws and regulations in the interest of establishing and operating the common market,[2] the Community enacted another broad body of law involving industrial norms, corporations, taxation, intellectual

---

1   298 U.N.T.S. 11.

2   Article 100 (now Article 94) (ECT).

property, financial services, public procurement, telecommunications and broadcasting. The Court of Justice accepted this extension of the Community's jurisdiction. Indeed the Court contributed to it by developing the theory of implied powers, which permitted the Court to interpret widely the provisions bestowing specific competences on the Community.[3]

The Single European Act (SEA)[4] confirmed and formalized the Community's competences in the areas of consumer protection, research and development, public health, the environment and regional policy. While the attribution of these specific competences to the Community was a positive step, it had one significant drawback. As Article 308 can only be used where the EC Treaty does not give the Community the necessary powers for action, it could no longer be used in these areas with the result that the Community's jurisdiction over them was crystallized by the SEA. However, the SEA stopped short of restricting the Community's jurisdiction to its attributed competences, which meant that it could continue to use Article 308 to extend its jurisdiction to other areas in which action by the Community was needed to achieve the objectives of the Treaty. It could also rely on the theory of implied powers to stretch its newly attributed competences to their limits. The SEA did not affect the Community's harmonizing power. Indeed, it made it easier to use by introducing qualified majority voting for some matters involving the internal market.[5]

IV.1.3 The Jurisdiction of the European Union

IV.1.3.a The Attributed Competences of the European Union

The Treaty on European Union (TEU)[6] created the European Union and formalized its jurisdiction over industrial policy, education and energy as well as attributing a number of new competences to the Union. The Treaty of Amsterdam[7] added more. As a result, the European Union now has an impressive array of attributed powers. The list includes the following: the internal market, which comprises the free movement of persons, services, goods and capital and more specifically liberalizing and harmonizing measures on financial services, taxation, telecommunications, broadcasting, commercial law, public procurement, corporations, industrial norms and intellectual property, Union citizenship, common foreign, security, defense, agriculture, fisheries, transport, external trade and monetary policies, visas, asylum, immigration and other measures involving non-EU nationals, anti-trust rules, economic policy, employment, customs cooperation, social policy, education, vocational training, culture, pub-

---

3   *See Einführ- und Vorratsstelle für Getreide und Futtermittel* v. *Koster*, 2/70, [1970] ECR 1161; *Massey-Ferguson*, 8/73, [1973] ECR 898.

4   OJ L169/87.

5   Article 100a (now Article 95) (ECT).

6   [1992] 1 C.M.L.R. 573.

7   OJ C340/97.

lic health, consumer protection, trans-European networks, industrial policy, regional policy, research and development, the environment and overseas development.

It is perhaps not surprising that, in the face of all these attributed competences, it was felt necessary to restrict the Union's ability to encroach further on areas of national jurisdiction. The TEU thus introduced into the EC Treaty three limits on the exercise by the Union of its legislative and executive powers[8] that have a significant impact on the basis and scope of its jurisdiction.

IV.1.3.b The Principle of Attributed Powers

The first limit on the Union is that it must act "within the limits of the powers conferred upon it by [the] Treaty and the objectives assigned to it therein."[9] On the surface, the new provision does not seem to change much as it retains a reference to the objectives of the Treaty, which, taken as the basis of the Community's jurisdiction, had enabled it to extend its competences continuously. Thus, Kapteyn and Themaat dismiss the provision as adding nothing to existing law,[10] while Mengozzi maintains that it in no way restricts the Union's jurisdiction to the competences that are attributed to it.[11] The Court of Justice, however, has interpreted the provision as introducing into Union law a new principle of the attribution of powers. In *Opinion 2/94*,[12] it takes the view that this changes the basis of the Union's jurisdiction by restricting it to the attributed competences. The jurisdiction of the European Union is thus now circumscribed by these enumerated powers and cannot be extended beyond them by the use of Article 308. This would indicate that this Article can henceforth only be used to enable the Union to act in areas of attributed competence where the EC Treaty does not provide the necessary means to do so. This applies only to energy, civil protection and tourism. At the same time, however, the Court in its judgment continues to support the theory of implied powers, which would at least permit a wide interpretation of the Union's jurisdiction under its attributed competences. Moreover, the new principle does not affect the Union's harmonizing power. It should be noted that the principle of attributed powers is not taken up by the TEU,[13] but this is not necessary as the Union is given no general power to

---

8   Article 5 (ECT).

9   This provision must be distinguished from the requirement in Article 7(1) that every institution must act within the limits of its powers. This requirement is concerned with the allocation of powers between the institutions of the Union and has no bearing on the Union's jurisdiction.

10   P.J.G. Kapteyn and P. Verloren van Themaat, *Introduction to the Law of the European Communities* (3rd edition by L.W. Gormley, 1998) at page 137.

11   P. Mengozzi, *European Community Law* (1999) at page 72.

12   [1996] ECR I-1759.

13   Article 2 refers only to the principle of subsidiarity, which includes that of proportionality. *See infra* in the text.

act in that Treaty and is therefore restricted in any case to its attributed competences.

IV.1.3.c The Principle of Subsidiarity

The second limit on the Union is that it can act only if and to the extent that the objectives of the proposed action cannot be sufficiently achieved by the Member States and can be better achieved by the Union. This is the principle of subsidiarity. The action must also not go beyond what is necessary to achieve the objectives of the Treaty. This is the principle of proportionality, and although it is a separate limit on the Union's exercise of its powers, it is to all intents and purposes part of the principle of subsidiarity.[14] This principle applies to both the EC Treaty and the TEU.[15]

The principle of subsidiarity comprises two conditions. The scale or effects of the proposed action be such that, firstly, individual Member States are incapable of dealing adequately with the problem and, secondly, the Union is able to achieve a better result. Although the two conditions are closely related, the Union must show that both are met.[16] The responsibility for doing this falls initially upon the Commission when it makes a proposal for action by the Union[17] but the Council and the European Parliament are also charged with ensuring that the principle is followed.[18] Even where action by the Union is justified, as much scope as possible must be left for national action.[19]

The principle of subsidiarity does not directly limit the Union's jurisdiction in the same way as that of the attribution of powers. Moreover, it does not apply to the exclusive competences of the Union, which reduces sensibly its effects. However, by preventing the European Union from acting in certain cases within its area of concurrent jurisdiction, it certainly curtails the effective scope of the Union's jurisdiction.[20] It also militates against any expansion of the Union's concurrent powers by way of the theory of implied powers. Thus, although subsidiarity

---

14 It is treated as such by the Protocol on the application of the principles of subsidiarity and proportionality, which is attached to the EC Treaty—*see* Article 6.

15 It is taken up into the TEU by Article 2 (TEU).

16 Article 5 of the Protocol on subsidiarity.

17 Article 9 of the Protocol on subsidiarity.

18 Article 11 of the Protocol on subsidiarity.

19 Article 7 of the Protocol on subsidiarity.

20 Kapteyn and Veloren van Themaat (fn. 10) maintain at page 142 that the principle of subsidiarity is unlikely to be very effective in limiting Union action as the Court of Justice is unlikely to go beyond a formal justification by the Commission for action. This ignores the fact that the Council and the European Parliament also review the Commission's proposals for compliance with the principle of subsidiarity. While the latter has been more tolerant of the Commission's justifications, the Council is stricter. In fact, the Commission has withdrawn many of its proposals because of failure to satisfy the principle of subsidiarity.

does not apply to the exclusive competences of the Union, it nevertheless limits their scope by making it virtually impossible for a concurrent power to become exclusive.[21] *A fortiori*, ancillary powers cannot become exclusive. Proportionality, by the way, does apply to areas of exclusive Union jurisdiction but, divorced from the principle of subsidiarity, it does not have a significant limiting effect.

IV.1.3.d Other Conditions Attached to Action by the European Union

The EC Treaty contains a number of other criteria that the Union must meet when it exercises legislative or executive power. They do not directly limit its jurisdiction, but, as with subsidiarity, some of the criteria may have this effect. Thus, the Union must respect fundamental rights and the national identities of the Member States.[22] In all its policies and activities, it is obliged to promote gender equality, ensure environmental, human health and consumer protection and contribute to economic and social cohesion within the Union.[23] It must also take into account the objective of a high level of employment, the cultural aspects of its actions and, with respect to policies likely to affect developing countries, objectives such as sustainable growth, integration into the world economy, eradication of poverty, democracy and the rule of law and respect for fundamental rights.[24]

IV.1.4 Types of Union Jurisdiction

IV.1.4.a Exclusive Jurisdiction

Strangely, the extent of the Union's exclusive jurisdiction is not clear, and it is perhaps incumbent upon the Court of Justice to clarify the issue.[25]

In principle, the European Union should have exclusive jurisdiction over those matters for which the Treaties provide a common policy, namely agriculture, fisheries, transport, external trade, monetary matters and foreign and security policy, including the new common policy on security and defense. To these may be added the coal and steel and atomic energy sectors, which are regulated by the ECSC and EAEC Treaties respectively. However, with the exception of monetary policy, where the Union exercises its jurisdiction to the full, none of the other areas is in practice the exclusive preserve of the Union.[26] This may be

---

21   *See* Mengozzi (fn 11) at pages 75-76.

22   Article 6(2),(3) (TEU).

23   Articles 3(2), 6, 152(1), 153(2) and 159 (ECT).

24   Articles 127(2), 151(4) and 178 (ECT).

25   This is certainly the opinion of Kapteyn and Verloren van Themaat (fn 10) at p. 139.

26   On this issue, *see* Point 116 of the Commission's communication to the Council of October 27, 1992 in the EC Bulletin (10). *See* also Kapteyn and Verloren van Themaat (fn 10) at page 139.

by the Union's choice or because of limitations placed on the Union's jurisdiction by the Treaties.

The Union has chosen to concentrate within the common agricultural policy on the common organization of product markets and on the conservation of stocks in the area of fisheries. As far as foreign, security and defense policies are concerned, the Union exercises jurisdiction only with respect to those matters on which it has chosen to act. By contrast, the common transport policy is formally restricted to certain, albeit essential, matters, such as international transport, cabotage (the right of non-resident carriers to operate in another Member State), safety and anti-trust rules.[27] The common commercial policy does not extend to the international regulation of intellectual property or trade in services.[28] The center of gravity for the EAEC has been research and its dissemination and safety matters.

Nevertheless, we can still talk of the Union's exclusive jurisdiction in areas where common policies exist. Monetary policy, of course, poses no problems. In the case of agriculture, fisheries and foreign, security and defense policy, it is important to note that the Union has the power to occupy these fields completely. The Member States are free to act within them only as long as the Union has chosen not to do so. There is, therefore, a potential for Union exclusivity. With respect to transport and external trade, the Union exercises jurisdiction to such a significant extent that it is effectively exclusive. This is also true of the coal and steel sector.

Certain other matters have been suggested as coming within the Union's exclusive jurisdiction. These are regional policy,[29] general anti-trust law and the internal market.[30] This suggestion cannot yet be accepted in the case of regional policy and anti-trust law. In both instances, there is still a clear line of demarcation between Union and national jurisdiction based on a the need for a Union dimension. Regional aid projects at the Union level and anti-trust matters that affect more than one Member State or involve transactions whose very size gives them a Union dimension are a matter for the Union. Otherwise, both matters fall within national jurisdiction. Perhaps, if the Union dimension came to dominate

---

27   Article 71(1) (ECT).

28   Article 133(5) (ECT). *See* also *Opinion 1/94*, [1994] ECR I-5276. Article 2(5) of the Treaty of Nice extends the Community's external trade powers to the negotiation and conclusion of agreements relating to trade in services and the commercial aspects of intellectual property. The Community's jurisdiction under this Article will not, however, include cultural and audiovisual services, educational services and social and human health services, which continue to fall within the shared competence of the Community and the Member States. The Treaty of Nice also provides for the Council to extend the Community's jurisdiction to all aspects of intellectual property.

29   Kapteyn and Verloren van Themaat (fn. 10) at page 139.

30   Point 116 of the Commission's communication to the Council of October 27, 1992.

to the extent that nearly all regional aid and anti-trust regulation were decided at Union level, we could, by analogy with transport and external trade, talk about Union exclusivity. This is, however, not yet the case although in some aspects of anti-trust law, such as mergers, it is not far off.

The issue of the internal market is more complex. Here we are dealing with a large and heterogeneous body of law, all of which aims at establishing the free movement of goods, persons, services and capital throughout the European Union. However, we can distinguish between two broad categories within this body of law. On the one hand, there are the general rules on the free movement of goods, persons, services and capital that establish the basic framework of the internal market. No Member State regulates such movement within its borders as there are no restrictions or discrimination that prevent it. It is a non-issue. Free movement in the generic sense thus has by its very nature only a Union dimension and as such falls within the exclusive jurisdiction of the Union. Accordingly, the Union is given specific powers to achieve it.[31] This area of Union exclusive jurisdiction will be extended by May 2004 to some matters involving non-EU nationals, namely visas, asylum, immigration and external border controls.[32] It will not impinge on the sole responsibility of the Member States for law and order and the safeguarding of internal security.[33]

The second category of internal market law involves harmonization and liberalization in specific sectors, such as banking, insurance, securities, taxation, public procurement, corporations, intellectual property protection, commerce, industrial standards, telecommunications and the audiovisual sector. Here the Union acts only to the extent necessary for the establishment and proper functioning of the internal market.[34] In many of these sectors, Union law is extremely important but it is never exclusive by virtue of its limited aim.

We may add one further matter to the Union's exclusive jurisdiction. Union citizenship is based on the possession of the nationality of a Member State and that Member State has the exclusive right to determine who are its nationals. However, this only permits Member States to decide who shall enjoy Union citizenship; it gives them no jurisdiction over the incidences of this citizenship. This is a matter exclusively for the Union.

---

31   Articles 14, 23-31 and 39-60 (ECT).

32   Articles 61-63 (ECT).

33   Article 64(1) (ECT).

34   Articles 90-97 (ECT). The Union's environmental and consumer protection policies both originated in this fashion before they were elevated by the SEA to the status of independent policies. Indeed, even now there is provision for action in these areas to be taken under the internal market provisions—see Articles 153(3)(a) and 175(2) (ECT).

To summarize therefore, we may conclude that the following matters come, actually or potentially, within the exclusive jurisdiction of the European Union:

agriculture
fisheries
coal and steel
atomic and nuclear energy
the essential elements of transport
almost all external trade
foreign, security and defense policy
monetary policy
the general rules on free movement within the internal market
visas, asylum, immigration and external border checks on non-EU nationals
Union citizenship

One final point is the exact significance of Union exclusivity. It means that the Union has the power to operate, by executive or legislative acts, within an area to the total exclusion of the Member States. Union law replaces national law completely. However, as we have seen, the Union rarely makes use of this power to the full, in which case the Member States have the power to act to the extent that the Union has not done so. To hold otherwise would mean that in important areas the law is likely to have gaps. Once the Union does act, the measures previously enacted by the Member States become inoperative and no new ones may be adopted.

IV.1.4.b Concurrent Jurisdiction

In many areas, the Treaties permits the Union to act concurrently with the Member States. The Union has a concurrent jurisdiction with respect to any matter where harmonization is needed to secure the establishment and good functioning of the internal market.[35] As we have seen, this has spawned a body of Union law dealing with a large array of matters: financial services, public procurement, taxation, telecommunications, audiovisual services, intellectual property, corporations, commerce, even consumer protection and the environment. A specific Treaty provision on judicial cooperation in civil matters permits the Union to act with respect to the cross-border service of documents, the taking of evidence, the recognition and enforcement of judgments, national rules on the conflict of laws and jurisdiction and the compatibility of national rules of civil procedure where this is necessary for the proper functioning of the internal market.[36] The Union also has the power to establish and enforce anti-trust rules to deal with measures that either disturb competition within the common market or affect trade between Member States.[37] In all these instances, the limit of the Union's

---

35   Article 93, 94 and 95(1) (ECT).

36   Article 65 (ECT).

37   Articles 81(1), 82 and 87(1) (ECT).

jurisdiction is the Union dimension. It would be possible for these areas of con-current jurisdiction to become exclusive to the Union if the Union dimension were to eclipse the national one. This is unlikely except possibly in the case of anti-trust rules.

In other areas, the Union has been attributed a specific power to act, both legis-latively and executively. In social and labor matters,[38] public health,[39] consumer protection,[40] vocational training,[41] industrial policy including trans-European networks,[42] regional development,[43] research and development,[44] the environ-ment[45] and overseas development,[46] there is provision for a Union policy that supplements, complements or contributes to national policies. Normally this in-cludes the power to harmonize national laws and regulations where this is nec-essary. Certain matters are reserved for the Member States[47] and they may also enact more stringent measures with respect to the protection of workers, public health, consumers and the environment.[48]

The extent of these specific concurrent competences is not always clear. Thus, the question arises as to whether the Union could impinge progressively on na-tional jurisdiction until it achieves exclusivity. Certainly, it could not encroach on the reserved powers of the Member States, but these are not extensive enough to prevent effective exclusivity. However, the principle of subsidiarity would seem to militate against this development.

Within the areas of concurrent jurisdiction, Union law takes precedence over national law.[49] This applies both in the case of existing national rules and those that are enacted subsequently. The principle *lex posterior derogat lege priori* can-not apply in the case of a conflict between Union and national law. This is the classic federalist situation.

---

38   Articles 136-148 (ECT).

39   Article 152 (ECT).

40   Article 153 (ECT)

41   Article 150 (ECT).

42   Article 154-157 (ECT).

43   Articles 158-162 (ECT).

44   Articles 163-173 (ECT).

45   Articles 174-176 (ECT).

46   Articles 177-181 (ECT).

47   These are the maintenance of law and order and the safeguarding of internal security, certain aspects of labor law such as pay, strikes and lock-outs and the organization and delivery of health services. *See* the discussion *infra* in Section IV.1.5.

48   Articles 137(5), 152(4((a), 157(5) and 176 (ECT).

49   The issue of the supremacy of Union law is discussed *infra* in Section IV.2.7. *See* also P. Ra-worth, "Article 177 of the Treaty of Rome and the Evolution of the Doctrine of the Supremacy of Community Law," 1977 *Canadian Yearbook of International Law* 276.

IV.1.4.c Ancillary Jurisdiction

In the areas of economic and employment policy, education, culture and PJC, the role of the European Union is restricted, entirely or substantially, to coordinating the national policies of the Member States. It can be said to exercise here an ancillary jurisdiction.

The most important area of the Union's ancillary jurisdiction is economic policy, where, despite economic and monetary union (EMU), there is only coordination of national policies on the basis of guidelines issued by the Council.[50] However, Member States are expected to follow these guidelines and in the budgetary area there are sanctions for not doing so.[51] A slightly different approach is taken to employment policy as here Member States are only expected to take into account the Council's guidelines.[52] Moreover, the Union is specifically precluded from harmonizing national rules and regulations.[53] This is also the case in the areas of education and culture, where the Union's action is limited to incentive measures and recommendations.[54] In the area of police and judicial cooperation in criminal matters (PJC), as the name suggests, the Union's major role is to coordinate the activities of the police and judicial authorities of the Member States, but it also has a power to harmonize national rules, including those relating to criminal law.[55]

The Treaties do not distinguish between the Union's concurrent and ancillary jurisdictions but there is a difference as we can see from the above discussion. In the case of PJC and economic policy, however, there is considerable potential for the Union's jurisdiction to become concurrent. In the other areas, this is unlikely because of the principle of subsidiarity. It is only in the case of harmonization within the area of PJC that there is a possibility of conflict between national and Union law, in which case the latter takes precedence.

IV.1.5 The Jurisdiction of the Member States

The Treaties attribute certain competences to the Member States. These are the maintenance of law and order and the safeguarding of internal security,[56] certain aspects of labor law such as pay, strikes and lock-outs,[57] the organization and delivery of health services[58] and systems of property ownership.[59]

---

50   Articles 99 and 100 (ECT).
51   *See* the discussion of economic and monetary union *supra* in Section II.3.2.e.
52   Article 128(2) (ECT).
53   Article 129 (ECT).
54   Articles 149(4) and 151(5) (ECT).
55   Articles 29 and 31 (TEU).
56   Articles 33 (TEU); 64(1) (ECT).
57   Article 137(6) (ECT).
58   Article 152(5) (ECT).
59   Article 295 (ECT).

The Court of Justice has added certain aspects of the international regulation of trade in services and intellectual property protection.[60]

The question here is not whether this list of competences is exhaustive, which it is clearly not, but whether all areas that are not specifically attributed to the European Union are reserved to the Member States. Prior to the TEU and its introduction of the concept of the attribution of powers, this was not the case. This is why the Community was able to impinge progressively on areas that originally came within the jurisdiction of the Member States. Mengozzi believes that the obligation of European loyalty contained in Article 10 of the EC Treaty continues to ensure that this situation will continue,[61] but this is not a convincing argument. European loyalty certainly prevents the Member States from enacting laws within their areas of jurisdiction that conflict with Union law or policy, but it does not give the Community a right to encroach on these areas. If, as now seems clear, the Union's jurisdiction is based on its attributed competences, surely this implies that all other areas are reserved to the Member States. However, within areas of concurrent jurisdiction, the line of demarcation between Union and national jurisdiction is not often clear.

IV.2 The Nature of European Union Law

IV.2.1 The Double Character of Union Law

A peculiar feature of the legal system of the European Union is that no formal distinction is made between executive and legislative powers. Indeed, the task of distinguishing them is made more difficult by the fact that the acts of the Union's bodies may on occasion have both an executive and a legislative character.[62] In addition, the instruments and procedures used by Union bodies overlap. Regulations, decisions and directives are used for both types of acts as are the Consultation and Co-Decision Procedures and to a lesser extent, the Council and Assent Procedures. The Member States also are involved in adopting both executive and legislative acts.

The closest that the Treaties come to making a distinction between executive and legislative powers is the provision in the EC Treaty that the results and explanations of votes as well as statements in the minutes must be made public when the Council acts in a legislative capacity.[63] It is left up to the Council, however, to define when this is the case,[64] and it has done so by defining legislative

---

60 *Opinion 1/94*, [1994] ECR I-5267. *See* the discussion *supra* in Section II.3.2.f.

61 Mengozzi (fn. 11) at pages 87-88.

62 *See* Articles 37(2), 40, 57(2), 63(3)(b), 65, 65(a), 65(c), 71(1)(d), 135, 137(1),(2), 150(2),(4), 152(4), 153(3)(b),(4), 155(1) and 156, 157(3), 159, 175(1), 175(3) and 308 (ECT).

63 Article 207(3) (ECT).

64 Article 207(3) (ECT).

acts as "rules which are legally binding in or for the Member States."[65] This is not particularly helpful as executive acts may also involve the laying down of binding rules. Nor does it obviate the need to analyze and categorize the provisions of the Treaties and the acts of the Union bodies to determine whether they constitute executive or legislative acts. At the same time, however, all these acts and Treaty provisions, whether executive or legislative, are part of the legal order of the Union and are considered to constitute Union law[66] as the term is used in this Chapter.[67] At this stage, it is not necessary to make the distinction. This is done later in Chapter VI.

IV.2.2 The Composition of Union Law

The law of the European Union can be divided into three component parts. Firstly, there is formal Union law, which consists of the Treaties upon which the European Union is based,[68] any amendments thereto and all acts done pursuant to them whatever their character. These acts include the specific acts undertaken by the European Council under the Treaties, such as common strategies in the common foreign and security policy (CFSP)[69] and the adoption of conclusions on the employment situation in the Community,[70] but probably not statements of policy emanating from its powers under the TEU to define general political guidelines.[71] Such statements, which take forms such as declarations, resolutions or conclusions, can be considered part of informal Union law, although there is room for debate.

Informal Union law, which is the second component part of Union law, consists of all the acts of the Member States and the bodies of the European Union that are adopted outside the framework of the Treaties.[72] They are inspired by the Treaties but they are not acts undertaken under their authority. They regulate matters for which the Treaties provide no authority for the Union to act with a

---

65   Rule 7 of the Council's Rules of Procedure, which are contained in Council Decision 00/396 (OJ L149/00), as amended by Council Decision 01/216 (OJ L81/01). One would think, however, that the final word on what constitutes a legislative act must lie with the Court of Justice.

66   I use this term throughout even though prior to the TEU it was called Community law. Because almost all Union law that is subject to judicial review emanates from the EC Treaty, the Court of Justice still refers to "Community" as opposed to "Union" law.

67   This does not include executive acts that have no permanent effect, such as a referral to the Court of Justice.

68   The various treaties are set out *supra* in Section II.2 and again *infra* in Section IV.2.3.

69   Pursuant to Article 13(2) (TEU).

70   Pursuant to Article 128(1) (ECT).

71   The European Council has a general power to define the political guidelines of the European Union under Article 4 (TEU), and a specific power to do so in the area of CFSP under Article 13(1) (TEU).

72   This law is sometimes called "soft" law—*see* K.C. Wellens and G.M. Borchardt, "Soft Law in European Community Law," 14 *European Law Review.* 267.

view to improving the functioning of the Union and furthering the process of European integration. This body of law exists parallel to formal Union law as a supplement to it. It has to be consistent with formal Union law.

Finally, set apart by its judicial nature, is the third component of Union law. The case law of the Court of Justice does not comprise legislative or executive acts done pursuant to the Treaties; on the other hand, this law does derive from specific powers given to the Court under the Treaties and is most certainly not outside the framework of the Treaties.

An expression that occurs often in the context of Union law is *acquis communautaire*. Few scholars bother to define it although its meaning is not self-evident. Most frequently, it is taken to describe the amalgam of all that has been decided and promulgated since the establishment of the Communities.[73] In other words, it embraces all three component parts of Union law. However, the sense of the French word *acquis* would suggest that the concept covers only that part of Union law which has been acquired by the action of the bodies and Member States of the Union. In this case, the *acquis* would not include the Treaties. It is in this sense that the word is used in this book.

IV.2.3 Primary and Subordinate Law in the European Union

Primary law emanates from a universal prescriptive authority entailing the right to enact rules of any type and scope for all domains of human activity. This authority is only restricted by constitutional limitations that either protect the rights of citizens or the division of power in a federal state. Subordinate law implements and applies superior law. The type and scope of its operations are determined by the superior law on which it depends. It may be prescriptive in that it can create new rules but only to the extent that this is permitted by the superior law and subject to any restrictions which this law places on it. Subordinate law is called secondary law when it is enacted pursuant to primary law and tertiary law when it is enacted pursuant to secondary law.

Universal prescriptive authority in the European Union is vested in the Member States acting individually in accordance with their internal constitutional procedures. The Treaties and any amendments thereto which they have adopted in this manner[74] constitute the primary law of the Union. This comprises the Treaties establishing the European Coal and Steel Community (ECSC),[75] the European Atomic Energy Community (EAEC)[76] and the EC, as amended by the First

---

73 *See* P.S.R.R. Mathijsen, *A Guide to European Union Law* (6th ed., 1995), note 7 on page 6.

74 The amendment processes are outlined in Section II.3.3.f.

75 261 U.N.T.S. 140.

76 298 U.N.T.S. 167.

and Second Budgetary Treaties (1970,[77] 1975[78]), the Treaty amending the Protocol on the Statute of the European Investment Bank (1975)[79], the Act concerning the Election of the Representatives of the European Parliament by Direct Universal Suffrage (1976),[80] the SEA (1986), the TEU (1992) and the Treaty of Amsterdam (1997)[81] as well as the Accession Treaties with new Member States.[82] Primary law does not include administrative amendments to protocols and statutes or extensions of the Union's jurisdiction decided by the Council without ratification by the Member States, as it is this ratification that transforms these amendments into primary law. Nor does it include agreements concluded between themselves by the Member States outside the framework of the Treaties. The Court of Justice has made it quite clear that any such agreements must follow the procedures set out in the Treaties in order to constitute an amendment or a supplement to the primary law of the Union.[83]

Secondary law enacted to implement and apply the Treaties is adopted primarily by the appropriate Union body[84] and on occasion by the Member States. The TEU and the EC Treaty both permit considerable discretion as to how their objectives are to be realized, which means that secondary Union law has a very broad scope. It does not, however, include the various acts adopted by the Union and the Member States outside the framework of the Treaties, as these acts are independent of the primary law of the Union.

The status of conventions that are concluded by the Member States, acting individually, under Article 34(2)(d) of the TEU and Article 293 of the EC Treaty is not entirely clear. They have the form of secondary legislative acts adopted by the Member States pursuant to the Treaties. On the other hand, where the Court is given jurisdiction, it is permitted only to interpret them and not pronounce on their validity.[85] This suggests that they are considered primary law. It may be, however, that narrower scope of the Court's jurisdiction over these conventions arises from the fact that it is bestowed specifically rather than emanating from the general power of judicial control which the Court exercises by virtue of various provisions of the EC Treaty, in particular Articles 230 and 234. The better

---

77 OJ L2/71.

78 OJ L359/77.

79 OJ L91/78. The Treaty only affects the EC Treaty.

80 OJ L278/76.

81 OJ C340/97.

82 The topic of accession is discussed *supra* in Section II.3.3.e.

83 *Defrenne* v. *SABENA*, 43/75, [1976] ECR 455 at 478.

84 The actors involved in the Union decision-making procedures are discussed *infra* in Section V.1.1.

85 *See* Article 35(1) (TEU) and the Protocol to the 1968 Brussels Convention on jurisdiction and enforcement of judgments in civil and commercial matters (OJ C27/98). The nature of judicial control in discussed *infra* in Section IV.2.5.

view is surely to view them as secondary law. The position is clearer with respect to the executive acts that the Member States adopt under the Treaties. Whether they are taken collectively or individually by the Member States, they are clearly secondary law.

International treaties that are concluded by or on behalf of the Union can also be considered secondary acts although their status is normally superior to that of other subordinate acts.[86] These treaties are concluded by the Council acting alone or in conjunction with the Member States.[87]

Tertiary law, which implements or applies secondary law, is enacted mainly by the Commission but in some cases by the Council. Where the Council reserves to itself the power to implement or apply its own secondary legislation, it must enumerate the special circumstances that justify this decision.[88] No such justification is needed when the Council implements conventions adopted by the Member States under Article 34(2)(d) of the TEU or closer cooperation arrangements. The Council is obliged to implement its own secondary decisions in PJC.[89] While more circumscribed than secondary law, tertiary law may nonetheless have quite large a scope, which may extend to establishing exceptions to the rules[90] and setting penalties where they are violated.[91]

IV.2.4 The Binding Nature of Union Law

Law consists by its very nature of binding rules, but not all Union rules are binding. Certain instruments are specifically said to have no binding force, others may or may not be binding and some are binding only on the Member States, certain institutions or the persons to whom they are addressed. It is thus easier to discuss this issue as we look at each instrument. There is no significant difference on this point between formal and informal Union law. The binding nature of the case law of the Court is a separate issue and is discussed in Section IV.5.2.

IV.2.5 The Nature of Judicial Control of Union Law

Where Union law is subject to judicial control, this means that the Court of Justice has the jurisdiction to interpret it and determine its legality. The Court's role is not exclusive as the national courts also have some role to play,[92] but the

---

86   *See* the discussion *infra* in Section IV.3.1.

87   See the discussion *supra* on the external competence of the European Community and the European Union in Sections II.3.2.f and II.3.3.c, respectively.

88   *See Commission v. Council*, 16/88, [1989] ECR 3457. An example is found in the 8th recital to the Preamble to Council Regulation 789/01 (OJ L116/01).

89   Article 34(2)(c).

90   *See SpA Eridania-Zuccherifici Nazionali et al v. Ministry of Agriculture and Forestry et al*, 230/78, [1979] ECR 2749.

91   *See Germany v. Commission*, 240/90. [1992] ECR I-5383.

92   The relationship between the role of national courts and the Court of Justice is discussed *infra* in Section VI.4.1.a.

Court of Justice is the final arbiter. An important point to note is that the Court has the right only to interpret primary law while it can both interpret and determine the legality of subordinate law. A detailed discussion of the role of the Court follows in Section VI.4.

Formal Union law is largely subject to judicial control, although this control does not extend to acts within the CFSP and is limited in the area of PJC.[93] Collective acts by the Member States are also exempt. Informal law is not subject to judicial control except to the extent that is necessary to determine whether the act in question belongs indeed to informal Union law.[94]

IV.2.6 The Direct Applicability and Direct Effect of Union Law

These two concepts were originally thought by many scholars to be interchangeable.[95] The early jurisprudence of the Court of Justice bears much responsibility for this confusion, although it was due in large part to the fact that the early cases on direct effect concerned exclusively provisions of Union law that were also directly applicable.[96] It was not until the *Grad* case[97] that direct effects were found to arise from a provision that was not directly applicable. Now it is established that the two concepts are quite distinct.[98] A provision of Union law may still be both, but it can also be directly applicable without having direct effect and directly effective without being directly applicable.

Direct applicability means that a provision of Union law takes effect in the legal orders of the Member States without the need for national or Union implementation[99] and as such is automatically binding throughout the European Union

---

93   *See* the discussion *infra* in Section IV.4.2.a.

94   *See Schlüter v. Hauptzollamt Lörrach*, 9/73, [1973] ECR 1135.

95   *See e.g.* K. Lipstein, *The Law of the European Community* (1974) at page 11; A.Parry and S. Hardy, *EEC Law* (1973) at page 142; Gerhard Bebr, "Directly Applicable Provisions of Community Law: the Development of a Community Concept," (1970), 19 *International Comparative Law Quarterly* 257. Mengozzi (fn. 11) still confuses the two concepts in his Chapter IV.

96   The most influential of these early cases was *NV Algemene Transport—en Expeditie Onderneming Van Gend en Loos v. Nederlandse Administratie der Belastingen*, 26/62, [1963] ECR 1. However, the Court was still confusing the two concepts as late as 1975—*see Defrenne v. SABENA*, 43/75, [1976] ECR 455.

97   *Grad v. Finanzamt Traunstein*, 9/70. [1970] ECR 825. *See* also *Van Duyn v. Home Office*, 41/74, [1974] ECR 1337.

98   *See* Kapteyn and Verloren van Themaat (fn. 10) at page 526 and Mathijsen (fn. 73) at page 138. This view is not, however novel. It was espoused quite early on by such scholars as J.A. Winter in "Direct Applicability and Direct Effect. Two Distinct and Different Concepts in Community Law," (1972), 9 *Common Market Law Rewview* 425 and D.Lasok and J.W. Bridge in the 1976 edition of *An Introduction to the Law and Institutions of the European Communities* at page 199.

99   Most legal writers emphasize national measures. However, in the case of Treaty provisions, it is often the need for Union implementing measures that prevents them from being directly applicable—*see* the discussion *infra* in Section IV.3.2.b.

from the time of its entry into force.[100] It should follow from this definition that any provision that requires national or Union implementing measures cannot be directly applicable, but, as we shall see later, the Court of Justice has taken a different view in the case of some Treaty provisions.

Direct effect refers to the capacity of a provision of Union law to create rights for natural or legal persons that can be enforced by national courts. In order to be directly effective, a provision of Union law, regardless of its nature, must meet the following conditions:[101]

a) the provision must establish rights for persons;

b) these rights must be clear and precise enough for the national courts to enforce;

c) these rights must be unconditional, in that they are not subject to any pre-condition that has not been fulfilled or any implementing measures or any delay that has not yet expired. In the case of implementing measures, this does not prevent unconditionality if the time for implementation has passed or the implementation has been done improperly;

d) the provision must not confer a discretion on the Member States or Union bodies with respect to enjoyment of the rights.[102] Negative obligations such as prohibitions are more easily seen as allowing no discretion, however this does not exclude positive obligations from having direct effect.

Whenever a provision of Union law is directly applicable, it will automatically and immediately have direct effect if it meets the above criteria. If it is not directly applicable because it needs to be implemented, it can only have direct effect once the time for its implementation has passed. Some decisions within PJC are specifically stated by the TEU to have no direct effect,[103] which means that they cannot be directly applicable either.

These enforceable rights arising under Union law derive first and foremost from the obligations it places on Member States. They extend vertically to include rights arising from obligations placed on subordinate state authorities[104] and

---

100 This concept must not be assimilated to the monist theory whereby international agreements entered into by a state are given effect within the legal order of that state without the need for national implementing measures—*see* the discussion *infra* in Section IV.6.

101 *See van Duyn v. Home Office*, 41/74, [1974] ECR 1337 and *Marshall v. Southampton and South-West Hampshire Area Health Authority*, 152/84, [1986] ECR 723.

102 This is a subtle distinction—*see* the Court's reasoning in *Ministère Public Luxembourgeois v. Hein (née Muller)*, 10/71, [1971] ECR 723 at 730.

103 Article 35(2)(b),(c). They are discussed in Section IV.3.2.dii and diii.

104 *See Marshall v. Southampton and South-West Hampshire Area Health Authority*, 152/84, [1986] ECR 723 (health authority); *Fratelli Constanzo SpA v. Comune di Milano*, C-188/89, [1989 ECR 4311 (territorial entities); *ECSC v. Acciaiere e Ferriere Busseni SpA*, C-221/88, [1990] ECR I-495 (fiscal authorities).

public enterprises.[105] Direct effect may also have a horizontal effect and create rights between persons where the obligations can be interpreted as binding the latter.[106]

Direct applicability is a Treaty concept[107] but as such it only applies to regulations. The Court applies it as well to Treaty provisions and international agreements concluded by the Union. This wider application like the concept of direct effect are creations of the jurisprudence of the Court of Justice. This jurisprudence only concerns the formal law of the European Union, and so the two concepts do not apply to informal Union law.

IV.2.7 The Doctrine of the Supremacy of Union Law

The final and most crucial characteristic of Union law is that it takes precedence over national law. The Court of Justice took the position early on that Union law must prevail over national law on grounds of jurisprudential logic:

> ... the law stemming from the [EC] Treaty could not, because of its special and original nature, be overridden by domestic legal considerations, however framed, without being deprived of its character as Community law and without the legal basis of the Community itself being called into question.[108]

However, the Court was faced with the reluctance of many national courts to override a provision of national law in favor of Union law, particularly if that provision was subsequent in time or part of an organic law. It nevertheless went about establishing a doctrine of the supremacy of Union law that applies to both prior and subsequent national legislation as well as to the effects of national constitutional provisions. Two cases stand out as landmark decisions on this topic.

The first is the *ENEL* case.[109] At issue was whether an Italian nationalization law passed subsequent to the EEC Treaty and conflicting with it could be allowed to stand. The position taken by the Italian government was that the national law should stand on the basis of the legal maxim *lex posterior derogat lege priori*. The Court rejected this contention in a clear statement of the principle of Union law supremacy:

> The transfer by the [Member] States from their domestic legal system to the Community legal system of the rights and obligations arising under the [EEC] Treaty carries

---

105   *See A. Foster et al v. British Gas plc*, C-188/89, [1990] ECR I-3313. Kapteyn and Verloren van Themaat (fn. 10) at page 549 criticize this case for obfuscating the distinction between vertical and horizontal effect by establishing a specious difference between public and private companies.

106   *See Walrave and Koch v. Association Union Cycliste Internationale*, 36/74, [1974] ECR 1405.

107   Article 249 (ECT).

108   *Costa v. ENEL*, 6/64, [1964] ECR 585 at 594.

109   *Ibid.*

with it a permanent limitation of their sovereign rights, against which a subsequent unilateral act incompatible with the concept of the Community cannot prevail.[110]

The second case is *Internationale Handelsgesellschaft m.b.H v. Einfuhr- und Vorratsstelle für Getreide und Futtermittel*.[111] Here the Court was faced with an EEC regulation that violated fundamental rights guaranteed by the German constitution. Building on the approach that it had taken in ENEL, the Court now went all the way and decreed that not even national constitutional provisions can prevail against Union law:

> . . . the validity of a Community instrument or its effect within a Member State cannot be affected by allegations that it runs counter to either the fundamental rights as formulated by the constitution of that State or the principles of a national constitutional structure.[112]

The Court has been equally clear and uncompromising about the effect of this doctrine of supremacy at the national level. It means that "every national court must, in a case within its jurisdiction, apply [Union] law in its entirety and protect rights which the latter confers on individuals and must accordingly set aside any provision of national law which may conflict with it. . . ."[113] Here the doctrine of supremacy meets and complements the concept of the direct effect of Union law.

Despite its breadth, the doctrine of the supremacy of Union law as elaborated by the Court of Justice has been generally accepted in the Member States. Initially, the Constitutional Courts of Italy and Germany had difficulty in accepting that Union law should prevail over constitutional guarantees on fundamental rights. The Italian *Corte Costituzionale* largely accepted the Court's position in the *Frontini* case[114] although it reserved the right to intervene in the unlikely event that Union law seriously violated fundamental rights. The German *Bundesverfassungsgericht* eventually took a similar approach in *Wünsche Handelsgesellschaft*[115] but only with respect to acts that come properly within the Union's jurisdiction. By thus reserving to itself the right to decide whether the boundaries of the Union's jurisdiction have been respected, it encroaches on the role of the Court of Justice, which is alone competent to decide this question.

The Court's doctrine of the supremacy of Union law can only apply to formal Union law, as that alone emanates from the transfer of the Member States' sovereign rights to the Union on which the doctrine is based. However, not all formal law benefits from this doctrine. Because of its more intergovernmental nature,

---

110   *Ibid* at 594.

111   11/70, [1970] ECR 1125.

112   *Ibid* at 1134.

113   *Amministrazione delle Finanze dello Stato v. Simmenthal SpA*, 106/77, [1978] ECR 629 at 644.

114   *Frontini et al v. Ministero delle Finanze*, [1974] 2 CMLR 386. *See* the discussion in Mengozzi (fn. 11), Chapter IV.

115   [1987] CMLR 225.

it has been suggested that decisions taken pursuant to the TEU in the areas of the CFSP and PJC do not share in this supremacy.[116] This is probably true of decisions within the CFSP but not those in PJC.[117]

IV.3 The Formal Law of the European Union

IV.3.1 The Hierarchy of Formal Union Law

Although there is no official hierarchy of the formal law of the European Union, it is possible to establish one by analogy with national legal systems. Clearly, primary law is paramount and secondary law must be consistent with it. Similarly tertiary law must be consistent with secondary law. Between the primary law and subordinate law of the Union are its international agreements.[118] On the one hand, these agreements must be consistent with the Treaties[119]; on the other hand, they are superior to other subordinate acts as the latter may not conflict with them.[120]

A list of the formal law of the Union in its hierarchical order would look like this:

1. The provisions of the Treaties and any amendments thereto that have been ratified by the Member States acting individually (Treaty law);

2. International agreements concluded by the Union and/or the Member States pursuant to the Treaties;

3. Binding secondary acts of the Member States and the Union bodies:

a) legislative acts (conventions) adopted by the Member States pursuant to Article 34(2)(d) of the TEU[121] and Article 293 of EC Treaty;[122]

b) executive acts of the Member States adopted pursuant to the Treaties;

c) executive and legislative acts adopted by the Union bodies, including the European Council, pursuant to the Treaties;

---

116 *See* Kapteyn and Verloren van Themaat (fn. 10) at page 68.

117 *See* the comments *infra* in Section IV.3.2.d.i.

118 These include agreements concluded by all the Member States prior to January 1st, 1958 that have been assumed by the Union according to the principle of substitution. An example is the 1947 General Agreement on Tariffs and Trade, which still exists as an appendix of the WTO Agreement.

119 Article 300(5),(6) (ECT). In the case of agreements concluded by the Member States prior to January 1st, 1958, any incompatibilities between them and Union law must be eliminated pursuant to Article 307 of the EC Treaty.

120 Article 300(7) (ECT).

121 These conventions are established by the Council and recommended to the Member States for adoption by them.

122 These conventions are drawn up directly by the Member States.

d) closer cooperation arrangements authorized under Articles 40 and 43 of the TEU and Article 11 of the EC Treaty;

4. Tertiary acts adopted by the Commission or the Council pursuant to:

a) secondary acts of the Union bodies;

b) conventions adopted by the Member States;

c) closer cooperation arrangements.

5. Non-binding executive and legislative acts adopted by the Union bodies, including the European Council.

IV.3.2 The Instruments of Formal Union Law

IV.3.2.a Introduction

In the following sections we shall be examining the instruments through which formal Union law is created. Each instrument will be described and its nature analysed with respect to its binding quality, judicial control, direct applicability, direct effect and precedence over national law. We shall also look at form and publication.

IV.3.2.b The Treaties

Treaty Law comprises the provisions of the various Treaties upon which the European Union is based.[123] They set out the scope and basic structure of the Union and the enabling provisions that bestow legislative, executive and judicial powers on Union bodies. They also regulate certain executive and legislative matters directly.

Treaty law is subject to judicial control in the sense that the Court of Justice has power to interpret it, but this control does not cover all Treaty provisions. Within the EC Treaty, the Court's jurisdiction is limited in only one instance. Under Article 68(1), a reference to the Court involving the interpretation of Title IV (visas, asylum, immigration and other policies related to free movement of persons) can only be made by national courts of last instance.[124] Within the TEU, the Court exercises no judicial control over the provisions on CFSP or PJC. By contrast, it has jurisdiction over the provisions on closer cooperation, amendment and accession.[125]

All Treaty law is, of course binding on the Member States but only the EC Treaty takes precedence over national law. Furthermore, provisions of the EC Treaty are directly applicable unless it can be shown that the provision has to be imple-

---

123   The various Treaties are set out *supra* in Sections II.2 and IV.2.3.

124   The normal rule under Article 234 is that any national court can request a preliminary ruling if it considers such a ruling necessary for it to give judgment.

125   Article 46(c),(e) (TEU).

mented by a Union institution. However, even in this case, the Court has indicated that such provisions of the Treaties become directly applicable once the period for implementation has passed.[126] The Court's view is that, not to hold these provisions directly applicable, would permit the Union bodies charged with their implementation, to evade their responsibilities. This approach is, in my view, unfortunate, as the effect has been to discourage the Union from adopting secondary legislation to facilitate the application of Treaty law.[127] It would have been wiser for the Court to hold the provisions to be directly effective, but it clearly meant directly applicable as it said there was no longer any need for secondary implementing legislation.

Where provisions of the EC Treaty meet the appropriate criteria,[128] they are directly effective. Such provisions are found among those setting out prohibitions, obligations to do a certain act, the definition of a legal position and conferring legal rights. This direct effect may be both vertical and horizontal.[129] Generally speaking, Treaty law setting out the scope and basic structure of the Union is not directly effective. Enabling provisions, however, may place an *obligation* on a Union body to act and thus bestow a corresponding right under Article 232 of the EC Treaty on the Member States, the Union institutions, the ECB within its area of competence and any natural or legal person who is the addressee of an act to bring an action for failure to act. To this extent, therefore, they are also in a sense directly effective.

IV.3.2.c. Regular Instruments Authorized by the Treaties

IV.3.2.c.i Introduction

In this section we shall discuss those subordinate instruments that are provided by Article 249 of the EC Treaty on a general basis for the adoption of acts by the Council, Commission and European Parliament acting jointly with the Council. These are regulations, directives, decisions, recommendations and opinions. The ECB may also use these instruments with the exception of directives.[130]

---

126 *See Reyners v. Belgian* State, 2/74, [1974] ECR 631; *van Binsbegen v. Bestuur van de Bedrijfsvereniging voor de Metaalnijverheid,* 33/74, [1974] ECR 1299; *Thieffry v. Conseil de l'Ordre des Avocats à la Cour de Paris,* 71/76, [1977] ECR 765. These decisions dealt specifically with provisions of the EC Treaty that had to be implemented by the end of the transitional period on Decembe 31, 1969, but the principle applies generally.

127 This same criticism is made implicitly in the 2nd recital to the Preamble to EP/Council Directive 99/42 (OJ L201/99), where it is noted that provisions of the redundant secondary legislation "should be retained, particularly where they usefully prescribe how obligations under the Treaty are to be discharged."

128 These are set out *supra* in Section IV.2.6.

129 *See Walrave and Koch v. Association Union Cycliste Internationale et al,* 36/74, [1974] ECR 1405; *Defrenne v. SABENA,* 43/75, [1976] ECR 455.

130 Article 110 (ECT). It can also issue recommendations and opinions.

Regulations, directives and decisions are subject to similar rules. They are all binding, albeit in slightly different ways.[131] Secondly, all three are fully subject to the judicial control of the Court except decisions taken in pursuance of the CFSP. In addition, under Article 241 of the EC Treaty, a party to legal proceedings before the Court of Justice may invoke a plea that the regulation at issue is illegal. However, the Court has extended this remedy to all three instruments.[132]

The rules as to form and publication are also similar. All three instruments must be reasoned, which the Court has interpreted to mean that they must mention the provisions of the Treaties or secondary legislation on which they are based,[133] the motives that prompted them and the proposals and opinions that were required under the enabling provision.[134] They do not have to indicate whether opinions were favorable or not, still less refute unfavorable opinions. Regulations, directives and decisions adopted pursuant to the Co-Decision procedure as well all other regulations and directives addressed to all Member States must be published in the *Official Journal of the European Communities*.[135] They enter into force on the date specified in them or, in the absence thereof, on the twentieth day following their publication. There is no obligation to publish other directives and decisions, but in practice most are published in the *Official Journal*.

Finally, all three of these instruments benefit from the Court's doctrine of the supremacy of Union law, except decisions in the area of the CFSP. In the case of directives, this supremacy applies to the national law that implements the directive.

The regular instruments can be used for the whole ambit of the Union's activities, including those which fall under the TEU,[136] to the extent that another, specific instrument is not prescribed for the act. The Treaties indicate in some instances which regular instrument should be used for a particular act.[137] Otherwise, it is up to the institution to choose that which is most appropriate.

---

131 Article 249 (ECT).

132 *See Simmenthal SpA v. Commission*, 92/78, [1979] ECR 777 at 800.

133 The topic of the legal base of Union acts is discussed *infra* in Section V.1.4.

134 *See e.g. Hoogovens v. High Authority*, 14/61, [1962] ECR 253; *Germany v. Commission*, 24/62, [1963] ECR 63; *R v. Minister for Agriculture, Fisheries and Food et al, ex parte Fedesa et al*, C-331/88, [1990] ECR I-4023.

135 Article 254(1),(2) (ECT).

136 *See* Articles 5 (TEU); 249 (ECT).

137 *See* Articles 13(3) (decisions) (TEU);40 (directives or regulations), 44(1) (directives), 46(2) (directives), 47(1) (directives), 47(2) (directives), 53 (recommendations), 77 (recommendations), 83(1) (regulations or directives), 86(3) (directives or decisions), 89 (regulations), 94 (directives), 95 (directives), 96 (directives), 97(1) (recommendations), 99(2) (recommendations), 99(4) (recommendations), 104(5) (opinions), 104(7) (recommendations), 119(1) (recommendations), 128(4) (recommendations), 132(1) (directives), 139(1) (directives), 148 (decisions), 149(4) (recommendations but optional), 151(4) (recommendations but optional), 152(4) (recommendations but optional)and 162 (decisions) (ECT).

IV.3.2.c.ii. Regulations

Article 249 bestows three characteristics on regulations. The first is that they have general application. This means that they must either apply to all persons throughout the Union or to "categories of persons viewed abstractly and in their entirety."[138] They cannot be aimed at specified or identifiable persons or groups. They also apply, where appropriate, to Union bodies and to Member States.

Regulations are binding in their entirety and cannot be applied by Member States in a selective or incomplete manner.[139]

Regulations are directly applicable. However, this does not mean that no national implementing measures are ever needed. In many cases, Member States need to adopt administrative and other measures in order for a regulation to becomes operative in their territories.[140] On the other hand, they may not reproduce the contents of a regulation in a national enactment. Not only is this unnecessary as the regulation is automatically part of the national legal order by reason of its direct applicability, it would also create confusion and obscure the direct Union character of the provisions.

It has been suggested that regulations are by their very nature directly effective.[141] This is not so, as regulations, like directives, decisions and Treaty provisions, can only be directly effective when they meet the necessary conditions.[142] For instance, they must establish rights for persons, which is most certainly not the case for all provisions in regulations.[143] Because of their direct applicability, regulations are, however, are part of the national legal order and thus can place obligations not only Member States but also on natural and legal persons. As a result they are capable of horizontal as well as vertical direct effect.

IV.3.2.c.iii Directives

Directives are addressed to the Member States. Article 249 does not require them to be addressed to all Member States, but this is their most common form.

---

138 *Confédération Nationale des Producteurs des Fruits et Légumes et al. v. Council*, 16&17/62, [1962] ECR 471 at 479.

139 *See Commission v. United Kingdom*, 128/78, [1979] ECR 419 at 428.

140 *See* the various national implementing measures for Council Regulation 2137/85 on the European Economic Interest Grouping (EEIG) (OJ L199/85), without which the regulation could not function.

141 *See* Mathijsen (fn. 73) at page 138.

142 These are set out in Section IV.2.6.

143 Thus a provision like Article 36 of Regulation 1408/71, which stipulates that a Member State which has paid out benefits in kind to a person covered by the social security scheme of another Member State can claim reimbursement from that State, can hardly be said to create a right for legal or natural persons susceptible of enforcement by a national court.

Essentially, directives are instructions issued by the Union to Member States requiring them to enact or modify national laws in accordance with the terms of the directive. They are said to be binding as to the result while leaving it up to the Member States to decide on the form and methods. In fact, many directives are so precise and detailed that all that is left for the Member States to do is transpose them textually into national law. Given that most directives also have general application, they resemble regulations in many instances. There remain, however, two important differences between the two instruments.

In the first place, directives are not directly applicable. They have to be transposed into the national legal order by national laws. Normally, Member States have two to three years to do this. Failure to do so is an infringement of the Treaties and one of the most frequent reasons why Member States are brought by the Commission before the Court of Justice. Two other consequences attach to a failure to implement directives properly. The first is that, if a provision of a directive meets the appropriate criteria, it has vertical direct effect once the time for national transposition has elapsed.[144] Secondly, Member States are liable in damages to persons who suffer loss as a result of a failure to implement a directive properly and in time.[145]

The second difference is the nature of the direct effect of directives. Unlike regulations, directives do not automatically have direct effect even where they meet the necessary criteria. It is only when they are not implemented properly or in time that they can acquire this quality. In addition, directives are addressed to Member States and are binding only on them and not directly on natural and legal persons. As a result, the Court of Justice has consistently maintained that they have only vertical effect against governments, subordinate state authorities and public enterprises. They do not have horizontal direct effect by creating enforceable rights against persons.[146]

IV.3.2.c.iv Decisions

There are two types of decisions. Here we are concerned with those that are provided for by Article 249. There are, however, other decisions that are made by Union bodies, often in connection with the operation of the Union, that do not have the same characteristics. These are usually called *sui generis* decisions.[147]

---

144 *Van Duyn v. Home Office*, [1974] ECR 1337; *Marshall v. Southampton and South-West Hampshire Area Health Authority*, 152/84, [1986] ECR 723.

145 *Francovich et al v. Italy*, C 6 and 9/90, [1991] ECR I-5357.

146 *Marshall v. Southampton and South-West Hampshire Area Health Authority*, 152/84, [1986] ECR 723 at 749; *Faccini Dori v. Recreb Srl*, C-91/92, [1994] ECR 3325 at 3355-3356. In fact, Miss Marshall was successful as she was looking for vertical direct effect against a health authority.

147 They are discussed *infra* in Section IV.3.2.d.

Decisions under Article 249 are described as binding in their entirety upon those to whom they are addressed. From this description we may infer two characteristics. Firstly, like regulations, they must be applied completely. Secondly, unlike regulations, they do not have general application but are addressed to specified or identifiable persons, groups, Union bodies or Member States. In order for an instrument to be a decision under Article 249, the Court of Justice requires that it be "of individual concern to certain persons."[148] Certain persons may include the Member States as a whole, for decisions are routinely addressed to all of them. This may seem to bring them close to directives but for the issue of direct applicability.

Decisions are not described in Article 249 as directly applicable. Nevertheless, their binding quality and the fact that they are not formally subject to national implementing measures suggests that they are directly applicable unless, in a particular case, they provide for national or Union implementation. It is odd how little attention has been given to this point. On the other hand, it is established that, where they meet the appropriate criteria, decisions can have direct effect.[149] This effect may be vertical and, where the decision places obligations directly on persons, horizontal as well.

IV.3.2.c.v Recommendations

According to Article 249, recommendations have no binding force They aim at obtaining voluntarily from the persons, bodies or Member States to which they are addressed a given action or behavior. They may also have general application. Because they are not binding, they are not subject to judicial control for legality under Article 230 of the EC Treaty. However, they may be the subject of a judicial interpretation in order to establish whether they are in fact a binding instrument under the guise of a recommendation, or indeed to decide whether they have any legal effects.[150]

This is all very clear, but it does not tell the whole story. Recommendations are not in fact without legal effects. They clarify Union law by legitimizing behavior that conforms to them and by making legal obligations more precise. More significantly, they may on occasion impose obligations on Member States backed by sanctions where the recommendation is not followed. Under Article 97(1) of the EC Treaty, the Commission may issue a recommendation to a Member State containing measures that it should adopt in order not to cause distortions in the conditions of competition in the common market. If the Member State does not follow the recommendation, the other Member States are not required to take any measures themselves to remedy the distortions. Under Article 99(2),

---

148 *Confédération Nationale des Producteurs des Fruits et Légumes et al. v. Council*, 16&17/62, [1962] ECR 471 at 479.

149 *Grad v. Finanzamt Traunstein*, 9/70, [1970] ECR 825.

150 *See Schlüter v. Hauptzollamt Lörrach*, 9/73, [1973] ECR 1135.

the Council adopts a recommendation setting out each year guidelines for the economic policies of the Member States. Member States are obliged to adapt their national economic policies to these guidelines and are open to public re-buke by the Council if they do not. In neither of these instances can Member States be brought before the Court for infringement of their obligations under the Treaty, nevertheless they are in a way bound to follow the recommendations in question.

The rules as to form and publication do not apply to recommendations, al-though they are often published in the *Official Journal*.

IV.3.2.c.vi Opinions

Like recommendations, opinions are said by Article 249 to have no binding force. They are merely the expression of a point of view although their impact depends on how they are adopted. Opinions that are issued *ad hoc* by Union bodies do not have as much weight as those that are issued as part of the legislative process. Many bodies can issue opinions including the Commission, the European Parlia-ment, the Economic and Social Committee, the Committee of Regions, the Eco-nomic and Financial Committee, the ECB and the Court of Auditors. Opinions are not subject to judicial control.

The rules on form and publication do not apply to opinions. Those that are is-sued as part of the legislative process are, however, normally published in the *Official Journal*.

IV.3.2.d *Sui Generis* Decisions

IV.3.2.d.i Introduction

The decisions provided for by Article 249 of the EC Treaty can only be taken by the Council, the Commission, the European Parliament acting jointly with the Council and the ECB. However, there are a number of acts that must be done by other Union bodies as well as the Member States acting collectively that also re-quire decisions. In addition, there are special decisions which are taken by the Council within the area of PJC. The nature of these various decisions differs from that of Article 249 decisions and also from that of each other. This is why they are called *sui generis*. Generally speaking, they are not bound by the rules on form and publication contained in Articles 253 and 254 of the EC Treaty, but they are normally published in the *Official Journal*. They must set out their legal base.

Many of these *sui generis* decisions deal with the functioning of the Union and so the doctrine of the supremacy of Union law is not relevant to them. However, where a conflict with national law is possible, they are probably covered by the doctrine as long as they are binding. Kapteyn and Verloren van Themaat, however, suggest that acts done within the context of PJC are not covered by the doctrine as the TEU adopts an intergovernmental model.[151] This is surely not the case with the framework decisions and other decisions taken under Article 34(2) as they are adopted under a Community procedure and are largely subject to judicial control like regular instruments

IV.3.2.d.ii Framework Decisions by the Council in PJC

Article 34(2)(b) of the TEU allows the Council to adopt framework decisions for the purpose of the approximation of the laws and regulations of the Member States in the area of PJC. These particular decisions are in fact identical to regular directives in that they are addressed to Member States and are binding upon them as to the result while leaving the choice of form and methods up to them. Neither are directly applicable. However, there are two important differences. Firstly, the Treaty specifically states that framework decisions cannot have direct effect. Secondly, there are some limits to the judicial control of these acts.[152]

IV.3.2.d.iii Decisions by the Council in PJC

Article 34(2)(c) of the TEU allows the Council to take decisions for all matters in PJC except approximation, which must be done by framework decisions. These decisions are binding but, unlike regular decisions, they do not have any particular addressee(s). Presumably, they may therefore have general application. They cannot have direct effect, which means also that they cannot be directly applicable. Tertiary acts implementing these decisions must be taken by the Council in the form of decisions of the same kind. The same limits with respect to judicial control apply as in the case of framework decisions.

IV.3.2.d.iv Decisions by Other Bodies of the European Union

Many bodies of the European Union other than the Commission, the Council, Parliament acting jointly with the Council and the ECB have the power to do certain acts. These are mainly connected with their internal organization, including the adoption of rules of procedure. This is the case, for example, with Parliament acting alone,[153] the Courts,[154] ECOSOC[155] and the Committee of Regions.[156] Parliament also sets up temporary committees of enquiry, appoints the Ombudsman and may pass a motion of censure on the Commission.[157] The

---

151 Kapteyn and Verloren van Themaat (fn 10) at page 68.

152 This topic is discussed *infra* in Section VI.4.2.a.

153 Articles 190(5) and 199 (ECT).

154 Articles 223, 224, 225(4), 245 and 247(3) (ECT).

155 Article 260 (ECT).

156 Article 264 (ECT).

157 Articles 193, 195 and 201 (ECT).

Court of Justice may dismiss Commissioners, members of the Court of Auditors and the Ombudsman.[158] The European Council has to draw up annual conclusions on the employment situation in the Union.[159] The Presidency of the Council convokes intergovernmental conferences.[160] All these acts require a decision. Usually it is called just that, but it may also be called a resolution in the case of Parliament and a conclusion, declaration or resolution in the case of the European Council.

These decisions are binding except in the case of the conclusions on unemployment adopted by the European Council. Only some of them are subject to judicial control. Decisions or resolutions of the European Parliament can be reviewed by the Court for their legality under Article 230 of the EC Treaty if they are intended to produce legal effect *vis à-vis* third parties. Acts of Parliament, the Court of Justice and the Court of Auditors can also be the subject of a preliminary ruling under Article 234 of the EC Treaty with regard to their interpretation or validity.[161] None of these decisions are directly applicable or have direct effect.

IV.3.2.d.v Decisions of the Member States

On a number of occasions, the Treaties require the Member States to act collectively in the performance of an executive act. Many have to do with the administration of the Union: appointment of the executive board of the ECB and of judges and advocates-general,[162] appointment and replacement of the President and members of the Commission[163] and establishment of the seats of Union bodies.[164] There are some other matters, however, that are also dealt with in this way. Under Article 20 of the EC Treaty, Member States are required to act collectively to secure the protection of nationals from other Member States in third countries where their home State does not have representation. Under this provision, the Member States have adopted a decision establishing an emergency travel document.[165] The Member States must also act to encourage

---

158 Articles 195(2), 213(2), 216 and 247(7) (ECT).

159 Article 128(1) (ECT).

160 Article 48 (TEU).

161 Article 234 only applies to the acts of institutions.

162 Articles 112(2)(b), 223 and 225(3) (ECT).

163 Articles 214 and 215 (ECT).

164 Article 289 (ECT). The Article refers only to "institutions" but in practice the Member States establish the seat of Union bodies as well. This is another example of the blurring of the distinction between bodies and institutions of the Union—*see* the discussion *supra* in Section III.2.

165 OJ L168/96.

the exchange of young workers.[166] Finally, they adopt general amendments to the Treaties and accession agreements acting collectively.[167]

As often in the European Union, nomenclature is a problem with these collective decisions of the Member States. In the first place, they go by a plethora of names. Here is a sample: Decision of the Representatives of the Governments of the Member States, Decision of the Representatives of the Governments of the Member States by Common Accord, Decision by Common Accord of the Governments of the Member States and Decision taken by Common Agreement between the Representatives of the Governments of the Member States. If the decision is taken at head of state or government level, this is normally mentioned. If the decision is taken in the course of a Council meeting, the words "meeting within (or "in") the Council" are added These decisions may also be styled "Acts." They state their legal base and are normally published in the *Official Journal* although this is not obligatory.

The second problem of nomenclature is that the same names are used to designate the collective acts of Member States taken *outside* the framework of the Treaties. It is essential to keep these two groups of decisions separate as they are quite different legally.[168]

The collective decisions taken pursuant to the Treaties are certainly binding but they are not subject to judicial control. However, if Member States violate the Treaties in making any of these decisions, they can be brought before the Court of Justice on that ground. The Court could then review the validity of the decision None of these decisions are directly applicable or have direct effect.

IV.3.2.e Special Instruments Authorized by the Treaties

IV.3.2.e.i Introduction

On some occasions, the Treaties specify a certain instrument to carry out a particular act. Regular instruments or *sui generis* decisions cannot be used instead. The legal nature of these acts is not uniform, and so it is discussed in context below. Common strategies, joint actions and common positions operate more like international commitments than Union law and so do not benefit from the doctrine of the supremacy of Union law.[169]

---

166 Article 41 (ECT).

167 Articles 48 and 49 (TEU). *See* the discussion on the amendment process *supra* in Section II.3.3.f.

168 The decisions taken outside the framework of the Treaties are discussed *infra* in Section IV.4.2.a.

169 *See* also Kapteyn and Verloren van Themaat (fn. 10) at page 68.

IV.3.2.e.ii Common Strategies

Article 13(2) of the TEU gives the European Council the power to decide on common strategies in the CFSP. Although the wording could indicate that these common strategies are adopted via a *sui generis* decision, they are in fact instruments in their own right with their own numbering.[170] As to form and publication, they state their legal base and are normally published in the *Official Journal* although this is not obligatory.

Common strategies set out the objectives, duration and means for dealing with a particular aspect of the CFSP. They are implemented by decisions, joint actions and common positions. The Treaty provision does not indicate that they are binding on Member States but the common strategies themselves normally include an obligation for Member States to ensure that their foreign policy conforms to the common strategy.[171] They are clearly not directly applicable or directly effective. Nor are they subject to judicial control.[172]

IV.3.2.e.iii Common Positions

The TEU provides for the Council to adopt common positions in the areas of the CFSP and PJC.[173] These define the approach of the Union to a particular matter. The former can stand on their own but normally implement common strategies. The latter are one of the instruments provided by Article 34(2) for realizing PJC. As to form and publication, both common positions state their legal base and are normally published in the *Official Journal* although this is not obligatory. Both bind the Member States to the extent that they must ensure that their national policies conform to the common position.[174] Common positions in the CFSP are not subject to judicial control.[175] In the area of PJC, the Court only has the power to rule on a dispute between Member States over the interpretation and application of a common position where the Council cannot settle the dispute within six months.[176] They are clearly not directly applicable or directly effective.

IV.3.2.e.iv Joint Actions

Article 14(1) of the TEU provides for the Council to adopt joint actions within the CFSP. These instruments set out the objectives, scope, means and duration of operational action by the Union to address a specific situation. They are normally used to implement common strategies. As to form and publication, they

---

170 *E.g.* Common Strategy 00/458 on the Mediterranean region (OJ L183/00).
171 *E.g. ibid*, Points 30 and 31.
172 This is implicitly excluded by Article 46 (TEU).
173 Articles 15 and 34(2)(a) (TEU).
174 Articles 15, 19 and 37 (TEU).
175 This is implicitly excluded by Article 46 (TEU).
176 Article 35(7) (TEU).

state their legal base and are normally published in the *Official Journal* although this is not obligatory. They bind Member States in the positions they adopt and in the conduct of their activity.[177] They are not subject to judicial control[178] and are clearly not directly applicable or directly effective.

IV.3.2.e.v. Individual Action by the Member States

The Treaties provide for the Member States to carry out certain acts pursuant to the Treaties on an individual basis. Here, they do not act collectively, but each makes the decision separately according to its national constitutional practices. The decisions may be published in a national gazette and they will often appear in the *Official Journal*. As national acts, they are not subject to judicial control by the Court of Justice unless this jurisdiction is conferred upon the Court by an express provision of the act itself.

The Member States act individually primarily in the legislative area. As we have already seen, they enact primary law in this way by ratifying amendments to the Treaties.[179] They also adopt secondary law in the form of conventions in the area of PJC[180] and with respect to a number of matters set out in Article 293 of the EC Treaty. These are the protection of persons, double taxation, mutual recognition of companies and the recognition and enforcement of judgments. Numerous conventions has been adopted in the field of PJC. One example is the Convention on Extradition.[181] Three conventions have been signed under Article 293: the Convention on the Mutual Recognition of Companies,[182] the Convention on Jurisdiction and the Enforcement of Judgments in Civil and Commercial Matters[183] and the Convention on the Elimination of Double Taxation.[184] The first has not yet entered into effect and the second will be superseded by Council Regulation 44/01 on March 1, 2002.

In many ways, these conventions are like acts of Union bodies despite the fact that they are adopted individually by each Member State. As to form and publication, they state their legal base and are normally published in the *Official Journal* although this is not obligatory. The conventions are binding and are subject to some judicial control, which is, however, limited to ruling on their interpretation. In the area of PJC, judicial control with respect to the interpretation of the

---

177 Article 14(3) (TEU).

178 This is implicitly excluded by Article 46 (TEU).

179 Articles 17(1), 42, 58 and 49 (TEU); 22 and 190(4) (ECT). *See* also the discussion *supra* in Section IV.2.3.

180 Article 34(2)(d) (TEU).

181 OJ C313/96.

182 Bull. EC Supp. 2/69.

183 OJ L299/72.

184 OJ L225/90.

conventions is conferred by Article 35(1) of the TEU subject to Member States accepting the Court's jurisdiction.[185] Judicial control of conventions adopted pursuant to Article 293 is conferred on the Court of Justice by the convention itself. It is suggested that, like international agreements concluded by the Union, all these conventions are directly applicable, capable of direct effect and take precedence over national law.[186]

The Treaties also provide for the Member States individually to carry out certain executive acts involving the appointment of national members to the Economic and Financial Committee and the Employment Committee.[187]

Member States also act individually to ratify decisions on their own resources[188] and international agreements involving the CFSP, PJC and free movement of workers from the Overseas Countries and Territories.[189] Here their acts are part of a Union decision-making procedure.

IV.3.2.f International Agreements of the European Union

The European Union has concluded a great number of international agreements although, as they mainly concern matters coming within the purview of the EC Treaty, they are mostly Community agreements. International agreements are concluded by the Council,[190] but the Member States also have a role to play. They must ratify agreements concluded pursuant to the TEU, otherwise they are not bound by them.[191] In addition, they are parties to all agreements that encroach on areas of national jurisdiction or entail expenditures by the Member States.[192]

The Union's agreements comprise world-wide multilateral agreements such as the WTO Agreement and the various commodity agreements, regional agreements such as the Lomé Agreement with developing countries and the agreements with the Andean Pact, Mercosur and the Central American Common Market and a whole range of bilateral agreements. These latter agreements include free trade agreements, association agreements, pre-accession agreements, trade and cooperation and scientific and technological cooperation agreements. There are also a number of sectoral agreements that have been concluded with countries on a bilateral basis. The sectors include customs cooperation, mutual recognition and conformity assessment, public procurement, nuclear energy,

---

185 Article 35(2) (TEU). This matter is discussed *infra* in Section VI.4.2.a.

186 *See Bresciani v. Amministrazione Italiane delle Finanze*, 87/75, [1976] ECR 129 at 141.

187 Articles 114(2) and 130 (ECT).

188 Article 296(ECT).

189 Articles 24 and 38 (TEU); 186 (ECT).

190 Articles 24 (TEU); 300(3) (ECT).

191 Article 24 (TEU). *See* also the discussion *supra* in Section II.3.3.c.

192 *See* the discussion *supra* in Section II.3.2.f.

public and animal health, textiles, transport, fisheries and steel products. Three important agreements between the European Union and the United States concern public procurement, anti-trust law and industrial standards.[193]

International agreements are appended to the Council decision approving them, and they are published with that decision in the *Official Journal.* The decision must follow the formal requirements that were set out above.[194] International agreements are binding on the Union and the Member States[195] but they must be consistent with the Treaties.[196] The Council, Commission or any Member State may refer an agreement to the Court of Justice to determine its consistency with the Treaties, and it cannot enter into force if it is inconsistent unless the Treaties are amended to accommodate it.[197] International agreements are also subject to the regular judicial control of the Court under Articles 230 and 234 of the EC Treaty with respect to their validity and interpretation. They are directly applicable, capable of direct effect in the appropriate circumstances and covered by the doctrine of the supremacy of Union law.[198]

IV.4 The Informal Law of the European Union

IV.4.1 Introduction

Unlike formal Union law, one cannot establish a hierarchy of informal Union law although one can perhaps list the various acts comprising it in order of importance:

- agreements between the Member States;

- collective decisions of the Member States;

- interinstitutional accords, and

- non-binding acts of Union bodies.

The very informality of this component of Union law means that the acts do not have to follow any set rules as to form and publication. The first three, however,

---

193 Council Decision 92/215 concerning the conclusion of an Agreement in the form of an exchange of letters between the European Community and the United States of America on government procurement (OJ L134/95); Agreement between the European Communities and the Government of the United States of America regarding the application of their competition laws (OJ L95/95); Agreement between the European Communities and the Government of the United States of America on the application of comity principles in the enforcement of their competition laws (OJ L173/98); and Council Decision 99/78 on the conclusion of an Agreement on mutual recognition between the European Community and the United States of America (OJ L31/99).

194 *See supra* in Section IV.3.2.c.i.

195 Article 300(7) (ECT).

196 Article 300(5),(6) (ECT).

197 Article 300(6) (ECT).

198 *See Bresciani v. Amministrazione Italiana delle Finanze,* 87/75, [1976] ECR 129 at 141.

have more in common with formal Union law. They are frequently published in the *Official Journal* and are usually binding at least on the parties that have adopted them. There are even circumstances under which some can be directly applicable, have direct effect and take precedence over national law. Some may be subject to some judicial control. The non-binding acts of the Union bodies have none of these characteristics although they may on occasion be published in the *Official Journal*. A last point to note is that all informal Union law must be consistent with formal Union law.

IV.4.2 The Instruments of Informal Union Law

IV.4.2.a Acts of the Member States Acting Outside the Framework of the Treaties

The Member States retain the right to regulate matters related to the Union in the absence of specific provisions of formal Union law dealing with the matter. This discretion is quite circumscribed and has diminished over the years as formal Union law has extended its scope. It is exercised by way of instruments adopted outside the framework of the Treaties that aim at improving the functioning of the Union, implementing the Treaties more efficiently and furthering the process of European integration. These instruments fall into two categories depending on whether the Member States act individually or collectively.

IV.4.2.a.i Agreements between the Member States Outside the Framework of the Treaties

On occasion, the Member States will conclude agreements between themselves on matters related to the European Union. These agreements are not concluded pursuant to any provision of the Treaties and are completely separate from them. They must be clearly distinguished from the agreements that the Member States adopt pursuant to Article 34(2)(d) of the TEU or Article 293 of the EC Treaty.

There have not been many such agreements. One example is the Convention on the Law Applicable to Contractual Obligations.[199] Two others were the Social Policy Agreement appended to the TEU and the Schengen agreements. Both these latter agreements aimed at furthering the process of European integration, but this is now possible within the framework of the Treaties by way of closer cooperation arrangements.[200] Agreements of this particular type will therefore be rare in the future.[201]

---

199 OJ C27/98. It is not yet in force.

200 Closer cooperation is discussed *supra* in Section II.4.

201 The Social Policy Agreement was incorporated into the EC Treaty by the Treaty of Amsterdam following its acceptance by the United Kingdom. The Schengen arrangement has been incorporated into the Treaties through the provisions on closer cooperation as Ireland and the United Kingdom still do not participate in it.

These are regular international agreements. They are negotiated by the Member States between themselves with each State acting in an individual capacity and adopting the agreement according to its constitutional requirements. They participate in the agreements as High Contracting Parties, not as Member States. The agreements are binding on the signatory states according to the rules of international law. If national law or tradition so provides, they may be directly applicable and even have direct effect in the signatory states as well as taking precedence over national law. However, let it be emphasized that these characteristics arise because of national law; they do not derive from Union law. Likewise, the agreements may provide for judicial control by the Court of Justice, which then exercises this control pursuant to the agreement and not under the Treaties.[202]

IV.4.2.a.ii Collective Acts of the Member States Outside the Framework of the Treaties

Rather than acting individually, the Member States will often act collectively with a view to improving the functioning of the Union, implementing the Treaties more efficiently and furthering the process of European integration. There have been a number of these acts. Some examples are the 1960 Luxembourg Accords,[203] the 1960 and 1962 Acceleration Decisions[204] and the 1992 Decision on Danish objections to the TEU.[205]

Generally speaking, these acts tend to be called "Decision of the Representatives of the Governments of the Member States meeting within the Council." If the decision is made within the European Council, the instrument is normally styled "Decision of the Heads of State or Government meeting within the European Council." The term "decision' may be replaced by "act." There is an obvious overlap with the name of those collective acts adopted by the Member States in pursuance of their executive obligations under the Treaties.[206] This is very confusing as the two types of instrument are quite different.

These decisions of Member States taken outside the framework of the Treaties have often been described as international agreements.[207] I disagree as their very name—*inter alia* Decision of the Representatives of the Governments of the Member States meeting within the Council—sets them apart from such agree-

---

202 Two protocols to the Convention on the Law Applicable to Contractual Obligations (OJ C27/98) confer on the Court the right to interpret the convention. They are not yet in force.

203 *9th General Report on the Activities of the EC* (1966), pp.31-33. The Luxembourg Accords are discussed *infra* in Section V.2.1.e.

204 OJ 1217/60 and OJ 1284/62. These decisions aimed at the earlier establishment of the customs union.

205 OJ C348/92.

206 *See* the discussion *supra* in Section IV.3.2.d.v.

207 *See* Kapteyn and Verloren van Themaat (fn. 10) at page 341.

ments. They exist in a sort of no-man's-land between Union and international law, and they have to be examined on a case-by-case basis to see whether they are intended to be binding on the Member States. In most cases, this is the case. A notable exception is the Luxembourg Accords, which is in essence an agreement to disagree.

It is a moot point whether these acts of the Member States are capable of binding the Union bodies or natural and legal persons.[208] Personally, I cannot see how this can be. These instruments are not adopted pursuant to the Treaties and thus cannot bind in any way the Union or persons that are not a party to them. By the same token, they cannot be directly applicable, have direct effect or take precedence over national law. They are not subject to judicial control.

IV.4.2.b Interinstitutional Accords Outside the Framework of the Treaties

On a number of occasions the European Parliament, the Council and the Commission have concluded agreements with each other on the way in which they exercise their powers. These are variously called joint declarations,[209] interinstitutional agreements or declarations,[210] agreements,[211] a modus vivendi[212] or codes of conduct.[213] They play a very important role in the decision-making procedures of the Union, and an argument could be made for considering them formal law. However, strictly speaking they are not as they are not adopted pursuant to the Treaties.

These accords are nonetheless acts within the meaning of Article 230 of the EC Treaty, and as such they are subject to judicial control. There is support in the ensuing case law of the Court for the view that they are binding on the

---

208 Mathijsen (fn. 73) at page 146 suggests that they may be so binding.

209 *E.g.* the Joint Declaration concerning the institution of a conciliation procedure between the European Parliament and the Council (OJ C89/75); Joint Declaration on fundamental rights (OJ C103/77); and Joint Declaration on practical arrangements for the new Co-Decision procedure (OJ C 148/99).

210 *E.g.* Interinstitutional Agreement on procedures for implementing the principle of susidiarity (OJ C329/93); Interinstitutional Declaration on democracy, transparency and subsidiarity (OJ C331/93); Interinstitutional Agreement on common guidelines for the quality of drafting of Community legislation (OJ C73/99); and Interinstitutional Agreement on budgetary discipline and improvement of the budgetary procedure (OJ C172/99).

211 *E.g* Agreement between the European Parliament and the Commission on procedures for implementing Council Decision 99/468 laying down the procedures for the exercise of implementing powers conferred on the Commission (OJ C256/00).

212 *E.g.* Modus Vivendi concerning the implementing measures for acts adopted in accordance with the procedure laid in Article 189b (now Article 251) of the EC Treaty (OJ C102/96)

213 *E.g.* Code of Conduct of the European Parliament and the Commission (OJ C89/95).

institutions that are a party to them.[214] This is logical as the institutions rely on them and expect the other institutions to act accordingly to their terms.

The issues of direct applicability, direct effect and precedence over national law are not relevant to these instruments, and, in any case, it is unlikely that any of the three doctrines would apply to them.

IV.4.2.c Non-binding Acts of Union Bodies Outside the Framework of the Treaties

These instruments comprise declarations, resolutions,[215] programs,[216] communiqués and conclusions[217] of Union bodies. Essentially, all these instruments define principles of Union policy although on occasion they can be more specific.[218] In addition, the Commission issues communications and notices, particularly in the area of anti-trust law and the approximation of laws, clarifying its approach to particular points of Union law.

These instruments are non-binding and hence the doctrines of direct applicability, direct effect and precedence over national law do not apply.[219] On the other hand, they may be subject to judicial control to the extent that the Court will look at them to see whether they have any legal effects and what these are.[220] It can, however, only do this when the instruments emanate from an institution.[221] This would exclude the European Council, for example.

IV. 5 The Case Law of the Court of Justice

IV.5.1 Introduction

The case law of the Court of Justice emanates from its various heads of jurisdiction.[222] The most important for establishing the administrative law of the Union

---

214   See *Andersen et al v. European Parliament*, 262/80, [1984] ECR 195 at 207-208. *See* also Kapteyn and Verloren van Themaat (fn. 10) at page 319.

215   Resolutions that are adopted by a *sui* generis decision are, however binding as are resolutions of Parliament that relate to its internal functioning. Both these types of resolution belong to formal Union law—*see Luxembourg v. European Parliament*, 213/88 and 39/89, [1991] ECR I-5643 at 5699.

216   Programs adopted by binding acts under Articles 166(1) of the EC Treaty on research and development and 175(3) on the environment are secondary acts within formal Union law.

217   The conclusions on employment that are adopted by the European Council pursuant to Article 128(1) of the EC Treaty belong to formal Union law.

218   *E.g.* the Code of Conduct for Business Taxation, which is set out in the Conclusions of Ecofin, (OJ C2/98).

219   *See Commission v. Luxembourg*, 90 and 91/63, [1964] ECR 625 at 631-632.

220   *See Schlüter v. Hauptzollamt Lörrach*, 9/73, [1973] 1135.

221   *See* Articles 230 and 234 (ECT).

222   These are discussed *infra* in Section VI.4.2.b.

are the control of the legality of secondary acts under Article 230 of the EC Treaty, the preliminary ruling on the interpretation and validity of Union law under Article 234 and the action against Member States for infringement of the Treaties under Article 228.

IV.5.2 The Nature of the Case Law of the Court of Justice

The court system of the European Union is not hierarchical in the sense that the judgments of the Court of Justice constitute binding precedents for national courts in the same way as the federal Supreme Court binds lower courts in the United States. However, the Court's decisions are binding on the parties before it, including the national court in a reference under Article 234 of the EC Treaty.[223] Furthermore, its case law has, in the words of the Italian Constitutional Court, "the character of a decision declarative of Community law, in the sense that the Court of Justice, as qualified interpreter of that law, authoritatively specifies its significance with its own decisions, and by such means, determines definitively the breadth and content of its possible application."[224] This means that national courts should follow the Court's rulings on Union law.[225] If they have any doubt as to the state of that law, they may, and in the case of the highest courts must, refer the matter to the Court of Justice for a preliminary ruling before making their decision on the matter before them.[226] In this way, the Court ensures that its jurisprudence is followed although it is not adverse on occasion to reconsidering its case law.[227]

Yet, despite all this, the system is not foolproof. In the first place, national courts are free to choose not to follow the Court's rulings. While it is true that a Member State could be taken to court for infringement of the Treaty if its national courts refused to follow the case law of the Court of Justice, the Commission has shown itself very reluctant to commence infringement proceedings on this ground. National courts can also avoid referring a matter to the Court under Article 234 by alleging that the issue has already been adjudicated satisfactorily by the Court (*acte éclairé*) or that the answer is self-evident *(acte clair)*. In the *CILFIT* case,[228] the Court sought to circumscribe the use of these devices, particularly the *acte clair*, which is more open to abuse. In order to evoke this principle, a national court must be "convinced that the matter is equally obvious to the courts of the other Member States and to the Court of Justice."[229] Fortunately, the national courts have in large measure cooperated with the Court of

---

223 *Milch- Fett- und Eierkontor GmbH v. Hauptzollamt Saarbrücken*, 29/68, [1969] ECR 165 at 180.

224 *Beca SpA e altri v. Amministrazione Finanziaria dello Stato*, 1985 Giur. cost. 694.

225 *See Brasserie du Pêcheur et al v. Germany et al*, C-46/93 and 48/93, [1996] ECR I-1029 at 1145.

226 Article 234 (ECT). Preliminary rulings are discussed *infra* in Section VI.4.2.b.i.

227 *See Keck and Mithouard*, C-267 and C-268/91, [1993] ECR I-6097.

228 *Srl CILFIT et al v. Ministry of Health*, 283/81, [1982] ECR 3415.

229 *Ibid* at 3430.

Justice. We may thus conclude by saying that, on balance, the case law of the Court of Justice is binding both in theory and practice.

To the extent that national courts must follow the case law of the Court of Justice and give effect to any rights in favor of natural or legal persons that it creates, it may also be said to be directly applicable and directly effective. Moreover, as this case law must be followed in preference to legal precedents from higher national courts, it can also be said to take precedence over national law.

IV. 6 The Nature of the Legal Order of the European Union

Hallmarks of the legal order of the Union are the susceptibility of Union law to direct applicability and direct effect and the doctrine of the supremacy of this law over national law. Yet, as long as Union law is considered traditional international law, it can only have these qualities in Member States that pass national enactments bestowing them on Union law or in those that, failing such an enactment, follow the monist approach to international law. Under this approach, international obligations accepted by a state automatically become part of national law and are considered superior to it.

Within the Union, some Member States have dealt with this issue by adopting appropriate constitutional provisions,[230] others by enacting ordinary statutes[231] and some by following the monist approach.[232] The Court of Justice does not consider this a satisfactory basis for the legal order of the Union. It is not hard to see why. As long as the hallmarks of the Union's legal order are secured by national enactments, they are at the mercy of a repeal of these enactments. They are particularly vulnerable where these national enactments are contained in regular rather than organic laws. Likewise, a state can always abandon a monist approach to its international obligations in favor of a dualist one, which requires such obligations to be enacted into national law before they can have any internal legal effect. Differences in approach between the Member States also endanger the uniformity of application of Union law, which the Court considers another essential hallmark of Union law.[233]

From the Court's perspective, it was essential to establish a secure basis for the legal order of the Union that was independent of the vagaries of national law.

---

230 *E.g.* the Netherlands and Luxembourg.

231 *E.g.* Germany, Italy and the United Kingdom. The relevant provisions in the United Kingdom are Sections 2 and 3 of the European Communities Act (1972).

232 *E.g.* Belgium and France.

233 In *Costa v. ENEL*, 6/64, [1964 ECR 585 at 594, the Court stated that "the executive force of Community law cannot vary from one State to another . . . without jeopardizing the attainment of the objectives of the Treaty . . . and giving rise to discrimination. . . ."

One of the first salvoes in the Court's quest came in the *van Gend* case.[234] Here, the Court differentiated Union law from traditional international law. It constituted, said the Court, "a new legal order in international law, for whose benefit the States have limited their sovereign rights, albeit within limited fields."[235] This statement contains the essence of the Court's concept of the legal order of the Union, which it developed further in *ENEL*.[236] Here, the Court asserted that the Member States have in fact transferred their sovereign rights to the Union in those areas where the Union has been given jurisdiction.[237]

Union law is thus no longer to be considered international law but the expression of a new legal order made up of sovereign rights that have been transferred to it from the Member States. The federalist overtones are unmistakable. The Member States have ceded their sovereign power in certain areas to the Union, which becomes as sovereign in those areas as the Member States that exercised power there before it. As a natural attribute of this sovereignty, Union law is capable of being directly applicable and directly effective within the national legal orders of the Member States. Furthermore, there can be no conflict between national and Union law because each is sovereign in its own area. Where one encroaches upon the other, it ceases to have validity. The doctrine of the supremacy of Union law is thus assimilated to the principle of federal paramountcy.

But the Court did not stop there in *ENEL*. It went on to assert that the new legal order is not just a reflection of the legal system that ceded the sovereignty; instead it is an autonomous order that has "its own institutions, its own personality and its own capacity in law."[238] The significance of this autonomy is immense.[239] By taking the various sovereignties ceded by the Member States and merging them into a new autonomous legal order, the Court is in effect placing them out of reach of the Member States that ceded them, for autonomy means independence. This has two far-reaching legal consequences.

It means firstly that the Member States can no longer recall the sovereignty which they have transferred. This transfer is irreversible to the extent that "the powers thus conferred could not . . . be withdrawn from the Community, nor could the objectives with which such powers are concerned be restored to the field of authority of the Member States alone, except by virtue of an express

---

234 *NV Algemene Transport- en Expeditie Onderneming van Gend en Loos v. Nederlandse Administratie der Belastingen,* 26/62, [1963] ECR 1.

235 *Ibid at 12.*

236 *Costa v. ENEL,* 6/64, [1964 ECR 585.

237 *Ibid at 594.*

238 *Ibid at 593.*

239 *See* Winter (fn. 97) at page 433.

provision of the Treaty."[240] Now, this does not mean that the Member States, acting in concert, can never restore powers back to the themselves. However, if they wish to do so, they must amend the Treaties according to the amendment process set out in Article 48 of the TEU, which requires the unanimous agreement of all of them.[241] Such an amendment is no different from a similar amendment to the constitution of a federation like the United States that is accepted by the requisite number of states.

The second consequence of autonomy is that, although the national systems that ceded the powers might only have been able to exercise them subject to certain constitutional limitations, the Union is not so restricted. The Court has asserted this right of the Union to exercise its powers freely quite categorically. In a passage that we quoted earlier, it stated that "the validity of a Community instrument or its effect within a Member State cannot be affected by allegations that it strikes at either the fundamental rights as formulated in that State's constitution or the principles of a national constitutional structure."[242]

Certainly, the Court has gone far in establishing the autonomous nature of the legal order of the Union. However, it is far from being completely independent. This issue is discussed in more detail in Chapter VII, but at this stage we can single out one particular problem. This is the ability of national courts to defy the Court of Justice. Although this has happened rarely, it nevertheless prevents the Union legal order from being self-enforcing. In the final analysis, the Union still has to rely on the traditional international remedy of bringing a Member State before the Court of Justice if it wishes to force a national court to follow the decisions of the Court. Such an action does not rescind the wrong decision of the national court and is inadequate as the underpinning of an autonomous legal order. Union law must apply uniformly and be protected by virtue of the Union legal order itself if the latter is to be considered truly autonomous.

---

240 *Commission v. France*, 7/71, [1971] ECR 1003 at 1018. *See* also Kapteyn and Verloren van Themaat (fn. 10) at p.81 and J. Usher, *European Community Law and National Law: The Irreversible Transfer?* (1981).

241 *See Defrenne v. Sabena*, 43/75, [1976] ECR 455 at 478. *See* the discussion *supra* in Section II.3.3.f.

242 *Internationale Handelsgesellschaft m.b.H v. Einfuhr- und Vorratsstelle für Getreide und Futtermittel*, 11/70, [1970] ECR 1125 at 1134.

CHAPTER V

THE DECISION-MAKING PROCESS IN THE EUROPEAN UNION

Chapter 2 Commentary

V.1 The General Framework

V.1.1 The Actors

The promulgation of legislation involves primarily the Council acting alone or the Council and Parliament acting jointly under the Co-Decision procedure and the budgetary procedure.[1] The only other actor is the Member States, who have a limited but nonetheless important legislative role. Acting individually, they alone have the power to amend the Treaties.[2] In addition, they may adopt conventions in the area of police and judicial cooperation in criminal matters (PJC) and for certain matters coming within the ambit of the European Community (EC) Treaty.[3]

The major actors in the adoption of executive acts are the Council acting alone, the Council and Parliament acting jointly under the Co-Decision procedure and the Commission. The Council is predominant although the role of the Commission is far from negligible. The Member States also carry out a number of executive acts.[4] Many have to do with the administration of the Union.[5] Others concern

---

1   I cannot agree with J. Usher in "The Commission and the Law" in G. Edwards and D. Spence (eds.), *The European Commission* (1994) at pages 153-154 that Article 86(3) bestows a secondary legislative power on the Commission. It permits the Commission to apply the competition rules against public undertakings, which is an executive act. It may entail the making of rules, but rule-making is not necessarily legislative in nature.

2   The amendment process is described *supra* in Section II.3.3.f.

3   298 U.N.T.S. 11. See also Articles 34(2)(d) (TEU); 293 (ECT). These conventions are discussed *supra* in Section IV.3.2.e.v.

4   *See* the discussion *supra* in Sections IV.3.2.d.iv and IV.3.2.e.v.

5   Articles 112(2)(b), 114(2), 130, 214(2), 215, 223 and 289 (ECT).

the implementation of the Treaty provisions for the protection of nationals from other Member States in third countries,[6] the exchange of young workers,[7] amendments to the Treaties[8] and accession agreements.[9] There are also other actors involved in specific matters. The European Central Bank (ECB) is responsible for conducting monetary policy;[10] the Presidency is active in the areas of PJC and the common foreign and security policy (CFSP) and also convokes intergovernmental conferences[11] and the European Council adopts common strategies in the CFSP[12] and sets overall policy on employment.[13] Other bodies also have the power to do certain executive acts. These are mainly connected with their internal organization, including the adoption of rules of procedure. This is the case, for example, with Parliament acting alone,[14] the Courts,[15] the Economic and Social Committee (ECOSOC)[16] and the Committee of Regions.[17] Parliament also has important other executive powers. It approves the nomination of the Commission,[18] sets up temporary committees of enquiry,[19] appoints the Ombudsman,[20] grants the Commission a discharge on its implementation of the budget[21] and may pass a motion of censure on the Commission.[22] It may also request the Commission to submit proposals for a Union act.[23] The Court of Justice may dismiss Commissioners, members of the Court of Auditors and the Ombudsman.[24]

---

6   Article 20 (ECT).
7   Article 41 (ECT).
8   Articles 17(1), 42 and 48 (TEU); 22 and 190(4) (ECT). *See* the discussion on the amendment process *supra* in Section II.3.3.f.
9   Article 48 (TEU).
10   Articles 105(2), 106, 110(3) and 114(2) (ECT).
11   Articles 18(1), 24, 37, 38 and 48 (TEU).
12   Pursuant to Article 13(2) (TEU).
13   Article 128(1) (ECT).
14   Articles 190(5) and 199 (ECT).
15   Articles 223, 224, 225(4), 245 and 247(3) (ECT).
16   Article 260 (ECT).
17   Article 264 (ECT).
18   Article 214(2) (ECT).
19   Article 193 (ECT).
20   Article 195(1) (ECT).
21   Article 276(1) (ECT).
22   Article 201 (ECT).
23   Article 192 (ECT).
24   Articles 195(2), 213(2), 216 and 247(7) (ECT).

V.1.2 The Right of Initiative

V.1.2.a Introduction

The right of initiative involves initiating legislative or executive action. The primary actor for initiating action is the Commission, although it is does not enjoy an exclusive right of initiative. However, only the Commission initiates action by way of proposals. Other actors use recommendations, requests or initiatives. This distinction has considerable legal significance, as proposals from the Commission within the EC Treaty can only be amended by the Council acting unanimously.[25] This rule does not apply where the Commission uses an initiative or a recommendation.[26]

V.1.2.b Legislative Acts

In the EC Treaty, the right to initiate legislative acts rests with the Commission. However, in the area of visas, asylum, immigration and other policies related to free movement of persons, it shares this initiative in many instances with the Member States until May 1, 2004.[27] After that date, it recovers its exclusivity but must consider requests from Member States to submit a proposal to the Council. In addition, both Parliament and the Council have a general right to request the Commission to submit proposals.[28] The Commission is not obliged to accede to these requests, but it may be ordered to do so by the Court of Justice if its refusal constitutes failure to act in infringement of the Treaty.[29] No-one, however, can dictate to the Commission the content of its proposals or prevent it from subsequently amending or withdrawing them.

The Commission has no initiatory exclusivity in the Treaty on European Union (TEU).[30] On the only occasion that the Council undertakes a legislative act, it acts on the *initiative* of the Commission *or* the Member States.[31] When the Member States adopt conventions in the area of PJC, they do so on the recommendation of the Council.[32] It is noteworthy too that Parliament can make recommendations directly to the Council for legislative acts in this area;[33] it

---

25   Article 250(1) (ECT).

26   *See* Articles 32(2) and 42 (TEU); 111(3) (ECT).

27   Article 67 (ECT).

28   Articles 192 and 208 (ECT).

29   Articles 232 and 233 (ECT).

30   [1992] 1 C.M.L.R. 573.

31   When it adopts framework decisions under Article 34(2)(b).

32   Article 34(2)(d) (TEU).

33   Article 39(3) (TEU). Legislative acts are not expressly mentioned, but there is no reason why they should be excluded.

does not need to request the Commission to act for it. This underscores the lesser role that the Commission plays as an initiatory organ in the TEU.

V.1.2.c Executive Acts

The Commission does not have an exclusive right of initiative for executive acts. In the EC Treaty it shares this right with the ECB,[34] the Council,[35] the Court of Justice[36] and the European Council.[37] Sometimes, no initiating proposal is required for action by the Council.[38] Both Parliament and the Council have the same right to request the Commission to make a proposal as in the case of legislation, and the same rules apply.

In the TEU, the situation is more complex. The Commission shares a right of initiative with the Member States with respect to the determination of a breach by a Member State of fundamental rights.[39] However, if the Council decides to take action against the Member State in question, it acts on its own initiative.[40] Similarly, no initiatory action is needed from the Commission for the Council to authorize closer cooperation.[41] In the area of PJC, the Council acts on the *initiative* of the Commission or the Member States.[42] Parliament may again bypass the Commission and make recommendations directly to the Council.[43]

There is no provision for a right of initiative in the area of the CFSP. The Council always acts unilaterally although the Commission has a general right to submit proposals to it.[44] It shares this privilege with the Member States. Parliament may again make recommendations directly to the Council.[45] There is, however, a somewhat odd provision that the Council may request the Commission to submit proposals relating to the implementation of a joint action.[46] It is not bound to request the proposal and so presumably may choose to follow or disregard it. It is not clear why this particular act has been singled out in this way.

---

34   Articles 107(5), 107(6), 110(3) and 111 (ECT).

35   Article 121(4) (ECT).

36   Article 225(2) (ECT).

37   Article 99(2) (ECT).

38   *E.g.* Articles 67(2), 72, 99(3), 128(4), 247(3), 290 and 309 (ECT).

39   Article 7(1) (TEU).

40   Article 7(2) (TEU).

41   Article 40(2) (TEU). It is, however, asked to present its opinion.

42   Article 34(2) (TEU). It is not entirely clear that the procedures set out in this Article apply to all the activities that the Council undertakes in this area. If this is not the case, then some acts may be carried out on the Council's own initiative.

43   Article 39(3) (TEU).

44   Article 22(1) (TEU).

45   Article 21 (TEU).

46   Article 14(4) (TEU).

V.1.2.d The Importance of the Initiatory Right

The right of initiative is very important for the Commission, particularly in the legislative area where it has no direct power. It enables the Commission to shape or at least influence the legislative and executive agenda of the Union. The European Council has confirmed that this right is not diminished in any way by the subsidiarity provisions that were introduced by the TEU.[47] Nonetheless, the Commission must respect the principle of subsidiarity as well as ensuring that any proposal it makes can be financed within the limits of the Union's own resources.[48] It should be noted that the Commission's right of initiative only applies to acts by the Council. The Commission has no right of initiative in the case of acts by the European Council, the Presidency or the Member States.

The Commission is given the express right to amend its proposals.[49] It would seem logical to assume that this includes the right to withdraw them as well. If the Commission has the power to alter a proposal completely, it is surely able to cast it aside. Certainly, the Rules of Procedure of Parliament provide for such an eventuality,[50] and the Commission has indeed withdrawn proposals.[51] What is less clear, however, is the scope of the Commission's right to amend or withdraw its proposals.

There is general agreement that, in the case of the Consultation Procedure, the Commission is free to act at any stage in the legislative process up to when the act is adopted by the Council. With respect to the Co-Decision and Cooperation Procedures, the issue is whether the Commission can still amend or withdraw a proposal once the Council has adopted a common position. The view taken by Parliament in its Rules of Procedure is that this should be possible in the case of the Cooperation Procedure.[52] The reason is clear enough. Whereas under the Co-Decision Procedure Parliament has an absolute right to reject the common position, its rejection under the Cooperation Procedure can be overruled by the Council acting unanimously. Thus, it may have to rely on the Commission withdrawing its proposal. Because the Commission's amending and withdrawing powers permit it to protect the integrity of the Union, I support the

---

47   Annex I to Part A, Point 10 of the Conclusions of the Edinburgh Summit. These provisions are discussed *supra* in Section IV.1.3.c.

48   Articles 5 and 270 (ECT)

49   Article 250(2) (ECT).

50   Rule 70(3) of the Consolidated Version of the Rules of Procedure of the European Parliament (14th ed., OJ L202/99), as amended by OJ L189/00.

51   In November 1986 the Commission withdrew the controversial Erasmus proposal. J Usher (fn. 1) at page 147 emits some doubts about the Commission's view.

52   EP Rule 79(4).

Commission's broader view that it should be able to amend or withdraw at any stage in any procedure. A number of academic writers have taken a similar position, but the issue is by no means settled.[53]

The Commission's broad initiatory powers are one of the most effective means it has for fulfilling its task of ensuring the proper functioning and development of the Union.[54] They have, however, been encroached upon by the European Council, which now regularly sets the legislative and policy agenda for the Union. Both the European Monetary System and the three-stage approach to economic and monetary union (EMU) were, for example, decided by the European Council, as was the 1992 program for the establishment of the internal market. In addition, the Council has made increasing use of its power under Article 208 of the EC Treaty to request the Commission to submit proposals, often on the basis of conclusions of the European Council.[55] Without doubt, the European Council has disturbed the institutional equilibrium of the Union but one could argue that it has done so to good purpose.[56]

V.1.3 Interaction of the Union Bodies and the Member States

Both executive and legislative decision-making in the European Union involve a wide degree of interaction between the various bodies as well as with the Member States. The most frequent type of interaction is consultation, but it can also take the form of submission of opinions, reports, observations, comments or views. Sometimes, an institution only has to be kept informed. It is the Council that carries out most of this interaction with the Commission, Parliament and European Council involved occasionally.

Apart from the consultation of Parliament as part of the official decision-making procedure, it is the ECB, ECOSOC and the Committee of Regions that are most frequently consulted. Consultations are also conducted with the Economic and Financial Committee (EFC), the Commission, and the Member States. Other

---

53   *See e.g.* R. Bieber, "Legislative Procedure for the Establishment of the Single Market," (1989), 26 *Common Market Law Review* 711 at 718 and 722. *Contra* J. Usher (fn. 1) at page 147.

54   It is given this task under Article 211 of the EC Treaty.

55   According to G. Edwards and D Spence in "The Commission in Perspective," in G. Edwards and D. Spence (eds.) *The European Commission* (1994) at page 8, this has enabled the Council "to set the agenda and undermine or usurp the intended role of the Commission." This is perhaps a little exaggerated.

56   See the discussion on the European Council *supra* in Section III.3.1. If I may be permitted a quote in French, the trade-off is well described by Béatrice Taulègne in *Le Conseil Européen* (1993) at page 414:

> Indéniablement, par essence et par destination, la creation du Conseil européen a provoqué un glissement progressif de la supranationalité vers l'interétatisme, ce qui ne lui interdit nullement d'être à l'origine de réalisations en faveur de l'Union européenne.

forms of interaction involve the EFC, Employment Committee, Commission, European Council, Parliament, Court of Auditors, Council and Member States. It is only with Parliament that interaction includes keeping it informed.

Some acts must be ratified by the Member States acting individually. These are international agreements in the areas of the CFSP and PJC,[57] agreements on freedom of movement within the Member States for workers from the associated countries and territories,[58] decisions on own resources[59] and some amendments to the Treaties that change their actual texts.[60] On two occasions, this involves ratification of a collective act of the Member States themselves.[61]

V.1.4 The Legal Base of Subordinate Acts

Under the principle of attributed powers, the Union can only act "within the limits of the powers conferred upon it" by the Treaties. This means that every decision must be based on a provision of the Treaties that confers, explicitly or implicitly, the power to do that act. The legal base of a Union act is thus very important, and the Court of Justice will annul a decision where the legal base is invalid or inappropriate.[62] It will do this even if the deadline for challenging the decision has passed.[63]

It is up to the Commission in its proposal to choose the legal base for a decision. If the parliamentary committee charged with examining the proposal disagrees with this legal base, it refers the matter to the Legal Affairs Committee for its opinion.[64] The Legal Affairs Committee may also act on its own initiative.[65] If Parliament accepts by plenary vote the need to change the legal base, it requests the Commission to modify its proposal accordingly. If the Commission

---

57   Articles 24 and 38 (TEU).

58   Article 186 (ECT).

59   Article 269 (ECT).

60   *See* Articles 17(1), 42, 48 and 49 (TEU); 22 and 190(4) (ECT).

61   In the case of general amendments to the Treaties under Article 48 (TEU) and accession agreements with a new Member State under Article 49 (TEU).

62   *See Commission v. France*, 131/87, [1991] 1 CMLR 780, where Council Directive 87/64 was annulled because the Council had used Articles 43 *and* 100 (now Articles 37 and 94) instead of just Article 43. The difference this made was that the Council had to act by unanimity under Article 100. On the other hand, in *Commission v. Council*, 165/87, [1990] 1 CMLR 457, the Council did not annul an act where the Council had erroneously added Article 235 (now Article 308) to the legal base, as it did not change the voting procedure.

63   *Commission v. France*, 6&11/69, [1970]CMLR 43.

64   EP RoP, 63(1).

65   EP RoP, 63(3).

does not oblige, Parliament may suspend examination of the substance of the proposal.[66]

The Council may also challenge the legal base chosen by the Commission.[67] This often happens when Member States are objecting to a legal base that permits legislation to be enacted by a qualified majority instead of unanimity. Sometimes, Member States will trade acceptance of a contested legal base for concessions on the substance of the proposal.[68] This is a practice of doubtful legality as no Union institution has the jurisdiction to make a definitive decision on the correct legal base of a decision. This is a matter exclusively for the Court of Justice.[69]

V.2 Voting Rules

V.2.1 Voting Rules in the Council

V.2.1.a Introduction

The Council may vote in one of three ways: by simple majority, qualified majority or unanimity. Under the EC Treaty, simple majority voting is supposed to be the norm,[70] but in fact it is rarely used. The most common method of voting is by a qualified majority for both executive and legislative acts, although unanimity is also required in many cases. A rough calculation yields around one hundred uses of qualified majority voting for executive acts and sixty for legislative acts. The respective figures for unanimity are around seventy and forty-eight.[71] The gap between the two is thus not as great as is sometimes assumed. Under the TEU, there is no prescribed norm. All three methods of voting are used with unanimity being by far the most common.

Qualified majority voting is the most complex as it is subject to special majorities, a safeguard mechanism and the so-called Ioannina compromise. Constructive abstentions are an issue in the case of unanimity. We shall also look at the 1966 Luxembourg Accords.

---

66   EP RoP, 63(6).

67   *See Greece v. Council*, 62/88, [1991] 2 CMLR 649.

68   These were the tactics used by the United Kingdom with respect to the Commission's proposal on the organization of working time—*compare* OJ C254/90 and OJ C124/91.

69   In *Commission v. Council*, 45/86, [1988] 2 CMLR 131 at 153, the Court of Justice declared: "the legal base for a measure may not depend simply on an institution's conviction as to the objective pursued but must be based on objective factors *which are amenable to judicial review*."

70   Article 205(1) (ECT).

71   Unanimity is also required for the Council to amend a proposal from the Commission—Article 250(1) (ECT).

The quorum needed before the Council can vote is a majority of the Council members, that is to say eight at present.[72] This applies to both the EC Treaty and the TEU.

V.2.1.b Simple Majority Voting

Simple majority voting requires only that a majority of Council members vote in favor of a measure. This means that a country like Luxembourg with 418,000 inhabitants has the same voting power as Germany with over eighty-two million. Theoretically it also means that the eight smaller Member States with a combined population of around fifty million could impose their will on the seven others with a combined population of around 320 million. It is therefore not surprising that this method of voting is used only for non-contentious matters such as procedural questions,[73] including establishing the Council's Rules of Procedure.[74] The Council also takes other administrative decisions by a simple majority, such as bringing an action before the Court of Justice. Likewise, within its Rules of Procedure, the Council votes by a simple majority except where the matter is more contentious. Thus, rules on security must be adopted by a qualified majority[75] and changes of venue for Council meetings by unanimity.[76]

V.2.1.c Voting by Unanimity

Voting by unanimity means that each member of the Council casts one vote in favor of adopting the measure in question. The major acts that must be taken by unanimity are the following:

- acts withing the CFSP with the exception of acts adopted on the basis of a common strategy and those that implement a joint action or a common position;[77]

- acts within PJC with the exception of measures implementing decisions and conventions;[78]

---

72 Article 11(4) of the Rules of Procedure of the Council, which are contained in Council Decision 00/396 (OJ L149/00), as amended by Council Decision 01/216 (OJ L81/01).

73 Articles 23(3) and 34(4) (TEU); 207(3) and 209 (ECT). One exception is that the Employment Committee can be set up by a simple majority under Article 130 of the EC Treaty. This is probably because agreement had already been reached on setting it up before this Article was inserted into the EC Treaty by the Treaty of Amsterdam.

74 Article 207(3) (ECT).

75 Article 24 of the Council's RoP.

76 Article 1(3) of the Council's RoP.

77 Articles 23 and 24 (TEU)

78 Articles 34(2) and 38 (TEU).

- certain areas within the EC Treaty (culture,[79] taxation,[80] social security,[81] industrial policy,[82] regional policy,[83] visas, asylum, immigration[84] and some measures relating to employment,[85] transport,[86] the environment,[87] EMU[88] and personal mobility[89]);

- determination of a breach of fundamental rights by a Member State;[90]

- most administrative amendments to the Treaties;[91]

- structural matters, including accession of new Member States;[92]

- residual power to take action to attain the objectives of the EC Treaty;[93]

- appointment of high officials in the Union administration;[94]

- some financial expenditures.[95]

In the EC Treaty, abstentions by any of the members do not prevent the adoption by the Council of an act by unanimity.[96] This is called a constructive abstention. Pursuant to Article 5 of the TEU, this rule on constructive abstentions also applies to decisions that are taken by unanimity in the TEU. However, with respect to decisions, common positions and joint actions adopted in pursuance of the CFSP, there are two differences in its application. In the first place, a Member State is not obliged to apply an act which is the subject of a formal

---

79   Article 151(5) (ECT).

80   Articles 93 and 95(2) (ECT).

81   Articles 42 and 137(3) (ECT).

82   Article 157 (3) (ECT).

83   Articles 159 and 161 (ECT). Some implementing measures are taken by a qualified majority under Article 162.

84   Title IV (ECT).

85   Articles 95(2) and 137(3) (ECT).

86   Article 71(1).

87   Articles 174(2) and 175(3),(5) (ECT).

88   Articles 105(6), 111(1)(4), 118 and 123(4),(5) (ECT).

89   Articles 18(2), 19(1),(2), 47(2), 95(2) and Title IV (ECT).

90   Article 7(1) (TEU).

91   Articles 42 (TEU); 22, 104(14), 107(5), 133(5), 190(4), 225(2) and 245 (ECT). The Council acts by a qualified majority when it extends the jurisdiction of the Union under Articles 49, 80 and 133(5) and when it is amending certain articles of the ESCB Statute on a recommendation from the ECB under Article 107(5) (ECT).

92   Articles 49 (TEU); 67(2), 133(5), 175(2), 202, 213(1), 221, 222, 290 and 296(2) (ECT).

93   Article 308 (ECT).

94   Articles 18(5) (TEU); 207(2), 247(3), 258 and 263 (ECT).

95   Articles 28(3) and 44(2); 100(2), 269 and 279(a),(b) (ECT).

96   Article 205(3) (ECT).

declaration by its representative in the Council qualifying the abstention.[97] The Member State concerned, however, must accept that the act commits the Union and refrain from any action likely to conflict with it. Secondly, if the number of qualified abstentions represents more than one third of the weighted votes, the act is not adopted. This constitutes a potential blocking minority of 30 votes.

In some instances, members are excluded from a unanimous vote. When a determination of the existence of a serious and persistent breach of fundamental rights by a Member State is made by the Council acting unanimously, the vote of the representative of that State is excluded.[98] For acts that are adopted pursuant to a closer cooperation arrangement, only the votes of those members that represent participating Member States are counted.[99] Some decisions by the Council in the area of monetary policy are taken without considering the votes of members representing Member States that have not entered the third stage of EMU.[100]

V.2.1.d Qualified Majority Voting

V.2.1.d.i Introduction

When the Council votes by a qualified majority, recourse is had to a procedure that allocates votes to the members according to the size of population of the Member State they represent and requires a certain majority for the act to be adopted. Qualified majority voting is used for all matters other than those which require simple majority or unanimous votes.

V.2.1.d.i The Basic Rules

At present, the votes of the members of the Council are weighted as follows:[101]

Luxembourg	2 votes (population 418,000)
Denmark	3 votes (population 5.3 million)
Ireland	3 votes (population 3.5 million)
Finland	3 votes (population 5.1 million)
Sweden	4 votes (population 8.9 million)
Austria	4 votes (population 8 million)

---

97 Article 23(1) (TEU). The provision only refers to "decisions" but this must surely be interpreted to include all acts taken by the Council for which no particular voting method is prescribed.

98 Article 7(1) (TEU).

99 Article 44 (TEU).

100 Articles 118 and 123(4),(5) (ECT).

101 Article 205(2) (ECT).

Belgium	5 votes (population 10.1 million)
Greece	5 votes (population 10.6 million)
Netherlands	5 votes (population 15.6 million)
Portugal	5 votes (population 9.9 million)
Spain	8 votes (population 39.6 million)
France	10 votes (population 58.5 million)
Germany	10 votes (population 82.1 million)
Italy	10 votes (population 57.4 million)
United Kingdom	10 votes (population 58.5 million)

Under the EC Treaty, the general rule is that sixty-two votes in favor are required to adopt an act that is based on a proposal from the Commission.[102] Where there is no such proposal, the sixty-two votes must be cast by at least ten members. This additional requirement applies to all acts that are adopted by the Council by a qualified majority under the TEU as on no occasion does the Council act on a proposal from the Commission. In the case of acts within the CFSP and PJC as well as authorizations for closer cooperation, this is explicitly stated.[103] In the case of decisions under Article 7(2) to suspend certain rights of a Member State that is in breach of fundamental rights or under Article 7(3) to vary or revoke such decisions, the requirement applies by virtue of Article 5 of the TEU. This Article states that the Council exercises its powers within the TEU under the conditions set down by the EC Treaty to the extent that there is not a contrary provision in the TEU.

V.2.1.d.ii The Ioannina Compromise

There is now a total of eighty-seven weighed votes in the Council, which means that the blocking minority stands at twenty-six votes. Prior to the accession of Austria, Finland and Sweden it was twenty-three. This increase concerned some Member States and the result is the Ioannina Compromise. This is a decision of the Council stating that if members of the Council representing between twenty-three and twenty-five votes indicate their opposition to a measure, the Council will endeavor to reach a satisfactory solution that can be adopted by at least sixty-five votes.[104] This search for compromise must not, however, prejudice any obligatory time limits set by the EC Treaty.

---

102 *Ibid*.

103 Articles 23(2), 34(3) and 40(2) (TEU).

104 Article 1 of Council Decision of 29 March 1994 (OJ L105/94).

V.2.1.d.iii Special Majorities

Sometimes, special majorities are required. For acts that are adopted pursuant to a closer cooperation arrangement, only the votes of those members that represent participating Member States are counted.[105] Similarly, the votes of the member representing the Member State in breach of fundamental rights are not considered by the Council in taking, modifying or revoking measures against that Member State under both the TEU and the EC Treaty.[106] In both these cases, the qualified majority is re-defined as the same proportion of weighted votes that is required rather than sixty-two votes. The provisions in the EC Treaty on measures to deal with an excessive deficit in a Member State stipulate that the Council acts by a majority of two-thirds of the weighted votes of its members, excluding those of the member representing the Member State in deficit.[107]

In the TEU, measures implementing a convention adopted by the Member States under Article 34(2)(d) are taken by the Council by a majority of two-thirds of the members from Member States who are Contracting Parties to the convention.[108] The votes are not weighted here, so it is not, in fact, an example of qualified majority voting.

V.2.1.d.iv Safeguard Mechanism

On certain occasions when a decision can be taken by a qualified majority,[109] a representative of a Member State on the Council may oppose the decision for important reasons of national policy that must be stated openly. In this case, the decision is not taken. However, the Council, acting by a qualified majority, may refer the matter to the European Council for a decision by unanimity.

V.2.1.d.v Reform of Qualified Majority Voting

Qualified majority voting is intended to ensure a balance of power between the smaller and larger Member States. By allocating forty-eight votes to the larger countries (France, Germany, Italy, Spain and the United Kingdom) and thirty-nine to the smaller countries, it ensures that neither group can push measures through on their own. There are, however, problems with this system.

In the first place, there is an imbalance in the way the votes are divided up between the two groups. The larger countries have forty-eight votes for a combined population of almost 300 million while the equivalent figures for the smaller countries are thirty-nine and around seventy million. This imbalance will

---

105   Article 44 (TEU).
106   Articles 7(4) (TEU); 309(4) (ECT).
107   Article 104(13) (ECT).
108   Article 34(2)(d) (TEU).
109   Articles 23(2) and 40(2) (TEU); 11(2) (ECT).

become even more pronounced as the Union acquires new Member States, some of which have quite small populations.

The second problem concerns the way votes are divided up among individual countries. The Netherlands with fifteen and a half million people, for instance, has the same number of votes as Portugal with less than ten million. Even more significant, Germany with over eighty million people has the same number of votes as France, Italy and the United Kingdom, all of which have populations in the mid-fifty million. With nearly twenty times the population of Luxembourg, Germany has only five times more weighted votes in the Council.

It is not surprising, therefore, that the Treaty of Nice attempts to rectify these imbalances. Although the Treaty is not yet in force and may never be, these new arrangements are likely to stand.[110] Under the new allocation, which is supposed to come into effect on January 1st, 2005, the larger states increase their percentage of the weighted votes from fifty-five percent to sixty percent of the total. There is still a disparity between the two groups, but it is attenuated. The new numbers are as follows:

Luxembourg	4 votes
Denmark	7 votes
Ireland	7 votes
Finland	7 votes
Sweden	10 votes
Austria	10 votes
Belgium	12 votes
Greece	12 votes
Portugal	12 votes
Netherlands	13 votes
Spain	27 votes
France	29 votes
Germany	29 votes
Italy	29 votes
United Kingdom	29 votes

These new figures represent a solution that is still far from perfect. The Netherlands at last acquires one more vote than Belgium, Greece and Portugal, which

---

110   They are contained in Article 3(1) of the Protocol on the Enlargement of the European Union (OJ C80/01), which is attached to the Treaty of Nice.

makes sense, but it is difficult to justify the award of twenty-seven votes to Spain. Logically, Germany should have been given more votes than the other three large nations, but this was opposed with particular vehemence by France, who hosted the conference that drew up the Treaty of Nice. The German imbalance thus remains. However, under a compromise arrangement, a member of the Council can request verification that the qualified majority represents at least sixty-two percent of the total population of the Union.[111] If this condition is not met, the act is not adopted. Verification is not automatic, it must be requested. With nearly twenty percent of the population of the Union, this provision clearly benefits Germany most.

In order for an act to be adopted on the basis of a proposal from the Commission using the new allocations, there must be at least 169 votes in favor cast by at least a majority of members. The latter requirement is new and is clearly intended to tighten up the procedure. Where there is no proposal from the Commission, two-thirds of the members must vote in favor. This is the same as at present where the accord of ten members is required, but it is a mechanism that will become more restrictive as the Union expands.

V.2.1.e The Luxembourg Accords[112]

The Luxembourg Accords or Compromise are nothing of the sort, but an agreement to disagree that ended up as a *diktat* by France. They stemmed from President De Gaulle's vehement opposition to the increase in qualified majority voting that was scheduled to take place on January 1, 1966. The French boycotted Council meetings and brought the Community to a halt. The result was the so-called Luxembourg Accords. All six Member States agreed that, where very important interests of a Member State were at stake, every effort should be made to secure unanimous agreement for action by the Council.[113] There was, however, no agreement on what should happen if it proved impossible to act by unanimity. The French view that discussion should continue until unanimous agreement was reached was recorded in the Accords[114] but did not bind the other Member States. However, due to France's preponderance at the time, it became the guiding principle of the Accords.

The Luxembourg Accords are part of informal Union law as there is no provision in the EC Treaty for the adoption of such an act. Moreover, as the way in which they have been interpreted conflicts with the provisions of the Treaty, they are probably illegal under Union law. Nevertheless, they were applied consistently

---

111   *Ibid*, Article 3(1)(ii).

112   Decision of the Council of January 28 and 29, 1966.

113   Point (b) 1 of the Luxembourg Accords.

114   *Ibid*, (b) II.

since 1966 and seemed even to have survived the advent of the SEA.[115] The better view is that the TEU, however, marked their demise.[116]

V.2.2 Voting Rules in the Commission

The only voting method that is set down for the Commission is an absolute majority of the Commissioners.[117] However, as all members of the Commission are required to attend its meetings and normally do so,[118] this effectively means a simple majority. The President votes. A tied vote means that the proposed act is rejected. However, the Commission is also enjoined by its Rules of Procedure to act collectively,[119] and so normally it makes its decisions by consensus and only votes if one of its members so requests. The quorum is constituted by the presence of a majority of the members of the Commission. At present, this means eleven.[120]

V.2.3 Voting Rules in the European Parliament

V.2.3.a Introduction

There are three methods of voting set down for Parliament. In some cases it is the Treaties that establish the method, in others the Rules of Procedure of Parliament. The quorum required before a vote can be taken is one third of the Members of the European Parliament (MEPs).[121] As of October 1, 2001 the number of MEPs totals 626, which means that the quorum is 209 MEPs.

V.2.3.b Voting by a Simple Majority

Article 198 of the EC Treaty provides that the normal way for Parliament to act is by a simple majority of votes cast.[122] In the case of a tied vote, the act is normally

---

115 *See e.g.* M. Vasey, "Decision-making in the Agriculture Council and the Luxembourg Compromise," (1988), 25 *Common Market Law Review.* 725.

116 *See e,g,* P.S.R.F. Mathijsen, *A Guide to European Union* Law (6th ed., 1995), footnote 46 on page 54. Kapteyn and Verloren van Themaat, *Introduction to the Law of the European Communities* (3rd edition by L.W. Gormley, 1998), on the other hand, state at page 1141 that it is still important in the area of agriculture.

117 Article 219 (ECT); Article 8 of the Commission's Rules of Procedure (OJ L308/00).

118 Article 5 of the Commission's RoP.

119 Article 1 of the Commission's RoP.

120 Article 7 of the Commission's RoP.

121 EP RoP, 126(2).

122 The wording refers to "an absolute majority of votes cast," which is very poor draftsmanship. When Parliament is approving or rejecting a motion before it, there is either a majority in favor of it or not. The "absolute" is quite redundant here and its use is misleading. On the other hand, when Parliament elects a President from more than two candidates, then the expression makes sense as it would possible in this situation for one candidate to have the most votes without having fifty percent plus one vote, which is an absolute majority. Parliament's Rules of Procedure correctly use the expression "absolute majority of the votes cast" in this situation—EP RoP, 14.

deemed rejected.[123] There are, however, some exceptions to this rule. Tied votes on the whole text of reports from committees and final votes on these reports are referred back to the committee.[124] In the event of a tied vote on Parliament's agenda, the minutes of a sitting of Parliament or on a text put to a split vote, the text is deemed adopted.[125]

Article 198 applies to the following acts by Parliament

- assent to the conferral by the Council on the ECB of specific tasks relating to prudential supervision of financial institutions with the exception of insurance undertakings;[126]

- assent to the amendment by the Council of certain articles of the ESCB Statute;[127]

- assent to the definition by the Council of the tasks, objectives and organization of the Structural Funds and the adoption of general rules applicable to them.[128]

Specific provisions in the EC Treaty or Parliament's Rules of Procedure or both provide for simple majority voting in the following cases:

- assent to the conclusion, renewal or amendment by the Council of association agreements and other international agreements involving cooperation procedures, important budgetary implications or the amendment of a Union act adopted under the Co-Decision Procedure;[129]

- adoption by Parliament of an Opinion under the Consultation, Cooperation or Co-Decision Procedures;[130]

- adoption by Parliament of the joint text agreed with the Council in the Conciliation Committee under the Co-Decision Procedure;[131]

- approval or rejection of the person nominated by the Member States for the position of President of the Commission;[132]

---

123   EP RoP, 128(3).
124   EP RoP, 128(1).
125   EP RoP, 128(2).
126   Article 105(6) (ECT).
127   Article 107 (5) (ECT).
128   Article 161 (ECT).
129   EP RoP, 97(7); Article 300(3) (ECT).
130   EP RoP 68(1). In the latter two procedures, this is referred to as the "First Reading."
131   EP RoP, 83(4); Article 251(5) (ECT).
132   EP RoP, 32(2).

– approval or rejection of the Commission as nominated by the Member States.[133]

V.2.3.c Voting by an Absolute Majority

When Parliament votes by an absolute majority, a majority of all MEPs must vote in favor of the act. As at October 1st, 2001, this means 314 votes.

The EC Treaty or Parliament's Rules of Procedure or both provide for voting by an absolute majority in the following cases:

– assent to accession treaties with new Member States;[134]

– rejection of or amendments to the common position of the Council under the Cooperation and Co-Decision Procedures;[135]

– assent to a recommendation by the Council to the Member States of an act on the procedure for electing MEPs by direct universal suffrage;[136]

– adoption by Parliament of a resolution asking the Commission to make a proposal to the Council under Article 192 of the EC Treaty.[137]

V.2.3.d Voting by a Double Majority

In certain cases, Parliament's Rules of Procedure or the Treaties or both provide for Parliament to act by an absolute majority plus a certain majority of the votes cast. The assent by Parliament to a determination by the Council of a serious and persistent breach by a Member State of fundamental rights and the adoption of a motion of censure on the Commission require an absolute majority and a majority of two-thirds of the votes cast.[138] Under the budget procedure, Parliament must on two occasions act by an absolute majority plus a three-fifths majority of the votes cast.[139]

V.3 Decision-Making Procedures

V.3.1 Introduction

This section is cast more widely than is usually the case with discussions of the decision-making procedures in the European Union. In addition to the five procedures used by the Council acting alone or with Parliament to adopt secondary acts pursuant to the Treaties, we also look at other procedures. These relate to

---

133   EP RoP, 33(4).

134   EP RoP, 96(6).

135   EP RoP, 79(1) and 80(4); Articles 251(b),(c) and 252(c) (ECT).

136   Article 190(4) (ECT).

137   EP RoP, 59(1); Article 192 (ECT).

138   38 EP RoP 108(3) and 34(7); Articles 7(1) (TEU) and 201 (ECT).

139   39 See the discussion supra in Section II.3.7

the conclusion of international agreements, the adoption by the Commission of tertiary acts, the way in which Member States use their powers under the Treaties and the methods by which other bodies of the Union take *sui generis* decisions. The budgetary procedure, however, has been discussed separately in Section II.3.7. The title of this section accommodates the fact that these procedures involve both legislative and executive acts.

V.3.2 Procedures for the Adoption of Secondary Acts by the Council Acting Alone or with the European Parliament

V.3.2.a Introduction

In the original EEC Treaty, there were only two procedures by which the Council, acting alone, adopted secondary acts. These were the Council Procedure and the Consultation Procedure. The Council is the sole decision-maker in both procedures. The Single European Act (SEA)[140] introduced the Cooperation Procedure, which did not impinge on the decision-making exclusivity of the Council but attenuated it by giving Parliament a greater say in the adoption of acts. Finally, the TEU introduced the Co-Decision Procedure, which, as revised by the Treaty of Amsterdam,[141] constitutes the Council and Parliament as equals in the decision-making process. The Treaty of Amsterdam also increases the scope of application of Co-Decision, mainly at the expense of the Cooperation Procedure. The Assent Procedure was introduced by the SEA and extended by the TEU and the Treaty of Amsterdam. Unlike Co-Decision, however, the Assent Procedure does not give Parliament an equal role in the actual decision-making process; instead, it has a veto over the end result.

Three further points can be made here as they apply to all the procedures. Firstly, where other actors have a right to initiate action by the Council, it is not bound to follow up on these initiatives, although it could be taken before the Court of Justice if its inaction constituted failure to act in infringement of the EC Treaty.[142] It can also amend the initiatives, although in the case of Commission proposals it can only do this by unanimity. [143]

Secondly, where the Council is required to interact with another institution or body, failure to do so normally constitutes infringement of an essential procedural requirement. Acts may be annulled on this ground by the Court of Justice under Article 230 of the EC Treaty.[144] However, no actor, not even Parliament,

---

140   OJ L169/87.

141   OJ C340/97.

142   *See* Article 232 (ECT).

143   Article 250(1) (ECT).

144   *See SA Roquette Frères v. Council*, 138/79, [1980] ECR 3333 at 3360-3361; *Maizena GmbH v. Council*, 139/79, [1980] ECR 3393 at 3424-3425.

can hold the Council up indefinitely by refusing to give its opinion.[145] The Council may set a time limit for responding of not less than one month for ECOSOC[146] and the Committee of Regions[147] and, in the case of PJC measures, three months for Parliament.[148] There is, of course, nothing to prevent the Council from interacting more widely if it chooses.

In the discussion that follows, we shall indicate which bodies apart from Parliament have to be consulted. However, it is the consultation of Parliament that is by far the most influential. This is not only because Parliament is the only directly elected body in the Union, but also because it has adopted certain Rules of Procedure that enable it to put pressure on both the Council and the Commission to take account of its opinions.

The third point concerns the Council's attitude towards opinions that it is obliged to take into consideration. The intention behind all forms of mandatory consultation is that the body give its opinion on the proposed measure before the Council acts. This means that any proposal or initiative should be transmitted to that body at the same time it is submitted to the Council. Where the Council acts on its own initiative, it must submit its proposed measure to a body before enacting it definitively. In giving its opinion, it is up to the bodies concerned to approve the measure, suggest amendments or even reject it. Unfortunately, the Council often begins its deliberations on a final text before receiving these mandatory opinions with the result that any amendments which are suggested may be politically unfeasible because of developments that have already taken place in the Council. It has even gone as far as making its final decision and then waiting to formalize it until consultation has taken place. However, as the Council is not bound to follow the input resulting from these consultations, the Court has sanctioned this doubtful practice.[149] This problem is not an issue in the Co-Decision Procedure.

V.3.2.b The Council Procedure

This procedure comprises the following steps:

1st stage: In some cases the Commission initiates the act, including the one occasion on which this procedure is used for a legislative act.[150] The Member

---

145 *Ibid*. In these two cases, the Council had enacted a regulation without waiting for Parliament to deliver its opinion. The Court of Justice held this to be a breach of an essential procedural requirement but only because the Council had not done enough to force Parliament to act. The clear implication is that the Council can act unilaterally if Parliament resists its best efforts and simply refuses to cooperate in the decision-making process.

146 Article 262 (ECT).

147 Article 265 (ECT).

148 Article 39(1) (TEU).

149 *Tunnel Refineries Ltd. v. Council*, 114/81, [1982] ECR 3107 at 3210.

150 Article 132(1) (ECT).

States both share this right of initiative with the Commission[151] and exercise it exclusively on some occasions.[152] The ECB twice shares it with the Commission.[153] In one instance, the Council acts on the basis of conclusions of the European Council.[154] Many times, however, the Council acts on its own initiative.[155]

2nd stage: On some occasions, the Council must consult or obtain an opinion from the Commission,[156] the ECB,[157] ECOSOC,[158] the EFC[159] or the Employment Committee.[160] There is no consultation of Parliament although it may be informed of the decision or even have its opinion taken into account.[161] The problem of the Council acting precipitately is particularly acute in this procedure.

3rd stage: The Council now proceeds to adopt the act in question, but it is by no means obliged to do so. It acts by unanimity, a qualified majority or a simple majority according to the provisions of the Treaties.

The Council Procedure is used under both the TEU and the EC Treaty but almost exclusively for the adoption of executive acts, including an administrative amendment to the EC Treaty.[162] It is only used once for a legislative act, but Parliament is not consulted here either.[163]

V.3.2.c The Consultation Procedure

This procedure consists of the following steps:

1st stage: Normally, the right of initiative in this procedure belongs to the Commission, which acts in most cases by submitting proposals to the Council. In a few cases, this right of initiative is shared with the Member States,[164] the

---

151 Articles 7(1) and 34(2)(a) (TEU). The Member States also share the Commission's right of initiative in the CFSP by virtue of Article 22(1) of the TEU.

152 Articles 40(2),(3) (TEU); 88(2) and 263 (ECT).

153 Article 111(1),(2) (ECT).

154 Article 99(2) (ECT).

155 *See* Articles 7(2),(3), 23, 18(5), 41(3) and 44(2) (TEU); 80(2), 120(3), 187, 207(2), 209, 210, 213(1), 215,, 247(8), 258, 290 and 300(2),(3) (ECT).

156 Articles 40(2),(3) (TEU); 209 (ECT).

157 Articles 59, 111, 114(3) and 123(5) (ECT).

158 Articles 75(3) and 144 (ECT).

159 Article 114(3) (ECT).

160 Article 128(4) (ECT).

161 *See* Articles 99(2), 111(1), 114(3) and 121(4) (ECT).

162 Article 49 (ECT).

163 Article 132(1) (ECT).

164 Articles 34(2)(b),(c),(d) and 42 (TEU); 67(1) (ECT) but note 67(3).

ECB[165] or the Court of Justice.[166] The Council also acts on its own initiative on three occasions.[167]

2nd stage: Under this procedure, Parliament is always consulted. On occasion, so are the ECB,[168] ECOSOC,[169] Committee of Regions,[170] Employment Committee[171] and Commission.[172] The consultation of Parliament remains, however, the most important and its Rules of Procedure try to ensure that its views are not disregarded. Parliament also has concerns that the Council will act before even considering its opinion or that the proposal will be amended after consultation with Parliament by the Commission or Council in a way it disapproves of. The two means that Parliament uses to bolster its position are supportive action by the Commission and re-consultation.

At its consultation, Parliament may approve, amend or reject the proposed act. Where the measure originates in a proposal from the Commission, Parliament tries to pressure the Commission into adopting its amendments to or rejection of the proposed measure. Its Rules provide for it to request the Commission to withdraw a proposal that is rejected by Parliament, which prevents the Council from enacting it.[173] As far as its amendments are concerned, they are more likely to be adopted by the Council if they have been incorporated into the Commission's proposal as the Council can only amend this proposal by unanimity. Thus, Parliament's Rules allow it to refer a proposal back to committee if the Commission does not accept its amendments.[174] In neither case is the Commission obliged to give way, so normally Parliament tries persuasion rather than force. It cannot anyway delay the process indefinitely and so coercive tactics have a limited use.

If, following consultation with Parliament, the Commission withdraws its proposal and introduces a new one, Parliament's Rules call for re-consultation except where this is done to accommodate Parliament's amendments.[175] This is generally accepted. Parliament, however, also insists on being re-consulted when the Commission or Council substantially amend a proposal for reasons

---

165   Articles 107(6), 110(3) and 111(1) (ECT).

166   Articles 225(2) and 245 (ECT).

167   Articles 67(2), 130 and 247(3) (TEU).

168   Articles 104(14), 107(6) and 111(1),(2),(3),(4) (ECT).

169   Articles 52(1), 71(2), 93, 94, 128(2), 137(3), 157(3), 159, 166(4), 172 and 175(2) (ECT).

170   Articles 128(2), 137(3), 159 and 175(2) (ECT).

171   Article 128(2) (ECT).

172   Article 107(6) (ECT).

173   EP RoP, 68(1).

174   EP RoP, 69(2).

175   EP RoP, 70(3) and 71(1),(2).

other than incorporating Parliament's amendments.[176] This normally happens as attempts are made, often with the Commission acting as honest broker, to forge the necessary agreement in the Council to enact the measure. Parliament's position is somewhat unreasonable as its opinion does not bind the Council and, without these necessary maneuvers, many measures would not be enacted. In any case, despite support from the Court of Justice, Parliament's view has not prevailed.[177] As a result, its Rules also permit it to request the Commission to withdraw a proposal where it has been substantially amended after consultation of Parliament.[178] This rarely happens unless the Commission also is dissatisfied with the Council's subsequent amendments to its proposal.

3rd stage: The Council is now free to enact the measure or not. It acts by unanimity, a qualified majority and, on one occasion, by a simple majority.[179]

The Consultation Procedure is used in both the TEU and the EC Treaty and in about equal measure for both legislative and executive acts. It is used for a number of administrative amendments to the Treaties, which must be ratified by the Member States acting individually if they change the main text of the Treaties.[180]

V.3.2.d Cooperation Procedure *Council is still legislative authority*

This procedure differs from the Consultation Procedure in that there are two consultations of Parliament and strict time limits once the Council has adopted its common position. It does not, however, place any obligation on the Council to act in the first place.

The procedure consists of the following steps as set out in Article 252 of the EC Treaty:

1st stage: The Commission has an exclusive right of initiative under this procedure, which it exercises by submitting a proposal to the Council. It also transmits the proposal to Parliament.

2nd stage: Parliament is now consulted and on one occasion the ECB as well.[181] This is Parliament's First Reading. It may approve, amend or reject the Commission's proposal. As it will have a second chance to vet the proposal, it might be thought that Parliament would be more sanguine about having the

---

176   *Ibid.*

177   In *ACF Chemiefarma N.V. v. Commission*, 41/69, [1970] ECR 661 at 662, the Court of Justice intimated that there was need for re-consultation where the final text differed substantially from that on which Parliament gave its opinion.

178   EP RoP, 70(3).

179   Article 130 (ECT).

180   *See* the discussion *supra* in Section II.3.3.f.

181   Article 106(2) (ECT).

Commission adopt its amendments. However, Parliament knows that it is much harder to change the Council's mind than to influence it initially. Moreover, although it can reject the proposed measure at its Second Reading, it will need an absolute majority to do so and the Council can override its decision. Thus, its Rules of Procedure make no distinction between a First Reading under the Cooperation Procedure and an opinion under the Consultation Procedure. It will still ask the Commission to withdraw a proposal that it has rejected or stall on a proposal until the Commission is prepared to come to some compromise on its first-round amendments. The Rules provide for re-consultation if a proposal is withdrawn and resubmitted and where it is substantially amended after the First Reading.[182] Nevertheless, on the question of re-consultation, Parliament seems to prefer to deal with any amendments that have been made since the First Reading during its Second Reading.[183] It did not, for example, ask for re-consultation in the case of the Public Offers Directive even though the common position differed substantially from the text Parliament had approved at its First Reading.[184]

3rd stage: It is now up to the Council to adopt a common position acting by a qualified majority, which it must communicate to Parliament along with a statement of the reasons why it did so in this form. This latter requirement may not remove the danger that the Council will act before receiving Parliament's views but at least it is now forced to justify its position. The Commission must also inform Parliament of its position.

The common position supplants the Commission's proposal as the basis for discussions and compromises leading up to the final enactment of the measure. For this reason, many Council jurists deny that the Commission has the right to withdraw or amend its proposal once the common position has been adopted. Neither Parliament nor the Commission share this view but the issue is not resolved.[185]

Once the Council adopts its common position, its First Reading is complete and the clock begins to run with strict time limits to be observed.

4th stage: Parliament now has a Second Reading in which it has three months to approve, reject or amend the common position. If it does not act at all, it is deemed to have approved the common position. The time limit may be extended by one month with the agreement of the Council.

Parliament may approve the common position by a simple majority but more frequently it is left up to the President of Parliament to declare the common

---

182 EP RoP, 71(1).

183 EP RoP, 80(2)(d).

184 *Cf* OJ C125/82 at p.177 and Co.Doc. 4017/1989.

185 *See* the discussion *supra* in Section V.1.2.d.

position approved where no motion to reject it or amendments to it have been adopted within the time limit.[186] It is somewhat unusual for Parliament to approve a common position without amendments except in the case of routine or other non-controversial matters. Where Parliament acquiesces in this way, there is no need for the Commission to react.

Parliament may reject the common position by an absolute majority.[187] Because this does not necessarily prevent the Council from enacting the common position, Parliament's Rules provide for it to ask the Commission to withdraw the proposal.[188] This, of course, assumes that the Commission has the right to do so at this late stage. In fact, Parliament has only rejected the common position once,[189] but the Commission did not withdraw the proposal.

If Parliament wishes to amend the common position on the Second Reading, it must do so by an absolute majority. Amendments are permitted only in the following situations:[190]

- to restore wholly or in part the text approved by Parliament on its First Reading;

- to reach a compromise with the Council;

- to amend those parts of the text that were added or amended subsequent to its First Reading but which do not amount to a substantial change ne-cessitating a re-consultation of Parliament;[191]

- to take account of a change in circumstances since the First Reading.

Parliament's Rules of Procedure allow it to put pressure on both the Commis-sion and the Council in order to reach some compromise on its second-round amendments by refusing to conclude its Second Reading until both have stated their positions.[192] It is particularly important for Parliament that the Commission include its amendments in the re-examined proposal, as this means that the Council will have to act by unanimity if it wishes to reject them on its Second Reading. Parliament cannot hold up the process beyond the time limit of three months under the Cooperation Procedure without tacitly

---

186 EP RoP, 77(2) and 78.

187 EP RoP, 79(1).

188 EP RoP, 79(4).

189 In October 1988, Parliament rejected the common position on a proposed directive dealing with the protection of workers exposed to benzene at work.

190 EP RoP, 80(2).

191 As mentioned earlier, Parliament now relies on its Second Reading rather than re-consulta-tion although this Rule preserves the rights that it believes it has in this regard.

192 EP RoP, 80(5).

approving the common position.[193] However, it can always choose to reject the common position altogether if it finds the position of the Commission and/or Council unacceptable.

5th stage: Where Parliament amends the common position, there is provision for an official response from the Commission in the form of a re-examined proposal. This document contains those of the amendments from Parliament that the Commission has accepted. It may not contain any new material. This limitation is suggested by the wording of Article 251(d) and is required by the inner logic of the Cooperation Procedure. The common position is a record of the Council's intentions which Parliament scrutinizes before they are enacted. If the Commission were to be allowed to introduce new material into the common position after Parliament's Second Reading, it would no longer have been the Council's intention that Parliament scrutinized and the whole basis of the Second Reading is called into question. If the Commission wishes to introduce new material, it would have to act by means of an amended proposal under the authority of Article 250(2) of the EC Treaty. However, if this is indeed possible, it would destroy the common position and the whole procedure would have to start all over again. The Commission has never done this although it has withdrawn proposals at this late stage. Because of the limited way in which the Commission can respond after Parliament's Second Reading, the issue of re-consultation does not arise.

The Commission has one month in which to produce the re-examined proposal as well as a supplementary document containing Parliament's amendments that it has rejected together with its opinion on them. This time limit cannot be extended.

6th stage: Now comes the Council's Second Reading. Article 251 provides that, where the common position has been approved by Parliament, the Council "shall definitively adopt the act in question in accordance with the common position." It has three months in which to act, which can be extended to four months with the agreement of Parliament. It is clear from the wording of Article 251 that the Council cannot change the text of the common position at this stage. This accords with the logic of the Cooperation Procedure for, if the Council can alter the common position after Parliament has approved it, the whole point of the Second Reading is lost.

On the other hand, academic opinion is not unanimous on whether the Council is obliged to adopt the act.[194] Certainly, Union law has always accepted that the Council can change its mind unless the Treaties specifically provide other-

---

193 It is unlikely in these circumstances that the Council would agree to extend the time limit!

194 Van Hamme in "The European Parliament and the Cooperation Procedure," (1988), 4 *Gestion 2000* at 135, *Contra* R. Bieber, "Legislative Procedure for the Establishment of the Single Market," (1989), 26 *C.M.L.Rev.* 711 at 718 and 723.

wise, which would, however, seem to be the case here. It is significant that Article 251 does not apply to this situation the rule that failure to act by the Council on its Second Reading means that the measure is deemed not to have been adopted. I would therefore incline to the view that the Council must enact the re-examined proposal. Certainly, this is Parliament's view for its Rules provide for an action against the Council for failure to act in infringement of the Treaty if it does not do so.

Where Parliament has amended the common position, the Council may enact the ensuing re-examined proposal from the Commission by a qualified majority. It requires unanimity for the Council to adopt any of Parliament's amendments that have not been accepted by the Commission. Again, the logic of the Cooperation Procedure would suggest that the Council cannot amend the common position beyond incorporating those parliamentary amendments that the Commission has rejected, but here the wording of the Treaty suggests otherwise. Parliament's Rules of Procedure provide for this eventuality by providing for re-consultation,[195] but, given that the Council has a maximum of four weeks in which to make its decision, this leaves little time for Parliament to be re-consulted. If the Council does not act within the time limit of three months, the measure is deemed not to have been adopted. This time limit may be extended to four months with the approval of Parliament.

Where Parliament has rejected the common position, the Council can nevertheless enact it as long as it acts by unanimity. It must do so within three months, which may be extended to four months with the agreement of Parliament. Otherwise, the measure is deemed not to have been adopted. The issue of whether the Council can enact the common position in a form different from that presented to Parliament arises again. The Treaty provision is quite neutral, but the logic of the Cooperation Procedure surely argues against this possibility. In practice, on the only occasion that Parliament rejected the common position, the Council did not attempt to override its veto.

The problem of the Council acting precipitately before it has the result of Parliament's Second Reading is still present but it is much attenuated. It would be difficult for the Council to proceed on elaborating a final text without knowing what will be in the Commission's re-examined proposal and whether it will have to act by unanimity. Moreover, it also has to wait to see whether Parliament approves the common position, in which case it must enact the text in the approved form.

---

195 The rules on re-consultation in Rules 70 and 71 apply only to the First Reading, but Rule 80(3) suggests that they can be extended to the Second Reading.

The Cooperation Procedure has been largely replaced by Co-Decision. It is now used only for four executive acts relating to EMU[196] and not at all in the TEU. Except where the Council is amending a proposal or re-examined proposal from the Commission or enacting the common position after its rejection by Parliament, it acts throughout the procedure by a qualified majority.

V.3.2.e The Co-Decision Procedure

There are still some similarities between the Cooperation and Co-Decision Procedures, but these are now much less since the latter was modified by the Treaty of Amsterdam. There will be, however, some repetition in the discussion below, but it is more convenient than requiring readers to search through the preceding section in order to understand how Co-Decision works.

Some major problems connected with other procedures are removed in Co-Decision. The Council cannot take precipitate action on either its First or Second Readings and the differences of opinion surrounding the enactment of the common position that plague the Cooperation Procedure are resolved.

The procedure consists of the following steps as set out in Article 251 of the EC Treaty:

1st stage: The Commission has an exclusive right of initiative under this procedure, which it exercises by submitting a proposal to the Council. Its practice of also transmitting proposals directly to Parliament becomes a formal requirement.

2nd stage: Parliament is now consulted and so are ECOSOC[197] and the Committee of Regions[198] on many occasions. The Court of Auditors is consulted once.[199] This is Parliament's First Reading. It can approve, amend or reject the Commission's proposal, and its opinion goes directly to the Council without any need for the Commission to incorporate it into an amended proposal. Nevertheless, Parliament may still request the Commission to withdraw a proposal that it has rejected. This may not seem necessary as Parliament will be able to reject the proposed measure definitively on its Second Reading. However, it will need to assemble an absolute majority of MEPs in order to do so whereas the request to the Commission requires only a simple majority in favor. It may also refer the proposal back to committee in order to pressure the Commission into amending it in accordance with Parliament's wishes. There is still an advantage for Parliament in having its amendments incorporated into the proposal as this forces the Council to amend the proposal if it de-

---

196   Articles 99(5), 106(2), 102(2) and 103(2) (ECT).

197   *See* Articles 40, 44(2), 71(1), 80, 95(1) and many others (ECT).

198   *See* Articles 71(1), 137(2), 150(4), 152(4) and many others (ECT).

199   Article 280(4) (ECT).

cides to adopt a common position that does not include Parliament's amendments. To do so, the Council must act unanimously.

Sometimes, subsequent to Parliament's First Reading, the Commission may replace its proposal with another one or substantially amend it for reasons other than incorporating Parliament's amendments. Parliament's Rules specifically call for a re-consultation in these circumstances.[200] This makes sense as, under Co-Decision, the Council bases its First Reading on Parliament's opinion, which the Commission's changes would have rendered obsolete. A new opinion is essential in order for the Council to proceed.

3rd stage: Once it has received Parliament's opinion, the Council starts its First Reading. It has the possibility of adopting the proposed act without further ado. If Parliament has adopted amendments to the Commission's proposal, this will entail including these amendments in the enactment. No intercession from the Commission is needed. Alternatively, where it does not approve of the Commission's proposal or disagrees with Parliament's amendments, the Council may adopt a different text as a common position, which it must communicate to Parliament along with a statement of the reasons why it did so in this form. Where the common position differs from the Commission's proposal, the Council must act by unanimity. The Commission must also inform Parliament of its position. *[handwritten marginal note: Council Adapted]*

The wording of Article 251 suggests that the Council is obliged to adopt a common position if it chooses not to adopt the act at its First Reading. This cannot be the case. In the first place, similar wording in Article 252 has never been interpreted in this way. Secondly, the Council has to assemble the necessary majority in order to act, which may not be possible.

The common position supplants the Commission's proposal as the basis for discussions and compromises leading up to the final enactment of the measure. For this reason, many Council jurists deny that the Commission has the right to withdraw or amend its proposal once the common position has been adopted. Neither Parliament nor the Commission share this view but the issue is not resolved.[201]

Once the Council adopts its common position, its First Reading is complete and the clock begins to run with strict time limits to be observed.

4th stage: Parliament now has a Second Reading in which it has three months to approve, reject or amend the common position. If it does not act at all, it is deemed to have approved the common position. It may extend the time limit unilaterally by one month.[202]

---

200 EP RoP, 71(1).

201 *See* the discussion *supra* in Section V.1.2.d.

202 The time limits can be extended at the initiative of either Parliament or the Council, rather than by the common accord of the two institutions as under the Cooperation Procedure.

Parliament may approve the common position by a simple majority but it is often left up to the President of Parliament to declare the common position approved where no motion to reject it or amendments to it have been adopted within the time limit.[203] In these circumstances, the act is now deemed to have been adopted in accordance with the common position without the need for a further reading in the Council. The issues of whether the Council is obliged to enact the common position in these circumstances or whether it can amend it thus no longer arise. It is somewhat unusual for Parliament to approve the common position without amendments except in the case of routine or other non-controversial matters.

Parliament may also reject the common position by an absolute majority, in which case the proposed act is deemed not to have been adopted and the decision-making procedure comes to an end.[204] There is no need for Parliament to ask the Commission to withdraw the proposal.

If Parliament wishes to amend the common position on the Second Reading, it must do so by an absolute majority. Amendments are permitted only in the following situations:[205]

– to restore wholly or in part the text approved by Parliament on its First Reading;

– to reach a compromise with the Council;

– to amend those parts of the text that were added or amended subsequent to its First Reading but which do not amount to a substantial change necessitating a re-consultation of Parliament;[206]

– to take account of a change in circumstances since the First Reading.

Parliament's Rules of Procedure allow it put pressure on both the Commission and the Council to reach some compromise on its second-round amendments by refusing to conclude its Second Reading until both have stated their positions.[207] It is particularly important for Parliament that the Commission issue a positive opinion on its amendments as the Council will have to act by unanimity if it wishes to adopt amendments that the Commission rejects. Parliament cannot hold up the process beyond the time limit of three or four months under the Co-Decision Procedure without tacitly approving the common position. However, it can always choose to reject the common position altogether if it finds the position of the Commission and/or the Council unacceptable.

---

203   EP RoP, 77(2), 78.

204   EP RoP, 79(1).

205   EP RoP, 80(2).

206   As mentioned earlier, Parliament now relies on its Second Reading rather than re-consultation although this Rule preserves the rights that it believes it has in this regard.

207   EP RoP, 80(5).

5th stage: Where Parliament amends the common position under Co-Decision, the Commission does not issue a re-examined proposal. Instead, it delivers an opinion to the Council on Parliament's proposed amendments. No time limit is set for the Commission to react, but it will have to act promptly as the Council is subject to a time limit of three months for its Second Reading, which it can unilaterally extend to four months. Alternatively, the Commission could possibly withdraw its proposal or introduce an amended proposal.[208] An amended proposal would destroy the common position and the whole procedure would have to start all over again. The Commission has never done this although it has withdrawn proposals at this late stage, which brings the process to an abrupt end.

6th stage: Now comes the Council's Second Reading. It receives Parliament's proposed amendments directly and has three or four months in which to approve them or not. It has to wait for the Commission to deliver its opinion on these amendments as it must act by unanimity if it wishes to approve those on which the Commission has expressed a negative opinion. Otherwise, it normally acts by a qualified majority. Presumably, it may operate of the basis of a positive opinion if the Commission fails to respond within a reasonable time.

Where the Council accepts *all* of Parliament's second-round amendments, including those rejected by the Commission, the act in question is deemed to have been adopted in the form of the common position as amended by Parliament without the need for any formal act by the Council. The issues of whether the Council is obliged to enact the common position in these circumstances or whether it can amend it thus no longer arise.

Where the Council does not accept *all* of Parliament's second-round amendments, the President of the Council must, if Parliament agrees, convene a meeting of the Conciliation Committee.[209] The Conciliation Committee meets at the latest six weeks after the expiry of the time limit for the Council to act on its Second Reading. This time limit may be extended to eight weeks by either the Council or Parliament. The Committee consists of the fifteen members of the Council (i.e. ministers from the Member States) or, more frequently, their representatives together with an equal number of MEPs.

7th stage: The Conciliation Committee has six weeks in which to reach agreement on a compromise text. This can be extended to eight weeks by either the Council or Parliament. This text requires for its joint adoption a qualified majority in the Council and a simple majority of the MEPs. The Commission

---

208 As to whether this is possible, see the discussion *supra* in Section V.1.2.d.

209 Article 251(3) is a little ambivalent, but RoP, 81 clearly gives the last word to the President of Parliament. *See* also Point III/1 of the Joint Declaration on Practical Arrangements for the New Co-Decision Procedure (OJ C148/99).

participates in the discussions and is empowered to act as honest broker in order to reconcile the positions of the Council and Parliament. The basis of these discussions is the common position and Parliament's proposed amendments to it, but this does not mean that a compromise text cannot introduce new material. Even where the joint text differs from the Commission's original proposal or incorporates parliamentary amendments on which it has expressed a negative opinion, the Council normally acts by a qualified majority. Where the Conciliation Committee does not approve a joint text within the time limit, the proposed act is deemed not have been adopted and the procedure comes to an inconclusive end.

8th stage: Where the Conciliation Committee approves a joint text, it is laid before the Council and Parliament for a Third Reading. At this stage, the text can either be approved or rejected; no amendments are permitted. Approval requires a simple majority in Parliament[210] and normally a qualified majority in the Council. The time limit for securing approval of the joint text is six weeks, but either institution can extend it to eight weeks.

The Co-Decision Procedure is used for both executive and legislative acts with the latter being the more frequent. It is used on one occasion to adopt an administrative amendment to the EC Treaty.[211] It is not used in the TEU. The Council normally acts by a qualified majority except where it amends the Commission's proposal on its First Reading and where it adopts parliamentary amendments on its Second Reading on which the Commission has expressed a negative opinion. On four occasions, however, the Council acts by unanimity throughout the procedure.[212]

V.3.2.f The Assent Procedure

The Assent Procedure in its true form occurs in the following cases:

- determination of a serious breach of fundamental rights by a Member State;[213]

- acceptance of an application by a European state to become a member of the European Union;[214]

- conferral of special prudential tasks on the ECB;[215]

- amendment of certain Articles of the ESCB Statute;[216]

---

210 EP RoP, 83(4).

211 Article 80 (ECT).

212 Articles 18(2), 42, 47(2) and 151(5) (ECT).

213 Article 7(1) (TEU).

214 Article 49 (TEU).

215 Article 105(6) (ECT).

216 Article 107(5) (ECT).

– implementation of the Structural Funds;[217]

– adopting an act providing for elections to Parliament by direct universal suffrage;[218]

– conclusion of international agreements under the EC Treaty.[219]

1st stage: Normally, the first step is for the Commission to submit a proposal to the Council. However, the act on elections to the European Parliament is initiated by a proposal from Parliament and accessions to the Union by an application from the interested state. In two instances, the Commission shares the right of initiative with the ECB or the Member States.[220]

2nd stage: The Council must sometimes consult the ECB,[221] ECOSOC,[222] Committee of Regions[223] or Commission[224] before drawing up the proposed act. Presumably it can modify the proposal or recommendation on which it is acting, although it would need to act by unanimity in the case of a Commission proposal. However, this is not a real problem as the Council almost always acts by unanimity in the Assent Procedure. Once the Council has decided on the proposed measure, it is put before Parliament.

3rd stage: Under the Treaties, Parliament may only approve or reject the proposed action, but it has given itself the right under its Rules of Procedure to approve recommendations to modify the act in question.[225] These recommendations require the same majority as that by which final assent must be given. Parliament may delay giving its assent until its objections have been met. It is under no formal time constraints here,[226] but in all probability it can no more hold the Council up indefinitely under this procedure than under the Consultation Procedure. Parliament acts by a simple majority,[227] an absolute majority[228] or a double majority[229] according to the provisions of the Treaties.

---

217 Article 161 (ECT).

218 Article 190(4) (ECT.

219 Article 300(3) (ECT).

220 Articles 107(5) (ECT) and 7(1) (TEU), respectively.

221 Articles 105(6) and, where the Council acts on a proposal from the Commission, 107(5) (ECT).

222 Article 161 (ECT).

223 *Ibid.*

224 Articles 49 (TEU) and 107(5) (ECT), where the Council acts on a recommendation of the ECB.

225 *See* EP RoP, 86(3), 96(4) and 97(5).

226 However, under Article 300(3) of the EC Treaty, the Council and Parliament may agree on a time limit for the latter to give its assent to an international agreement.

227 Articles 105(6), 107(5), 161 and 300(3) (ECT).

228 Article 49 (TEU) and EP RoP, 96(6).

229 Article 7(1) (TEU) and EP RoP, 108(3).

4th stage: Having obtained the assent of Parliament, the Council may enact the measure. It acts by unanimity except in the case of amendments to the ESCB Statute adopted on a recommendation from the ECB.[230] In the case of elections to the European Parliament, the Council does not adopt the final act but recommends it to the Member States for them to adopt according to their own constitutional arrangements. They must all adopt it for the act to enter into force.

The Assent Procedure is used in both the TEU and the EC Treaty but exclusively for executive acts. Certain administrative amendments to the EC Treaty are adopted under this procedure.[231] Where they change the main text of the Treaties, they must be ratified by the Member States acting individually.[232] The procedure for Parliament to approve the appointment of the Commission can be assimilated to the Assent Procedure.[233]

V.3.2.g The 1975 Conciliation Procedure

In 1975, a Joint Declaration of Parliament, the Council and the Commission inaugurated a conciliation procedure.[234] It was supposed to be used whenever the Council intended to depart from Parliament's opinion under the Consultation Procedure,[235] but Parliament's Rules also provided at one time for its use in the context of a First Reading under the Cooperation Procedure. The procedure functioned somewhat like the new Conciliation Committee under Co-Decision with representatives from the Council and Parliament and the Commission acting as honest broker.[236]

The procedure was not, in fact, very effective. In the first place, its scope was very narrow as it operated only in the case of acts with appreciable financial implications, the adoption of which was not required by virtue of acts already in existence.[237] The way in which the procedure operated was also flawed. The committee was empowered to operate for three months, but there was no provision for dealing with a failure of the Council and Parliament to come to an agreement. Worse still, Parliament did not even have a right to re-consultation unless

---

230   Article 107(5) (ECT).

231   Articles 107(5) and 190(4) (ECT).

232   *See* Article 190(4) (ECT).

233   Article 214(2) (ECT). The procedure for appointing the Commission is discussed *supra* in Section III.3.3.a.

234   OJ C89/75.

235   Point 4 of the Joint Declaration.

236   *Ibid*, Point 5.

237   *Ibid*, Point 2.

the positions of the two institutions were "sufficiently close."[238] This meant that, if conciliation failed badly, Parliament was powerless to react.

Given its flaws, it is perhaps understandable that the 1975 conciliation procedure now seems to have fallen by the wayside. Certainly, Parliament's Rules no longer make reference to it. It is mentioned here so that readers are aware of it and do not confuse it with the conciliation committee procedure under Co-Decision.

V.3.3 Procedures for the Conclusion of International Agreements by the Union

V.3.3.a International Agreements under the TEU[239]

When the Union wishes to conclude an agreement with third countries or international organizations in the area of the CFSP or PJC, the Council authorizes the Presidency of the Council to open negotiations.[240] The Presidency is assisted by the Commission, but it is the former and not the latter that makes the recommendation to the Council that the agreement be concluded. The Council acts throughout by unanimity. Where this is required by national constitutional law, the agreement must be ratified by a Member State before it can be bound by it.

V.3.3.b International Agreements under the EC Treaty[241]

This procedure is more complex than that under the TEU and also involves Parliament. The steps are as follows:[242]

The Commission recommends to the Council that negotiations be opened with third countries or international organizations with a view to concluding an agreement on a matter coming within the purview of the EC Treaty. The Council may authorize the Commission to open negotiations, which it conducts in consultation with a special committee appointed by the Council and within the framework of any directives that it receives from the Council. The Council acts throughout by a qualified majority unless the proposed agreement is an association agreement as defined in Article 310[243] or one that covers an area for which

---

238   *Ibid*, Point 7.

239   *See* the discussion *supra* on the international competence of the Union in Section II.3.3.c.

240   Articles 24 and 38 (TEU).

241   *See* the discussion *supra* on the international competence of the Community in Section II.3.2.f.

242   *See* Articles 133 and 300 (ECT).

243   It is an agreement that involves reciprocal right and obligations, common action and special procedures.

unanimity is required for the adoption of internal rules. In these two cases, the Council acts by unanimity.

If the negotiations are concluded satisfactorily, the Commission will submit a proposal to the Council for the conclusion of the agreement. The Council makes its decision by a qualified majority or unanimity according to the rules set out in the preceding paragraph. The Council must first consult Parliament before concluding any agreement except in the case of trade agreements that come within the common commercial policy. The Council may lay down a time limit within which Parliament must render its opinion. Association agreements, agreements establishing a specific institutional framework, agreements having important budgetary implications and agreements entailing the amendment of an act adopted under the Co-Decision Procedure require the assent of Parliament before they can be concluded by the Council. This includes trade agreements that fall into one of these categories. Parliament acts by a simple majority in giving its assent. Parliament and the Council may agree on a time limit for Parliament to act where the situation is urgent.

Where an agreement requires the EC Treaty to be amended, this must be done under the amendment procedure in Article 48 of the TEU before the agreement can be concluded. Member States, the Commission or the Council may refer a proposed agreement to the Court of Justice where there is a question of its compatibility with the EC Treaty.

The conclusion of an agreement may be accompanied by a decision by the Council on provisional application before its entry into force. The application of an agreement may also be suspended by the Council on a proposal from the Commission. The Council acts by a qualified majority in these situations unless it is dealing with an association agreement or one that covers an area for which unanimity is required for the adoption of internal rules. In these two cases, the Council acts by unanimity. Parliament must be informed of any suspension or decision on provisional application. The same rules apply to the establishment by the Council of the Community position in a body set up by an association agreement when that body has the power to adopt decisions having legal effects.

When it concludes an agreement, the Council may authorize the Commission to approve modifications on behalf of the Community where the agreement provides for them to be adopted by a simplified procedure or by a body set up by the agreement. The Council may attach conditions to this authorization.

V.3.4 The Commission Procedure

V.3.4.a Secondary Acts

The Commission adopts a considerable number of secondary executive acts under the EC Treaty. It has no such role under the TEU. The Commission acts by way of decisions,[244] directives,[245] recommendations,[246] opinions,[247] reports[248] and communications.[249] All these acts are adopted by a majority of members of the Commission although there is always an attempt to reach a consensus.[250] On most occasions, the Commission acts on its own initiative but twice it acts on that of Member States.[251] It does not consult widely although some provisions call for consultation of the Member States,[252] the EFC[253] or ECOSOC.[254] On occasion, the Commission is assisted by a committee.[255]

V.3.4.b Tertiary Acts

An important part of the Commission's executive role is concerned with the implementation of secondary acts adopted by the Council. The Council is explicitly given the authority to confer such tertiary powers on the Commission under Article 202 of the EC Treaty. It may impose certain requirements governing the way in which the Commission exercises these powers and, where it can be justified, it may reserve the right to adopt implementing measures itself.[256]

The Council subjects the exercise of the Commission's tertiary powers to a system of committee procedures, which goes by the general name of "comitology." There is also a procedure to supervise the Commission's use of safeguard measures. All these procedures are set out in their actual form in Council Decision 99/468,[257] but, despite the declarations appended to that decision,[258] the more restrictive procedures from repealed Council Decision 87/373[259] still apply widely.

---

244 *See* Articles 15, 38, 75(4), 76(1),(2), 85(1),(2), 86(3), 88(2), 95(6), 119(3), 134, 185 and 218(2) (ECT).

245 *See* Articles 39(3)(d) and 86(3) (ECT).

246 *See* Articles 53, 77, 97(1) and 199(1) (ECT).

247 *See* Articles 11(3), 104(5), 140 and 226 (ECT).

248 *See* Article 104(3) (ECT).

249 *See* Article 272(9) (ECT).

250 Article 219 (ECT) and Articles 1 and 8 of the Commission's RoP.

251 Articles 85(1) and 185 (ECT).

252 Articles 75(4), 76(2), 88(9) and 97(1) (ECT).

253 Article 104(3) (ECT).

254 Article 140 (ECT).

255 *See* Article 147 (ECT).

256 *See* Preamble, 8th recital of Council Regulation 789/01 reserving to the Council implementing powers with regard to certain detailed provisions and practical procedures for examining visa applications (OJ L116/01).

257 OJ L184/99.

258 OJ C203/99 on page 1.

259 OJ L197/87.

The European Parliament also exercises some control over the Commission. It may indicate by means of a resolution that it considers that implementing measures proposed by the Commission exceed the powers granted by a secondary instrument that was adopted under the Co-Decision Procedure.[260] The Commission must then re-examine the draft measures but it is not obliged to amend them. It must, however, give reasons to Parliament for the action it takes. The Commission has to submit draft implementing measures to Parliament where the secondary instrument was adopted under Co-Decision or is of particular interest to Parliament.[261] Parliament is obliged to adopt its resolution within one month from receiving these draft measures.[262]

We shall now look at the supervisory procedures. All the committees consist of representatives from the Member States and are chaired by a representative from the Commission.

V.3.4.b.i Advisory Procedure[263]

The advisory procedure is the least restrictive on the Commission. It is, however, used only when the Council considers appropriate, which means that it is the least used of the procedures.[264] It occurs either on its own or as an alternative to other procedures.[265]

The chairperson submits a draft of the implementing measures proposed by the Commission to the advisory committee and sets a time limit within which the committee must render its opinion on them. It may make its decision by consensus or simple majority vote. The chairperson may vote.

The decision of the advisory committee is not binding on the Commission, which is obliged merely to take the utmost account of it and to inform the committee of the manner in which it has done so. If the committee does not render its opinion within the time limit, the Commission is dispensed from taking it into account.

V.3.4.b.ii Management Procedure

This procedure is used for management measures, particularly with respect to the common fisheries and agricultural policies or the implementation of pro-

---

260   Council Decision 99/468, Article 8.

261   *Ibid*, Article 7(3); Points 1 and 2 of the Agreement between the European Parliament and the Commission on procedures for implementing Council Decision 99/468 laying down the procedures for the exercise of implementing powers conferred on the Commission (OJ L256/00).

262   *Ibid*, Point 6.

263   Council Decision 99/468, Article 3.

264   *Ibid*, Article 2(c).

265   The list of committees involved in comitology and the procedures they use are set out in OJ C225/00 at pages 2-18.

grams with substantial budgetary implications.[266] It occurs almost twice as often as the advisory procedure, either on its own or as an alternative to other procedures.

The chairperson submits a draft of the implementing measures proposed by the Commission to the management committee and sets a time limit within which the committee must render its opinion. It makes its decision by a qualified majority vote. The votes of the representatives of the Member States are weighted according to Article 205(2) of the EC Treaty, and sixty-two votes in favor are required. The chairperson does not vote.

Once the management committee has rendered its opinion or the time limit for doing so has expired, the Commission proceeds immediately to adopt the proposed implementing measures. However, if these measures are not in accordance with the committee's opinion, they must be communicated to the Council, which may decide on different measures within the time limit laid down in the secondary instrument. This period may not exceed three months from the date of the communication.

Under Decision 99/648, the Commission is free to suspend the application of its implementing measures during the Council's deliberations if it so wishes. Under Decision 87/373, there is a variant, under which the Commission is obliged to suspend. This variant still applies to many management committees.

V.3.4.b.iii Regulatory Procedure

This procedure is used for measures of general scope designed to apply essential provisions of secondary instruments that are being implemented.[267] It is used almost three times as frequently as the advisory procedure and half as many times as the management procedure. It occurs either on its own or as an alternative to other procedures.

The chairperson submits a draft of the implementing measures proposed by the Commission to the regulatory committee and sets a time limit within which the committee must render its opinion. It makes its decision by a qualified majority vote. The votes of the representatives of the Member States are weighted according to Article 205(2) of the EC Treaty, and sixty-two votes in favor are required. The chairperson does not vote.

If the regulatory committee approves the draft, the Commission adopts the measures. If the opinion is negative or if no opinion is delivered before the expiry of the time limit, the Commission must submit a proposal to the Council on which implementing measures to take and inform Parliament. Presumably, this proposal may incorporate all or some of the changes suggested by the regula-

---

266   Council Decision 99/468, Article 2(a).

267   *Ibid*, Article 2(b).

tory committee in its opinion. If Parliament considers that the implementing measures submitted by the Commission pursuant to a secondary instrument adopted under Co-Decision exceed its authority, it must inform the Council.

The Council now considers the Commission's proposed measures in the light of any information it has received from Parliament. It must act within the time limit laid down in the secondary instrument, which may not exceed three months from the date of the submission of the proposal by the Commission. The Council may reject the proposal by a qualified majority comprising sixty-two weighted votes, in which case the Commission can submit an amended proposal or the same proposal or make a proposal based on its own secondary powers under the Treaties. If the Council neither adopts nor rejects the proposal within the time limit, the Commission may enact its proposal. It is not clear, however, whether this must be the original proposal or that which the Commission submitted to the Council.

Under Decision 87/373, there is a variant to the procedure, under which the Council, acting by a simple majority, may prevent the Commission from adopting implementing measures where the Council has not actually rejected the proposal. This variant still applies to many regulatory committees.

V.3.4.b.iv Safeguard Procedure[268]

Some secondary instruments confer on the Commission the power to take safeguard measures. When it does so, it must notify the Council and the Member States and, where stipulated in the secondary instrument, it also consults with the Member States before making its decision. Any Member State may refer the Commission's decision to the Council within a time limit that is set by the secondary instrument. The Council may deal with this referral in one of two ways depending on what is laid down in the secondary instrument, which also establishes the time limit for the Council to act. The first variant calls for the Council to make a different decision from the Commission, in default of which the Commission's decision stands. The second variant calls for the Council to confirm, amend or revoke the Commission's decision. If the Council fails to act, the Commission's decision is deemed to be revoked. The Council acts by a qualified majority in both cases. The Commission has criticized the second variant as it can lead to a situation where no decision is taken and the problem remains unaddressed.

V.3.5 Member State Procedures

The Member States are empowered under the Treaties to adopt certain executive and legislative acts. They do this in one of two ways.

---

268 *Ibid*, Article 6.

Where the governments of the Member States are summoned to act by common accord, they act collectively in the form of a decision that is most commonly called a "Decision of the Representatives of the Governments of the Member States (meeting within the Council)."[269] On one occasion, they act collectively at the level of heads of state or government.[270] They invariably initiate the act themselves and do not have to consult with any body of the Union. However, their appointment of the Commission is subject to the approval of Parliament.[271] These collective acts are all executive in nature.[272] The same procedure is used for the adoption of collective acts outside the framework of the Treaties.[273]

Where the Member States are called upon to act in an individual capacity, they are governed by their own internal constitutional rules.[274] These individual acts are both executive and legislative in nature. Where amendments to the Treaties are ratified, they constitute primary Union law. When acting in this individual capacity, the Member States are responding in certain cases to the Council,[275] the European Council[276] or themselves acting collectively.[277] Member States also act in this way outside the framework of the Treaties.[278]

V.3.6 *Sui Generis* Procedures[279]

Sui generis decisions adopted by Parliament are taken according to rules that have already been mentioned. The European Council acts by consensus. Other bodies of the Union adopt *sui generis* decisions according to their own rules of procedure.

---

269 These decisions are discussed *supra* in Section IV.3.2.d.v.

270 Article 112(2)(b) (ECT).

271 Article 214(2) (ECT).

272 Article 23(1) (TEU). The provision only refers to "decisions" but this must surely be interpreted to include all acts taken by the Council for which no particular voting method is prescribed.

273 *See* the discussion *supra* in Section IV.4.2.a.ii.

274 These individual decisions are discussed *supra* in Section IV.3.2.e.v.

275 Articles 34(2)(d) and 42 (TEU); 22 and 190(4) (ECT).

276 Article 17(1) (TEU).

277 Articles 48 and 49 (TEU).

278 *See* the discussion *supra* in Section IV.4.2.a.i.

279 *See* the discussion *supra* in Section IV.3.2.d.

CHAPTER VI

THE EXERCISE OF STATE POWER IN THE EUROPEAN UNION

VI.1 Introduction

State power is legislative, executive or judicial. Judicial power is clearly distinct from the other two within the European Union, but, as we indicated earlier,[1] no formal distinction is made in the Treaties between legislative and executive acts. When the Council defines legislative acts in its Rules of Procedure as rule-making,[2] it is in fact making a distinction between policy-making, which is not subject to judicial control, and rule-making, which normally is. It does not establish a criterion for differentiating between legislation and executive acts as the latter also can involve rule-making.

As long as one regards the European Union as an international organization regulated by traditional treaties, this confusion is not a problem. It is possible to consider the Treaties as law and all acts done pursuant to them as executive in nature. The whole assembly of rules can then be conveniently labeled "Union law," which is what we have done until now in this monograph.

Such an approach, however, is no longer possible nor desirable. The European Union may not yet be a full-blown federation, but it is now much closer to being a state than an international organization. Accordingly, we must treat it as such in analyzing its legal system, which means distinguishing between the executive and legislative powers of the Union and establishing their allocation between the bodies of the Union and between the Union and the Member States. Only by understanding how state power is exercised in the Union can we appreciate its real nature and perceive the reforms that are increasingly necessary to ensure its proper, democratic functioning.

---

1   *See* the discussion *supra* in Section IV.2.1.

2   Article 7 of the Council's Rules of Procedure, which are contained in Council Decision 00/396 (OJ L149/00), as amended by Council Decision 01/216 (OJ L81/01).

In the discussions that follow, we attempt to make this distinction between the legislative and executive acts that are adopted pursuant to the Treaties by the Union bodies and the Member States. Unfortunately, the distinction is not always clear, particularly as one can allot fields of activity in different ways. In some countries, for example, the regulation of commerce is the sole prerogative of the executive, in others it is allotted to the legislature. Executive acts that implement primary or secondary legislation may resemble legislation. Thus, we may not all agree on what is a legislative and what is an executive act in the context of the European Union. What is important, however, is to understand that the two powers exist separately within the European Union and that one cannot fully appreciate the way it functions without some idea of how they are allotted.

VI.2 The Exercise of Legislative Power in the European Union

VI.2.1 Executive or Legislative Power?

A legislative act sets down basic norms that either regulate human activity or establish the organization of society. Based on this definition of legislation, one could take the view that there is no legislative power in the Union, only an executive power to implement the Treaties. After all, apart from when the Member States enact primary law acting individually, all acts by the Union are subject to the principles of the attribution of powers and, where the Union does not have exclusive jurisdiction, subsidiarity.[3] However, whatever merits such a view may have had in the early days, it is now much too narrow and ignores the nature of the Union legal order.

In the first place, the Council, acting alone or with the European Parliament, has considerable discretion in implementing the Treaties, as do the Member States when they act collectively to draw up conventions pursuant to the Treaties. In many areas where the Union has exclusive or concurrent jurisdiction, it has used this discretion to establish a substantial body of basic norms that must be considered legislative in nature. Just because the legislative power is subject to certain constraining principles does not take away its legislative nature. In nation-states as well, the legislative power is often not absolute but must observe fundamental rights and respect the division of power in a federal state.

The nature of the Union legal order as established by the jurisprudence of the Court of Justice also militates against this narrow view.[4] The legal order is based on the transfer by the Member States to the Union of their sovereign power in certain areas. Clearly, if sovereignty is transferred, both legislative and executive power are part of the transfer; otherwise it is not complete. The Union legal order is also autonomous, which means that the Treaties upon which it is based

---

3   *See* the discussion *supra* in Section IV.1.3.
4   *See* the discussion *supra* in Section IV.6.

can only be altered according to the procedures set out in Article 48 of the Treaty on European Union (TEU).[5] These Treaties thereby lose one of the salient features of international agreements, which is the right of signatory states to modify them by the conclusion of a new treaty, and become more like constitutional documents with an amending formula. Once they are seen in this light, it is a short step to treat the attribution of powers to the Union as just another example of the division of legislative power in a federation.

VI.2.2 Nature of Legislative Power in the European Union

Legislative acts are either primary or subordinate. Many provisions of the Treaties as well as individual acts of the Member States ratifying amendments to them are primary legislative acts. Secondary legislative is enacted primarily by the Council, acting alone or with the European Parliament. The Member States exercise secondary legislative power on two occasions when they adopt conventions pursuant to the Treaties.[6] There can be no tertiary legislative power as tertiary acts implement secondary legislation and are therefore executive in nature.

The procedures that are used by the Council, either alone or with the European Parliament, for the adoption of legislative acts are the Consultation and Co-Decision Procedures. On one occasion, the Council Procedure is used.[7]

VI.2.3 Scope of the Legislative Power in the European Union

The legislative power in the European Union is primarily a Community power. In the TEU, there are a number of instances in which the Member States exercise a primary legislative power to ratify amendments to the Treaties, but there are only two instances in which the Union exercises secondary legislative power. These are both in the area of police and judicial cooperation in criminal matters (PJC).[8] All remaining legislative acts are adopted pursuant to the European Community (EC) Treaty,[9] and this includes the budget. However, even in the Community, there are areas where the Union has no legislative power. This is the case in economic and monetary matters and the common commercial policy as well as in employment, culture and education, but in the latter three areas the Community exercises only an ancillary jurisdiction.

---

5   [1992] 1 C.M.L.R. 573.

6   Articles 34(2)(d) (TEU); 293 (ECT).

7   Article 132(1) (ECT).

8   Article 34(2)(b),(d) (TEU).

9   298 U.N.T.S. 11.

VI.2.4 Treaty Law

As we have already mentioned, there are certain provisions in the Treaties that are part of the legislation of the Union. These can be divided into provisions that set out the constitutional and administrative structure of the Union and those that regulate matters of law directly instead of leaving them up to the Union.

The constitutional and administrative law of the Union can be divided into three main categories: scope of the Union, structure of the Union and enabling provisions. The provisions setting out the scope of the Union can be further divided into four sub-categories:

a) Objectives and activities of the Union.[10] In both Treaties, general objectives and areas are set out which are then complemented by titles dealing with specific areas;

b) Geographical scope of the Union;[11]

c) Relationship of the EC Treaty and the TEU with other treaties;[12]

d) Matters reserved for the Member States and their institutions.[13] This category also contains some derogations that remove a matter from the jurisdiction of the Union.[14]

The provisions dealing with the structure of the Union can be sub-divided as follows:

a) Nature of the Union:

i) basic structure of the Union[15]

ii) general conditions for the exercise of Union powers[16]

iii) responsibility of Member States and Union institutions towards the Union ("loyalty principle");[17]

---

10 Articles 2, 11(1), 29, 30(1) and 31 (TEU); 2, 3(1), 4(1),(2), 32(1),(4), 33(1), 34(1),(3), 35, 39(1), 61, 70, 80(1), 127(1), 149(1),(3), 150(1),(3), 151(1),(3), 152(2),(3), 153(1),(3), 154(1),(2), 155(3), 157(1), 158, 163(1),(2), 164, 177(2), 174(1),(4), 177(1), 302, 303, 304 and 310 (ECT).

11 Articles 182 and 299 (ECT). Strangely, the TEU contains no provisions on this topic.

12 Articles 47 (TEU); 305(1),(2), 306 and 307 (ECT).

13 Articles 33 and 35(5) (TEU); 64(1), 68(2), 137(6), 152(5), 181, 240 and 295 (ECT).

14 Employment in the public service is excluded by a derogation in Article 39(4) (ECT), self-employed activities connected with the exercise of official authority by Articles 45 and 55 (ECT) and Title IV of the EC Treaty as regards Denmark and the United Kingdom by Article 69 (ECT).

15 Articles 1, 3, 6(1) and 51 (TEU); 1, 17(1), 23(1), 281 and 312 (ECT).

16 Articles 6(2)(3) (TEU); 3(2), 5, 6, 127(2), 151(4), 152(1), 153(2), 159 and 178 (ECT).

17 Articles 11(2), 14(3), 19(1),(2), 37 and 43(2) (TEU); 10, 86(1), 98, 105(4), 126(1), 133(3), 137(4), 159, 170, 174(4), 181, 228(1), 233, 237(d), 256, 280(1),(2), 282, 291, 292, 300(7) and 307 (ECT). This principle is discussed in some detail *supra* in Section II.3.8

b) Bodies of the Union (establishment, composition, tasks, procedures);[18]

c) Procedures in the Union:

   i) acts and means available to accomplish the tasks of the Treaties[19]

   ii) decision-making procedures[20]

   iii) special voting rules[21]

   iv) interaction between Union bodies and also with Member States (consultations, reports, questions, information)[22]

   v) cooperation between Member States and between Member States and the Union to accomplish the tasks of the Treaties[23]

   vi) judicial procedures;[24]

d) Financial Arrangements of the Union;[25]

e) Closer Cooperation between certain Member States.[26]

The enabling provisions are a substantial part of the two Treaties. They bestow legislative, executive and judicial power on Union bodies as well as on the Member States and set out the procedures for using these powers. Only the judicial power of the Court of Justice is set out in the Treaties; that of the Court of First Instance is at present established by secondary legislation.[27]

---

18   Articles 4, 18(3), 21, 25, 26, 36(1) and 46 (TEU); 7, 8, 9, 68(1), 79, 105(2),(4),(5), 107(1)-(4), 108, 112(1),(2), 113(1),(2), 114(2),(4), 123(1),(3), 128(5), 130, 146, 160, 189, 190(1)-(3), 192, 195(1)-(3), 196, 197, 198, 201, 202, 203, 204, 205(1)-(3), 206, 207(1)-(3), 211, 212, 213(1),(2), 214(1), 215, 219, 220, 221, 223, 225(1), 238, 247(1)-(5),(9), 248, 257, 258, 261, 262, 263, 265, 266, 267, 284 and 287 (ECT); 9(1)-(5) (TA); Act concerning the Election of Representatives of the European Parliament by Direct Universal Suffrage.

19   Articles 12 (TEU); 110(1),(2), 249, 253 and 254 (ECT).

20   Articles 44(1), 67(1)-(4), 133(2),(4), 137(4), 201, 251, 252 and 300(1)-(5) (ECT).

21   Articles 23(1),(2) and 34(2)(d),(3) (TEU); 122(5) and 309(1) (ECT).

22   Articles 4, 14(5), 21, 22(1), 27, 36(2), 39(1)-(3) and 45 (TEU); 22, 99(3),(4), 105(4), 113(3), 115, 121(1), 122(2), 128(3),(5), 130, 138, 143, 159, 192, 208, 218(1), 248(4), 250(1),(2), 262 and 265 (ECT).

23   Articles 16 and 34(1) (TEU), 99(1), 125, 126(2), 152(2), 155(2), 157(2), 159, 165(1), 180(1) and 280(3)(ECT).

24   Articles 35(4) (TEU); 234, 241, 242, 243, 244 and 256 (ECT).

25   Articles 28(2)-(4), 41(2)-(4) and 44(2) (TEU); 175(4), 268, 269, 270, 271, 272(1),(4)-(6),(9), 273; 275 and 280(1)- (3),(5).

26   Articles 40(1), 43(1) and 44(1) (TEU); 11(1) (ECT)

27   Council Decision 88/591 (OJ L318/98) as amended and corrected. The Treaty of Nice places the enabling provisions for the Court of First Instance in the EC Treaty and repeals the secondary legislation. The judicial power is discussed in more detail *infra* in Section VI.4.

Finally, there are various matters of law that are regulated directly by the Treaties:

– prohibitions on the Member States, the Union and sometimes persons from doing something;[28]

– obligations on Member States or the Union to do a certain act;[29]

– definitions of terms[30] or legal positions;[31] and

– the conferral of rights on legal and natural persons.[32]

This last type of Treaty law replaces legislative acts by Union bodies.

VI.3 The Exercise of Executive Power in the European Union

VI.3.1 Nature of Executive Power in the European Union

Primary executive acts are those provisions in the Treaties that replace acts by the Union bodies or the Member States.[33] The latter are secondary acts and the major role in their adoption is played by the Council acting alone. The Commission also adopts many executive acts. The Member States have an executive role as does the European Parliament, both in conjunction with the Council and acting alone. Other bodies involved in the adoption of executive acts are the European Central Bank (ECB), the Presidency, the European Council, the Courts, the Economic and Social Committee (ECOSOC) and the Committee of Regions.

All decision-making procedures are used by the Council to adopt executive acts, acting either alone or with the European Parliament. The Cooperation, Assent and Council Procedures are even used exclusively for this purpose except for one exception in the case of the Council Procedure.[34]

---

28 Articles 12, 25, 28, 29, 31(2), 43, 49, 56(1), 75(1), 76(1), 77, 81(1), 82, 86(1), 87(1), 90, 91, 92, 101(1), 102(1), 118 and 184(1),(2),(5) (ECT).

29 Articles 14(1), 31(1), 41, 77, 104(1), 109, 116(2)(a),(4),(5), 123(1), 124(2), 132(1), 141(1), 142, 183(1),(2),(3) and 294 (ECT).

30 Articles 14(2), 17(1), 24, 32(1), 39(2), 43, 48, 50, 55, 81(1)(a)-(e) and 141(2) (ECT).

31 Articles 32(2),(3), 48, 55, 73, 81(2),(3), 88(3), 103(1), 116(1), 119(4), 120(4), 121(1),(4), 122(6), 132(2), 183(5), 225(2), 286(1), 288 and 311 (ECT).

32 Articles 18(1), 19(1),(2), 20, 21, 39(3)(a)-(d), 50, 183(4), 194 and 255(1) (ECT).

33 For a discussion of the actors in the adoption of executive acts, *see* the discussion *supra* in Section V.1.1.

34 It is used once to adopt a legislative act under Article 132(1) (ECT).

VI.3.2 Scope of the Executive Power in the European Union

VI.3.2.a Introduction

Executive power is difficult to define as it is so diffuse. Its most important component is the power to set policy and to initiate legislation where that policy requires the amendment, repeal or creation of legal rules. However, it also includes authority to apply and enforce legal rules although, strictly speaking, this is a judicial power. The executive power may also extend to a certain control over the functioning of the state. The implementation of primary or secondary legislation is also part of the executive power.

In the European Union, all these matters can be said to come within the executive power, the components of which are discussed below. It has been said that the executive power is limited in the EC Treaty,[35] but this is not so. On the other hand, in the TEU it is certainly much more in evidence than legislative power.

VI.3.2.b Implementation of Treaty Rules and Secondary Legislation

The implementation of Treaty rules is carried out by the Council in most instances.[36] On two occasions it is the Member States acting collectively[37] and on another, the Commission.[38] The Commission is mainly responsible for enacting tertiary acts to implement the secondary legislation of the Council, although the Council may reserve this responsibility to itself.[39] The Council implements the secondary conventions adopted by the Member States in the area of police and judicial cooperation in criminal matters (PJC).[40]

---

35 *See* P.J.G. Kapteyn and P Verloren van Themaat, *Introduction to the Law of the European Communities* (3rd edition by L.W. Gormley, 1998) at page 71.

36 Articles 34(2)(d) (TEU); 102(2), 103(2), 139(2) and 187 (ECT).

37 Articles 20 and 41 (ECT).

38 Article 39(3)(d). In fact, the Commission enjoys considerable discretion in implementing the rules on Union nationals remaining in another Member State after having worked there. However, it makes more sense to characterize this as an executive act that implements a Treaty rule. Firstly, the Treaty talks specifically in Article 39(3)(d) of implementing measures by the Commission. Secondly, to consider it a legislative act would create an awkward exception by giving the Commission a legislative power that it does not otherwise possess under the TEU and EC Treaty.

39 Article 202 (ECT). *See* the discussion *supra* in Section V.3.4.b.

40 Article 34(2)(d) (TEU).

VI.3.2.c Application of Union Rules

VI.3.2.c.i Derogations[41]

The typical derogation is a permission to apply national rules or not to apply Union rules in a certain situation on an open-ended basis in favor of any Member State that meets the pre-conditions. It exists only in the EC Treaty. The derogation is mostly set out as Treaty law and can be used unilaterally by Member States subject to the Commission's general monitoring power under Article 211. There are sometimes limits placed on the duration of the derogation, which may on occasion be granted by the Council or the Commission instead of directly by the Treaty. Some derogations are provided for in the secondary legislation of the Council and administered by the Commission.

VI.3.2.c.ii Safeguard Measures[42]

The typical safeguard measure is a permission to apply national rules that infringe Union rules in order to deal with a particular problem caused by the latter. The measure applies only to Member States that suffer the problem and only for as long as it persists. On two occasions, they are limited to six months duration. Safeguard measures exist only in the EC Treaty. They normally have to be authorized by the Commission or the Council. In the one case that they are permitted directly by Treaty law, they are tightly controlled by the Council.[43]

VI.3.2.c.iii Exceptional Measures[44]

The typical exceptional measure is one that is permitted in order to deal with an exceptional situation whether or not it infringes Union law. The measure applies only to a Member State that is in the exceptional situation and only for as long this situation persists. On one occasion, the Union may take an exceptional measure.[45] Exceptional measures are found in the EC Treaty and once in the TEU. They may be authorized by the Treaty or the Council, acting on one occasion with Parliament. In all cases there is tight Community control.

---

41   Articles 15, 19(1),(2), 30, 39(3),(4), 45, 46(1), 57(1), 58(1), 69, 72, 76(1), 86(2), 92, 95(4),(5),(10), 101(2), 122(1), 137(5), 141(4), 152(4)(a), 153(5), 174(2), 175(5), 176, 184(3) and 296(1) (ECT).

42   Articles 38, 59, 64(2), 119(3), 120(1) and 134 (ECT).

43   Article 120(1) (ECT).

44   Articles 14(6) (TEU); 60(2), 87(2), 87(3), 88(2), 175(5) and 297 (ECT).

45   Article 175(5) (ECT).

VI.3.2.c.iv Ensuring the Observance of Union Rules by Member States[46]

Ensuring the observance of Union rules by Member States involves three elements:

- monitoring the application of Union rules
- establishing the existence of a breach of these rules
- consulting with the Member State concerned to remedy the breach without conflict

The major role in ensuring the observance of rules within the EC Treaty falls to the Commission. It has both a general responsibility to do so[47] and specific responsibility on a number of occasions. The Council plays a lesser role and often acts in conjunction with the Commission. In the TEU, on the other hand, it is the Council that ensures the observance of the Union rules in the area of foreign and security policy (CFSP) and which determines the existence of a persistent breach of rights guaranteed by Union law.

VI.3.2.d Enforcement of Union Rules

VI.3.2.d.i Introduction

The enforcement of Union rules is primarily the responsibility of the Council and the Commission. However, actions may be brought before the Court of Justice for this purpose by the Member States, Parliament, the ECB, the Court of Auditors and natural and legal persons. Union rules may be enforced, where appropriate, against the Council, Commission and Parliament as well as the Member States. The enforcement measures can be broken down into four distinct actions. Only non-pecuniary sanctions are possible in the TEU.

VI.3.2.d.ii Measures to Eliminate the Breach[48]

Having established that a Member State is in breach of Union rules, the Council or the Commission, as the case may be, may lay down concrete measures to be taken by that state in order to remedy the breach. The nature of the measures depends on the breach. Measures may be instituted after failure to reach a solution through consultation or they may be imposed at the very outset.

---

46   Articles 7(1) and 11(2) (TEU); 44(2)(h), 75(4), 76(2), 77, 85(1), 86(3), 88(1), 95(6), 96, 97(1), 99(3)(5), 104(2),(3),(5),(6), 128(4), 211, 226, 228(2), 298 and 300(6) (ECT).

47   Article 211 (ECT).

48   Articles 60(2), 75(4), 76(2), 85(1), 88(2), 96, 99(4), 104(7),(9), 119(3), 120(3) and 134 (ECT).

VI.3.2.d.iii Non-Pecuniary Sanctions Against a Member State[49]

Where a Member State does not respond to requests or take concrete measures in order to cure a breach of Union rules, the Council, and on one occasion the Commission,[50] may invoke non-pecuniary sanctions against the offending state. These sanctions can range from a suspension of rights to a public rebuke to an authorization for other Member States to take remedial action. This type of sanctions can be invoked under the TEU in the case of a violation of fundamental rights.

VI.3.2.d.iv Pecuniary Sanctions Against a Member State

Pecuniary sanctions in the form of non-interest-bearing deposits or fines may be imposed directly by the Council on Member States that fail to follow measures recommended by the Council for the reduction of an excessive government deficit.[51] On a general basis, the Commission may request the Court of Justice to impose a lump sum or penalty payment on a Member State that fails to comply with a judgment of the Court that it has infringed the EC Treaty.[52] It will not do so as a matter of course but only where a fine is considered to be the most appropriate way of securing compliance as rapidly as possible.[53] The Commission calculates the amount of the fine on the basis of three fundamental criteria: the seriousness of the infringement, its duration and the need to ensure that the fine itself is a deterrent to further infringements.

VI.3.2.d.v Action Before the Court of Justice

On a general basis, the Commission or any Member State may bring another Member State before the Court of Justice for failure to fulfill its obligations under the EC Treaty.[54] If the Court agrees, the Member State at fault is required to comply with the judgment of the Court or face a fine.[55] The Member States or the Commission may also bring this action specifically in cases of illegal state aids, improper use of derogations and abuse of the security exceptions.[56] An action may also be brought before the Court by the Member States, the Council and the Commission to strike down illegal subordinate acts of the Council, Parliament, the Commission or the ECB.[57] Parliament, the Court of Auditors and

---

49   Articles 7(2) (TEU); 85(2), 96, 99(4), 104(8),(11) and 309(2),(4) (ECT).

50   Article 85(2) (ECT).

51   Article 104(11) (ECT).

52   Article 228(2) (ECT).

53   Memorandum from the Commission on applying Article 171 (*now Article 228*) of the EC Treaty (OJ C242/96).

54   Articles 226 and 227 (ECT).

55   Article 228 (ECT).

56   Articles 88(2), 95(9) and 298 (ECT).

57   Article 230 (ECT).

the ECB can bring the same action but only in order to protect their prerogatives. The Member States, the Council, the Commission, Parliament and the Court of Auditors can bring an action against Parliament, the Council or the Commission if they fail to act in infringement of Union law.[58] In bringing actions before the Court, the Member States act individually.

VI.3.2.e The Formulation and Execution of Union Policies

The executive power over policy in the European Union covers both the CFSP and PJC from the TEU and most areas of Union competence in the EC Treaty. It is exercised mainly by the Council acting alone or with the European Parliament although it is the European Council that defines the general political guidelines of the Union.[59] It also defines the guidelines for the CFSP and decides on common strategies in that area[60] as well as directing employment policy.[61] There are also provisions in the EC Treaty that set down the direction of a number of Union policies.[62] The Commission has a smaller policy role. It negotiates international treaties except for those in the areas of the CFSP and PJC, which are negotiated by the Presidency of the Council,[63] and is active in some other areas.[64] The ECB is responsible for monetary policy.[65] The Member States have no direct policy role.

VI.3.2.f The Initiation of Legislative and Executive Acts

The right of initiative is a very important facet of executive power. It is exercised frequently but by no means exclusively by the Commission, at least in the EC Treaty and in particular for legislative acts. This topic is discussed above in Section V.1.2.

VI.3.2.g The Functioning of the Union

VI.3.2.g.i Introduction

Finally, the executive power includes a number of acts that are needed to ensure the proper functioning of the Union. This power is wielded by a number of bodies but again it is the Council that predominates, acting mostly alone. The Member States have a small but important role, as does Parliament.

---

58 Article 232 (ECT).

59 Article 4 (TEU).

60 Article 13(1),(2) (TEU).

61 Article 128(1) (ECT).

62 Articles 4(1),(3), 15, 16, 33(2), 34(2), 44(2)(a), 47(3), 55, 95(3), 98, 105(1), 131, 133(1), 136, 174(2), 174(3) and 285(2) (ECT).

63 *Cf* Articles 133(3) and 300(1) (ECT) *with* Article 24 and 38 (TEU).

64 Articles 53, 119(1), 140, 147 and 185 (ECT).

65 Article 105(2) (ECT).

VI.3.2.g.ii Operation of Existing Union Bodies

Where the Treaties sets up bodies, they usually give a subordinate executive power to deal with their operation. This power may concern the jurisdiction of these bodies, their rules of procedure and composition, their organization, the rules governing the performance of their members and even the setting up of subsidiary bodies within them. Often it is the Council that makes the decisions, but bodies like Parliament,[66] the Courts,[67] ECOSOC[68] and the Committee of Regions[69] have the right to decide on their own internal organization. The Member States decide collectively the location of the bodies of the Union.[70]

VI.3.2.g.iii Appointment and Dismissal of Officials

The power granted by the Treaties to appoint and dismiss senior officials is a very important aspect of executive power. The appointment and dismissal of lesser officials within bodies is governed by the appropriate Rules of Procedure.

Under the Treaties, the power of appointment is exercised in the European Union in the following ways:

a) The Member States, acting collectively, appoint the following people:

- the President and Members of the Commission, subject to the approval of Parliament;[71]

- the President, Vice-President and other Members of the Executive Board of the ECB;[72]

- the Judges and Advocates-General of the Court of Justice;[73]

- the Judges of the Court of First Instance.[74]

b) The Council appoints the following people:

- the special representative for a particular policy issue in the CFSP;[75]

---

66   Articles 190(5) and 199 (ECT).

67   Articles 223, 224, 225(4), 245 and 247(3) (ECT).

68   Article 260 (ECT).

69   Article 264 (ECT).

70   Article 289 (ECT). They have not always decided wisely. Parliament's monthly plenary sessions take place in Strasbourg, while its committees meet in Brussels and the General Secretariat is based in Luxembourg. Needless to say, this bizarre arrangement hampers Parliament's efficiency.

71   Article 214(2) (ECT). The procedure for appointing the Commission is discussed *supra* in Section III.3.3.a.

72   Article 112(2)(b) (ECT).

73   Article 223 (ECT).

74   Article 225(3) (ECT).

75   Article 18(5) (TEU).

- the Secretary-General and Deputy Secretary-General of the Council;[76]

- the members of the Court of Auditors;[77]

- the members of ECOSOC;[78]

- the members of the Committee of Regions.[79]

c) The Court of Justice appoints the President and the Registrar of the Court of Justice.[80]

d) The European Parliament appoints the Ombudsman.[81]

e) The Commission appoints its own Vice-Presidents.[82]

f) ECOSOC appoints its President and officers as does the Committee of Regions.[83]

g) The Commission and the Member States each appoint two members to the Employment Committee,[84] and the Commission, the ECB and the Member States each appoint two members each to the Economic and Financial Committee (EFC).[85] The Member States act individually.

The power under the EC Treaty to dismiss officials is exercised by the Court of Justice. It may dismiss the Ombudsman,[86] Commissioners,[87] judges of the Court of Justice and the Court of First Instance[88] and members of the Court of Auditors.[89]

VI.3.2.g.iv The Supervision of Executive Acts

The supervision of executive acts is carried out in most countries by the legislature although it is an executive and not a legislative act. In the European Union,

---

76 Article 207(2) (ECT. Per Article 26 of the TEU, the Secretary-General acts as the High Representative for the CFSP.

77 Article247(3) (ECT).

78 Article 258 (ECT).

79 Article 263 (ECT).

80 Articles 223 and 224 (ECT).

81 Article 195(1) (ECT).

82 Article 217 (ECT).

83 Articles 260 and 264 (ECT).

84 Article 130 (ECT).

85 Article 114(2) (ECT).

86 Article 195(2) (ECT).

87 Article 213(2) and 216 (ECT).

88 Articles 6 and 44 of the Statute of the Court of Justice, which is attached to as a protocol to the EC Treaty and was last amended by Article 6 III 3(c) of the Treaty of Amsterdam.

89 Article 247(7) (ECT).

this task is carried out by Parliament but only with respect to the Commission. On a general basis, it may pass a vote of censure on the Commission, in which case the Commission must resign as a body.[90] Parliament also supervises the Commission's implementation of the budget, in respect of which it alone can give a discharge.[91] The Court of Auditors, however, is responsible for auditing the accounts of the Union.[92] There is no formal supervision by Parliament of the executive acts of the Council, the Member States or any other body of the Union.

VI.3.2.g.v Structural Changes

We have already discussed the administrative amendments to the Treaties that the Member States, the European Council and the Council may adopt.[93] There are also other acts that may be adopted under the Treaties that cause or have the potential to cause structural change to the Union without necessitating an actual amendment of the Treaties in themselves. One such act is the decision of the Council to accept a state into the Union.[94] Other acts are the provision for a system of own resources for the Union,[95] the convocation by the Presidency of an intergovernmental conference[96] as well as minor changes to existing procedures and bodies[97] and the establishment of new bodies and procedures.[98] These latter acts are all adopted by the Council, normally acting alone but on one occasion with Parliament.[99] Provisions relating to own resources must be ratified by the Member States acting individually.

VI.3.2.g.vi Authorization of Closer Cooperation[100]

The authorization of a closer cooperation arrangement is another executive act related to the functioning of the Union. The decision is taken by the Council, but it may be referred to the European Council.[101]

---

90   This mechanism is discussed *supra* in Section III.3.3.a.

91   Article 276(1) (ECT).

92   Articles 246 and 248(1) (ECT).

93   *See* the discussion *supra* in Section II.3.3.f.

94   Article 49 (TEU). This decision is followed, of course, by an Accession Agreement that adjusts the Treaties, which must be ratified by the Member States.

95   Article 269 (ECT).

96   Article 48 (TEU).

97   Articles 67(2), 175(2), 213(1), 221, 222 and 296 (ECT).

98   Articles 111(3), 111(4), 130, 161, 171, 269 and 286(2) (ECT).

99   Article 286(2) (ECT).

100 Articles 40(2),(3) and 44(2) (TEU); 11(3) (ECT).

101 Closer cooperation is discussed *infra* in Section II.4.

VI.3.3 Treaty Law

As with legislative power, there are certain provisions in the Treaties that are part of the body of executive acts of the Union. They have been mentioned in context above. They relate to policy directions,[102] derogations,[103] safeguard measures[104] and exceptional measures.[105]

VI.4 The Exercise of Judicial Power in the European Union

VI.4.1 The Nature of Judicial Power in the European Union

VI.4.1.a The Court of Justice and the National Courts

The role of judicial power is to establish what the law is and to apply it. This also involves deciding upon the validity of the measure that is at issue. The judicial branch has, however, to rely upon the executive branch to enforce its judgments as this requires use of the coercive powers of the state.

In the European Union, the Court of Justice is given the role of ensuring the interpretation and application of Union law.[106] This is an exclusive power to the extent that Member States agree not to submit any dispute regarding the Treaties to any other method of settlement.[107] It is not, on the other hand, exclusive as regards national courts, which also interpret and apply Union law. In fact, their role is primordial for the everyday application of Union law is done by them as they apply national law of which Union law is an integral part. Moreover, given that the European Union lacks its own coercive powers, the enforcement of judgments of the Court of Justice, including any that impose pecuniary obligations, is governed by national rules of civil procedure,[108] which normally involves authentification of the judgment by a national court. Except where jurisdiction is conferred exclusively on the Court, disputes involving the European Community may also be heard by national courts.[109] The judicial branch in the European Union thus comprises the Court of Justice and the national courts. This obviously raises the question of the relationship between them.

---

102   Articles 4(1),(3), 15, 16, 33(2), 34(2), 44(2)(a), 47(3), 55, 95(3), 98, 105(1), 131, 133(1), 136, 174(2), 174(3) and 285(2) (ECT).

103   Articles 30, 39(3), 39(4), 45, 55, 57(1), 58(1)(a),(b), 69, 86(2), 95(4),(5), 101(2), 122(1), 137(5), 141(4), 152(4)(a), 153(5), 176, 184(3) and 296(1)(a),(b) (ECT).

104   Article 120(1) (ECT).

105   Articles 14(6) (TEU); 60(2), 87(2), 87(3) and 297 (ECT).

106   Article 220 (ECT). The provision applies to the TEU, as far as the Court has jurisdiction in that Treaty, by virtue of Article 46 (TEU).

107   Article 292 (ECT).

108   Article 256 (ECT).

109   Article 240 (ECT).

It is said that the Court of Justice is not placed hierarchically above the national courts, but this widely-held view is not really correct. Certainly, the Court of Justice is not an appellate court to which parties before national courts can appeal if they disagree with the judgment and whose rulings are precedents that bind inferior courts. In other words, national courts are not systemically inferior to the Court of Justice. In practice, they are inferior albeit with a very important proviso.

National courts interpret and apply Union law as part of their national role, but, left to their own devices, it is very likely that differences would emerge between them with the result that Union law would not be applied consistently throughout the Union. The same problem exists in a federal state like Canada, where the courts of the various provinces all interpret and apply federal law as they think appropriate. There is thus need for a higher court to ensure that the interpretation and application of federal or Union law is done in a consistent manner, that is to say in accordance with its rulings. This is the role in Canada of the Supreme Court of Canada as it is the role in the European Union of the Court of Justice.[110] The only difference is the way in which this supervisory role is played. In the case of the Court of Justice, it is not by way of an appeal from the parties before the national court but by a reference from the court itself before which the issue involving Union law has been raised. The result is essentially identical. The Court of Justice gives a decision that binds the court making the reference just as the Supreme Court of Canada makes a decision that binds the inferior court from which the appeal has come.[111] Furthermore, the case law of the Court of Justice is also generally accepted as binding on national courts in the same way that precedents set by the Supreme Court of Canada are binding on inferior courts.[112] National courts must follow this case law even if it means disregarding national laws that are incompatible with it.[113]

In some ways, the position of national courts vis-à-vis the Court of Justice may be inferior to their position vis-à-vis federal supreme courts as they cannot impugn the validity of a Union measure. Only the Court of Justice can do this. In Canada, by contrast, the courts in a province can dispute the validity of a federal law. So, if a national court has doubts about the validity of a Union measure, its only recourse is to refer the matter to the Court of Justice.[114] Otherwise, it is obliged to apply the measure. An additional limitation on national courts is that

---

110   *See* the comments of the Court of Justice in *Rheinmühlen-Düsseldorf v. Einfuhr- und Vorratsstelle für Getreide und Futtermittel*, 166/73, [1974] ECR 33 at 38.

111   *See Milch- Fett- und Eierkontor GmbH v. Hauptzollamt Saarbrücken*, 29/68, [1969] ECR 165 at 180.

112   *See Brasserie du Pêcheur et al v. Germany et al*, C-46/93 and 48/93, [1996] ECR I-1029 at 1145.

113   *Simmenthal SpA v. Commission*, 92/78, [1979] ECR 777.

114   *Foto-Frost v. Hauptzollamt Lübeck-Ost*, 314/85, [1987] ECR 4199 at 4232.

they cannot follow national procedures if these would render impossible or fruit-less the application of Union law.[115]

The argument that the Court of Justice and national courts are equals is based on the idea that national courts are supreme in the area of national law in the same way that the Court is in the area of Union law. Thus, so goes the argument, the Court of Justice cannot interpret or apply national law and must rely on the co-operation of the national courts. Certainly, it is true that the Court has nothing to do with national law where it is truly national without any Union dimension. However, where the issue is the compatibility of a national law with Union law, it is for all practical purposes the Court of Justice that makes the decision. It leaves the final decision up to national courts, thus preserving their so-called suprem-acy in the area of national law, but its rulings rarely leave a national court in any doubt as to what do.

There is, therefore, an informal hierarchical relationship between the Court of Justice and national courts, subject, however, to one important proviso. In a fed-eral country like Canada or the United States, the inferior courts have no choice but to follow the rulings of appellate courts and cannot prevent a matter being heard by them. This is a crucial difference, for in the European Union it is the na-tional courts themselves that decide whether or not to refer to the Court of Jus-tice. Even those courts of last instance that are obliged to refer can avoid it by using the *acte clair* or *acte éclairé* doctrines.[116] Likewise, national courts cannot be forced to follow the Court's rulings. So, in the final analysis, the Court of Justice must indeed rely on cooperation with national courts. To this extent, we can consider them equals, although it is an equality based on an infringement of the principle of Union loyalty set out in Article 10 of the EC Treaty, for which the Member State in which the recalcitrant court is situated could be brought before the Court of Justice.

VI.4.1.b The Court of First Instance

Article 225 of the EC Treaty provides for a Court of First Instance to be attached to the Court of Justice with a right to hear and determine certain matters subject to a right of appeal to the Court on points of law. The Treaty provision prohibits the Court of First Instance from being given the right to hear references from na-tional courts under Article 234.

---

115   *See Hans Just I/S v. Danish Ministry for Fiscal Affairs*, 68/79, [1980] ECR 501 at 522-23.

116   *See* the discussion of these devices *supra* in Section IV.5.2.

The Council established the Court of First Instance in Council Decision 88/591.[117] Article 2 of this Decision[118] sets out the jurisdiction of the Court of First Instance within the European Community as covering:

- disputes under Article 236 between the Community and its servants;

- actions brought under Article 230 by natural or legal persons to contest the validity of a decision addressed to them;

- actions brought under Article 232 by natural or legal persons for failure of Parliament, the Council or the Commission to address a binding act to them;

- actions brought under Article 235 by natural or legal persons for compensation for damage caused to them by the institutions or servants of the Community;

- actions brought under Article 238 by natural or legal persons for judgment pursuant to an arbitration clause contained in a contract concluded by the Community.

The Court of First Instance has no jurisdiction under the TEU.

VI.4.2 The Scope of the Judicial Power in the European Union

VI.4.2.a The Jurisdiction of the Court of Justice

The judicial power is a Union power in that the Court of Justice has jurisdiction over matters coming within both the TEU and the EC Treaty. However, in both cases, there are limitations on the Court's jurisdiction.

Within the EC Treaty, the Court's jurisdiction is limited in only two instances. Under Article 68(1), a reference to the Court involving the interpretation of Title IV (visas, asylum, immigration and other policies related to free movement of persons) or the interpretation and validity of secondary acts based on this Title can only be made by national courts of last instance.[119] Secondly, the Court does not have jurisdiction to rule on any measure within the purview of Title IV that relates to the maintenance of law and order and the safeguarding of national security.[120]

Within the TEU, the Court exercises no judicial control over the CFSP. In PJC, it has jurisdiction over framework decisions, decisions and conventions, together with any implementing measures.[121] However, its right to give a preliminary

---

117   OJ L 241/89.

118   As amended by Article 1 of Council Decision 93/350 (OJ L144/93).

119   The normal rule under Article 234 is that any national court can request a preliminary ruling if it considers such a ruling necessary for it to give judgment.

120   Article 68(2) (ECT).

121   Article 35(1),(6) (TEU).

ruling in a reference from a national court is subject to the Member State in question giving its consent to this jurisdiction.[122] Moreover, Member States may choose whether the request for a ruling comes from a national court of last instance or any national court.[123] On the other hand, the Court has full jurisdiction to rule on the legality of framework decisions and other decisions. It may also rule on the interpretation and application of common positions, framework decisions, decisions and conventions in PJC in the case of disputes between Member States that cannot be resolved by the Council.[124] The Court has no jurisdiction, however, over operations carried out by the police or matters pertaining to a Member State's responsibility for the maintenance of law and order and the safeguarding of internal security.[125] It does have jurisdiction over the provisions on closer cooperation, amendment and accession and, to the extent that it concerns a matter that falls within its jurisdiction and involves a Union act, fundamental rights.[126]

VI.4.2.b The Fields of Jurisdiction of the Court of Justice

VI.4.2.b.i Interpretation and Application of Union Law

Preliminary Rulings

Under Article 234 of the EC Treaty, national courts may, and in the case of courts of last instance must, refer to the Court for a preliminary ruling any question of Union law that is raised before them where a decision on the matter is necessary for them to give judgment. The question may concern the interpretation of the Treaty, the validity and interpretation of subordinate acts of the Community institutions and the ECB or the interpretation of the statutes of bodies set up by the Council to the extent provided in the statute. Subordinate acts include any instrument that is subject to judicial control, which means regulations, directives, decisions, *sui generis* decisions and international agreements concluded under the EC Treaty. Even mixed agreements that are concluded jointly by the Community and the Member States are included.[127]

If the Court determines that an act of a Community institution or the ECB is invalid, it will not declare it void on a preliminary ruling.[128] This is because this procedure is intended to ensure the uniform application of Union law rather

---

122　Article 37(2) (TEU).

123　Article 35(3).

124　Article 35(7) (TEU).

125　Article 35(5) (TEU).

126　Article 46(c),(d),(e) (TEU).

127　*See Office National de l'Emploi (Onem) v. Kziber*, C-18/90, [1991] ECR I-199.

128　*Firma C. Schwarz v. Einfuhr- und Vorratsstelle für Getreide und Futtermittel*, 16/65, [1965] ECR 877 at 886.

than constitute a judicial control of the legality of subordinate acts. However, the national court is unlikely to enforce the act under these circumstances, and the institution concerned will obviously amend or repeal it.

The definition of a national court is quite broad and covers all but administrative tribunals that do not operate independently of the entity against which the action has been brought. It is not entirely clear which national courts are obliged to refer. The abstract view is that the obligation apples only to the highest court in the land, but it would seem more sensible to make it the highest court in a particular case. Not all matters are susceptible of being heard by the former. Even the second view is not without problems as it may not be clear during the proceedings before a lower court whether any appeal from it would be granted, in which case that lower court itself becomes the court of last instance. In the case of matters that come within Title IV of the EC Treaty,[129] only courts of last instance may make a reference, but they are obliged to do so.[130] The Court may not rule on the validity of measures taken under Title IV that relate to the maintenance of law and order or the safeguarding of internal security.[131]

In the area of PJC, the Court may give preliminary rulings on the validity and interpretation of framework decisions and decisions adopted by the Council under Article 34(2)(b) and (c), on the interpretation of conventions adopted by the Member States under Article 34(2)(d) and on the interpretation and validity of the measures taken by the Council to implement these conventions.[132] However, the jurisdiction of the Court must be accepted by a Member State in the form of a declaration appended to the Treaty of Amsterdam.[133] In making its declaration, a Member State also specifies whether any court or only courts of last instance may make the reference.[134] The Court may not rule on the validity of measures carried out by the police or those related to the maintenance of law and order or the safeguarding of internal security.[135]

Article 68(3) Rulings

Under Article 68(3) of the EC Treaty, the Council, the Commission or a Member State may ask the Court to give a ruling on the interpretation of Title IV of the Treaty involving visas, asylum, immigration and other policies related to the free

---

129 Visas, asylum, immigration and other policies related to free movement of persons.

130 Article 68(1) (ECT).

131 Article 68(2) (ECT).

132 Article 35(1) (TEU).

133 Article 35(2) (TEU).

134 Article 35(3) (TEU).

135 Article 35(5) (TEU).

movement of persons. These rulings are binding but do not apply to rendered judgments of national courts.

Disputes involving Member States

Member States may submit any dispute between them regarding the interpretation of the EC Treaty to the Court of Justice.[136] They are not obliged to do so, but they may not submit the dispute to any other method of settlement.[137]

Disputes between Member States regarding the interpretation or application of acts adopted in the area of PJC by the Council or the Member States under Article 34(2) of the TEU are first referred to the Council. It is only if the Council fails to settle the dispute within six months that the matter comes before the Court of Justice.[138] It is not clear whether a Member State has to refer it or whether the Court can act on its own initiative. It is worth noting that this provision also applies to common positions adopted under Article 34(2)(a), which are not otherwise subject to the judicial control of the Court.

The Court has jurisdiction to rule on disputes between the Member States and the Commission on the interpretation or application of the conventions adopted by the former in the area of PJC pursuant to Article 34(2)(d). Presumably, it acts at the request of one of the parties involved.

VI.4.2.b.ii Control of the Legality of Union Acts

Acts of the Council, Commission, European Parliament and ECB

Under Article 230 of the EC Treaty, the Court has jurisdiction to review all acts adopted by the Council, Commission, Parliament and ECB pursuant to the Treaty in order to determine whether they are illegal on certain grounds. These grounds are lack of competence, infringement of an essential procedural requirement, infringement of the EC Treaty or any rules relating to its application and misuse of powers. Primarily, this means that an act will be declared void under Article 231 if it infringes the principles of attribution of powers or subsidiarity, if its adoption does not follow the procedures set out in the Treaty, if its content violates fundamental rights or if it represents a use of the powers given by the Treaty for means other than those contemplated by it. In some cases, provisions in an act that are not illegal will be upheld.[139] Acts again include all instruments that are subject to judicial control. In the case of Parliament, this means instruments adopted with the Council under the Co-Decision Procedure as well as other acts intended to produce legal effects for third par-

---

136 Article 239 (ECT).

137 Article 292 (ECT).

138 Article 35(7) (TEU).

139 Article 231 refers only to regulations, but the Court interprets such provisions to mean any act of general application—*see Simmenthal SpA v. Commission*, 92/78, [1979] ECR 777at 800.

ties. The Court may not rule on the legality of measures taken under Title IV of the Treaty that relate to the maintenance of law and order or the safeguarding of internal security.[140]

Under Article 35(6) of the TEU, the Court may also rule on the legality of framework decisions and decisions adopted by the Council under Article 35(2) to the extent that they do not involve measures carried out by the police or those related to the maintenance of law and order or the safeguarding of internal security.[141]

The Court acts under Article 230 primarily at the request of the Member States, the Council or the Commission. The European Parliament, Court of Auditors and ECB can also bring actions but only to protect their rights. Natural or legal persons can bring an action before the Court of First Instance with respect to acts that are of direct and individual concern to them. Under the TEU, the Court acts at the request of a Member State or the Commission.

Actions must be brought within two months of the publication or notification of the act, or in the absence thereof, of when it came to the knowledge of the plaintiff. Bodies whose act has been declared void must take the necessary measures to comply with the judgment of the Court.[142]

Acts of the European Investment Bank (EIB)

At the request of a Member State, the Commission or Board of Directors of the EIB, the Court can review an act of the Board of Governors of the EIB under Article 237(b) of the EC Treaty to establish whether it is illegal on one of the grounds set out in Article 230. Under Article 237(c), the Court can likewise review acts of the Board of Directors at the request of a Member State or the Commission. However, illegality can only be established in this instance on grounds of non-compliance with certain provision of the Statute of the EIB relating to the granting of loans.[143] Where an act is found to be illegal, it can be voided by the Court under Article 231.

VI.4.2.b.iii Control of the Applicability of Union Acts

Preliminary Rulings

In its preliminary rulings, which are discussed above, the Court may review the validity of Union acts. It will not void them if it finds them illegal but declare

---

140 Article 68(2) (ECT). The wording refers only to "validity," but if the Court cannot rule on validity, it certainly cannot rule on legality.

141 Article 35(5) (TEU). The wording refers only to "validity," but if the Court cannot rule on validity, it certainly cannot rule on legality.

142 Article 233 (ECT). This provision must also apply to rulings by the Court under Article 35(6) (TEU).

143 Article 21 (2),(5),(6) and (7) (ECT).

them invalid. The result is that the national court is unlikely in these circumstance to apply the act.

Plea of Inapplicability

Under Article 241 of the EC Treaty, a party to a proceeding before the Court of Justice may invoke in its defense the inapplicability of an act of general application[144] of the Council, acting alone or with Parliament, the Commission or the ECB on the grounds of illegality as set out in Article 230. This may be done even if the time limit for bringing an action under Article 230 has expired. The Court does not declare the act void but will not apply it.[145]

Inapplicability of an International Treaty under the EC Treaty

Under Article 300(6) of the EC Treaty, a Member State, the Council or the Commission may request the Court to rule on the compatibility with the EC Treaty of an international agreement that is envisaged by the Community. If the Court finds that there is incompatibility, the agreement cannot be applied until the Treaty has been appropriately amended under Article 48 of the TEU.

VI.4.2.b.iv Non-Fulfillment of Obligations under the EC Treaty

Non-Fulfillment of Obligations by Member States

At the suit of the Commission or a Member State, the Court can rule under Article 228(1) of the EC Treaty that a Member State has failed to fulfill an obligation under the Treaty. The Member State is obliged to take the necessary measures to comply with the Court's judgment. Otherwise, the Court, at the specification of the Commission, may impose a lump sum or penalty payment on it.[146]

The procedure differs depending who brings the action.[147] The Commission may bring an action after first giving the Member State concerned the opportunity to comply with its opinion on the matter. Member States must first bring the matter before the Commission for it to deliver an opinion to the offending Member State. It is only if the Commission does not do this within three months that they can bring the matter themselves before the Court. In the case of violations by Member States of the rules on state aids or the abuse by them of derogations from approximation directives or the security exceptions, both the Commission and the Member States can bring the matter directly before the Court.[148]

---

144 Article 241 refers only to regulations, but the Court interprets such provisions to mean any act of general application—*see Simmenthal SpA v. Commission*, 92/78, [1979] ECR 777at 800.

145 *See Milchwerke Heinz Wöhrmann & Sohn et al v. Commission*, 31 and 33/62, [1962] ECR 501 at 507.

146 Article 228(2) (ECT).

147 *Cf* Articles 226 and 227 (ECT).

148 Articles 88(2), 85(9) and 298 (ECT).

Where the non-fulfillment concerns a Member State's obligations under the Statute of the EIB, it is the Board of Directors of the EIB that brings the action before the Court under Article 237(a) of the EC Treaty. It acts in all ways like the Commission above except that it may not ask for pecuniary sanctions against a recalcitrant Member State.

Non-Fulfillment of Obligations by National Central Banks

At the suit of the Governing Council of the ECB, the Court may rule under Article 237(d) of the EC Treaty that a national central bank has failed to fulfill an obligation under the Treaty or the Statute of the ESCB, in which case the bank must take the necessary measures to comply with the Court's judgment. The Governing Council acts in all ways like the Commission above except that it may not ask for pecuniary sanctions against a recalcitrant bank.

Non-Fulfillment of an Obligation to Act by Union Bodies (Failure to Act)

The Member States and the other institutions of the Community[149] may bring an action before the Court under Article 232 of the EC Treaty against the European Parliament, Council, Commission or ECB where they consider that the body has failed to act in infringement of the Treaty. The ECB can also bring an action where the failure involves a matter in its area of competence. Natural or legal persons may bring an action before the Court of First Instance in the case of a binding act that should have been addressed to them. If either Court finds in favor of the plaintiff, the institution concerned must take the necessary measures to comply with the Court's judgment.[150]

VI.4.2.b.v Plenary Jurisdiction of the Court

Compensation for Non-Contractual Liability of the Community

The Court has full jurisdiction under Articles 235 and 288 of the EC Treaty to rule on disputes concerning compensation for damage arising out of tortious acts by the European Parliament, Council, Commission, Court of Auditors, Court of Justice and ECB and by the Community's employees. It must, however, rule in accordance with the general principles common to the laws of the Member States. Actions brought by natural or legal persons are heard by the Court of First Instance. An action may not be brought after a period of five years from the occurrence of the event giving rise to it.[151]

---

149   The relevant Community institutions are the Council, Commission, Parliament and Court of Auditors.

150   Article 233 (ECT).

151   Article 43 of the Statute of the Court of Justice.

Disputes between the Community and its Employees

The Court has full jurisdiction under Article 236 of the EC Treaty over cases involving a dispute between the Community and its employees. It, must, however, act within the limits and conditions of the Staff Regulations or the Conditions of Employment. These cases are heard by the Court of First Instance.

VI.4.2.b.vi Accorded Jurisdiction of the Court

Penalties provided for by Council Regulations

Regulations adopted by the Council, acting alone or jointly with the European Parliament may, pursuant to Article 229 of the EC Treaty, give the Court unlimited jurisdiction with regard to the penalties provided for therein. The Court's authority in these cases flows from the regulation in question and not directly from the Treaty.

Jurisdiction to Give Judgment pursuant to an Arbitration Clause in a Contract

Pursuant to Article 238 of the EC Treaty, a contract concluded by or behalf of the Community, whether governed by public or private law, may contain an arbitration clause giving the Court jurisdiction to rule on disputes over the contract. The Court's authority in these cases flows from the clause in the contract and not directly from the Treaty. Where the dispute is brought by natural or legal persons, it is heard by the Court of First Instance.

Judicial Control of Agreements Concluded by the Member States under Article 293 of the EC Treaty

Conventions concluded by the Member States pursuant to Article 293 of the EC Treaty may contain a provision conferring jurisdiction on the Court of Justice to interpret them.

VI.5 The Separation of Powers and the Constitutional System of the European Union

VI.5.1 The Doctrine of the Separation of Powers

The doctrine of the separation of powers was enunciated in the eighteenth century by the French philosopher, Montesquieu, as a model for the reform of the absolutist monarchical regime of pre-revolutionary France.[152] Observing the constitutional regime of Great Britain, Montesquieu concluded that it avoided tyranny by separating out the three powers of government—legislative, executive and judicial—and subjecting their relationship to a system of checks and balances.

---

152 *Esprit des Lois*, Book XI, chapter 6.

In fact, the name of the doctrine is a misnomer. A strict separation of the *powers* of the state would mean that the legislature alone make rules, the judiciary has the exclusive right to interpret, apply and enforce them and the executive restricts itself to the formulation and enactment of policy, initiating legislation where that policy requires the amendment, repeal or creation of rules.

Such a rigid system does not operate even in the United States, whose constitution is inspired by the doctrine. The US Congress, for example, has judicial powers of impeachment and trial as well as executive powers, such as the right to initiate legislation, declare war, regulate commerce with foreign nations and confirm presidential appointments. In turn, the President's power to execute the laws of the United States involves both the legislative role of making rules to implement these laws and the judicial role of applying and enforcing them. The common law tradition inherited from England embodies a judicial power to create rules.

Far from undermining the doctrine, this intermingling of functions is necessary in order to provide the checks and balances that are an important part of it. What we must do is to distinguish between the separation of *powers* and that of the *branches* of state governance.[153] It is the independence and separate identity of the three branches that is the essence of the doctrine. The extent to which the doctrine in this form is put into practice determines whether a country follows the US presidential model or the British parliamentary one.[154] In Europe, the latter is the norm, although France has a hybrid system with an executive President presiding over a parliamentary system.[155]

---

153 I use the word "governance" deliberately as meaning the whole system comprising the three branches. The term "government" for me connotes more the executive branch alone.

154 I discount the French Revolution as a source of constitutional inspiration. It never elaborated a coherent system of government and soon degenerated by turns into the terror of the Jacobins, the cupidity of the Directorate and the military despotism of the First Empire. If it has bequeathed any constitutional legacy to France, it is a radical cleavage between right and left and a facile belief that the state, as long as it drapes itself in republicanism, can do no wrong. This legacy explains in large part the partisanship and corruption of present-day French politics.

155 Where the President's allies control the National Assembly, the President is the major executive figure and the Prime Minister is relegated to the role of executor of the President's policies. When the opposition controls the National Assembly, it is the Prime Minister who runs the executive and the President becomes little more than a non-executive head of state. He retains, however, the personal power to dissolve the National Assembly and to have a voice in France's foreign and defense policies. It is a rather bizarre system.

VI.5.2 The British and US Models

VI.5.2.a The British Parliamentary Model

The starting point for both the US and British models is the revolutionary settlement in England that took place between 1688 and 1700.[156] This settlement put an end to the century-long battle between the Crown and Parliament by creating a constitutional monarchy. It was based on the separation of the branches of government. However, it has developed in different directions in Great Britain and the United States. This was due to the atrophy of the personal powers of the British monarch during the eighteenth century, which placed executive power in the hands of the monarch's ministers. This development left the judiciary independent and separate but it has had a decisive impact on the relationship between the legislature and the executive within the British system of governance.

The most important consequence of the demise of royal power in Great Britain is that the executive, freed from its responsibility to the monarch, has become responsible to Parliament and can only remain in office as long as it retains its support.[157] This is the distinguishing feature of the parliamentary system, which is why it is sometimes referred to as "responsible government."[158] The executive is no longer independent but placed under the ultimate control of the legislature. At least, this is the theory, but two other common features of the parliamentary system dilute and can even reverse it.

The revolutionary settlement envisaged a complete separation of the executive and legislative branches by banning the monarch's ministers from sitting in the House of Commons.[159] This provision, which probably would have changed the constitutional development in Great Britain, was repealed before it came into effect and the contrary came to pass. By convention if not by law, ministers in the British government have to sit in Parliament. The result is an overlapping of the identities of the executive and the legislature, though not a fusion. Not all persons sitting in Parliament are in the government. In some countries that have adopted the parliamentary system, government ministers have to resign their seats in the legislature but they are still present in the chamber.

The presence of the executive in the legislature, as members or as a presence, certainly permits the legislature to supervise more closely the activities of the

---

156   The two most important statutes are the Bill of Rights (1688), 1 Wm 3 & Mary, c.6 and the Act of Settlement (1700), 12 and 13 Wm3, c.2.

157   The British Parliament consists of the House of Lords, which is now appointed by the executive, and the House of Commons, which is elected. It is the support of the House of Commons that is crucial.

158   This expression in no way precludes the policies pursued from being totally irresponsible.

159   They could not prevent them sitting in the House of Lords if they were peers of the realm.

executive. More significantly, however, with the growth of political parties and the discipline they exercise over their members, it has also enabled the executive to gain control of the legislature. In most parliamentary countries, it is the executive that sets the legislative agenda and decides what laws will be passed. It is rare that private members' bills are enacted into law and impossible in the face of the executive's opposition. Even where the support of the legislature is lost, the executive may have recourse to another feature of the parliamentary system, which is the power of the executive to dissolve the legislature and call for new elections in the hope of obtaining a new majority. This ability to dissolve the legislature at any time also helps maintain party discipline, which further strengthens the executive's control. However, there are differences in the ease with which a legislature can be dissolved. In Great Britain, the power to do so is part of the royal prerogative that is exercised at the discretion of the executive. In Germany, on the other hand, strict conditions must be met before the legislature can be dissolved. These two features are very common in parliamentary systems, but they are not its essence, which remains the principle of responsible government.

One other consequence of the demise of royal power in Great Britain is that the Crown, shorn of its personal powers, has become a non-executive head of state, who stands above the political fray as a symbol of national unity. This, too, is an intrinsic feature of parliamentary systems, all of which are presided over by a monarch or president with no or very limited executive powers.[160]

VI.5.2.b The US Model

Under the US Constitution, all the branches of government are kept separate and independent, not just the judiciary. The legislature, or Congress, is elected at fixed intervals and cannot be dissolved by the executive.[161] It alone has the formal power to initiate and make laws. Neither the President nor any other member of the government sit in Congress and thus have not over time managed to attain control over it.[162] The absence of disciplined political parties along the European model has also played a role. Executive power is vested in the President who is elected separately from Congress and who holds office for

---

160   Where the political system is fragmented and alliances within the legislature shift continually, the non-executive head of state becomes an umpire and acquires more power. This has tended to be the case with the Dutch monarch and the Italian President. Other non-executive heads of state have varying degrees of informal political authority, which may emanate from their longevity in office (Elizabeth II) or their historical importance (Juan Carlos I). The German President and the King of Sweden are examples of non-executive heads of state that are assigned a strictly representative role.

161   Among the countries who have adopted the US model, only Chile permits the President to dissolve the legislature. The French President may also dissolve the National Assembly, but this is a hybrid system.

162   The Vice-President does, however, preside over the Senate, but he has no vote except in the case of a tie.

a fixed term of four years regardless of whether he or she has the support of Congress. The President is not answerable to Congress although he or she can be impeached for "high crimes and misdemeanors." The other members of the executive are responsible to the President and not to Congress. The President combines the functions of head of the executive and head of state as did the British monarch at the beginning of the eighteenth century. In short, the US model is much more faithful to the revolutionary settlement than the British one.

VI.5.3 The Constitutional System of the European Union

The only branch of governance in the European Union that has coherence is the judicial branch, which is clearly separate from the other branches. Moreover, judges of the Court of Justice are appointed by the Member States and can only be dismissed by a decision of their own colleagues, which gives the Court a certain independence. The appointments are only for six years and one could argue that, although judges are eligible for re-appointment, they do not enjoy the security of tenure that is perhaps necessary for real independence. In practice, however, the Court of Justice has shown great independence and so we should not belabor this point.

When it comes to separating out the legislative and executive branches, the task is much more difficult. Even leaving aside the Member States, which one can regard as exogenous to the internal Union system of governance, we are confronted with a more or less complete fusion of the two branches. Executive power is wielded by the Council, acting alone or with Parliament, and the Commission. There are other executive organs for specific matters but the general executive power belongs to these three institutions. Legislative power is wielded by the Council, acting alone or with Parliament. Thus, while the Commission wields only executive power, Parliament and the Council have both executive and legislative powers.

Nevertheless, on closer inspection, it is possible to perceive the outline of a separation of the executive and legislative branches in the European Union. As we pointed out above, the Commission is a purely executive body. Moreover, despite its executive role, the European Parliament is essentially a legislative body. If ever a clear distinction were made between executive and legislative acts, as we have suggested in this chapter, it should be possible to hive off the executive acts, which are a matter for the executive and not the legislature. The question we must now ask is what is the constitutional relationship between these two institutions; parliamentary or presidential.

There are certainly presidential-style aspects to this relationship. Parliament is separate from the Commission as Commissioners may not be MEPs. It is also independent of the executive as it is elected for a fixed term and cannot be dissolved prematurely. The Commission is separate from Parliament; its members are appointed by the Member States and they may not be MEPs. However, the salient point in the relationship is that the Commission is responsible to Parliament, which has the power to dismiss it by passing a vote of censure. Commissioners also appear frequently before parliamentary committees and there is a general supervision on the part of Parliament of the Commission's activities.[163] This control of the executive is the hallmark of the parliamentary system.

Viewed in this light, the European Union can be seen as an inchoate parliamentary regime with an executive that is responsible to Parliament. The fact that the Commissioners do not sit in Parliament and cannot dissolve it is not decisive, although it does mean that the executive will not end up controlling the legislature as frequently happens in a parliamentary system. However, it should be noted that it is the Commission and not Parliament that enjoys the right of legislative initiative, which is another parliamentary feature.

Can we say, then, that the European Union has the potential to develop into a parliamentary state? The problem is the Council. Its executive role is as important as its legislative role, so that it is impossible to separate out the two branches and give the Council a particular identity. As a logical consequence of its dual identity, the Council is responsible to itself rather than Parliament. It is, in short, an anomaly within the constitutional structure of the Union and one that prevents its development into a parliamentary system. As long as the Council exists in its present form and remains as powerful as it is, there can no meaningful separation of the executive and legislative branches of state governance in the European Union. Without such separation, it is impossible to institute responsible government, for without separate identities there can be no relationship between the executive and legislative branches. If the Union is to progress from this situation, it will be necessary to distinguish between the executive and legislative acts of the Council and make a decision as to what branch of state governance it should belong. The choice that is made will determine in large measure the future constitutional system of the Union. Such a decision could also involve transforming the Council into a permanent body.

One possibility is for the Council to renounce its executive powers and become in effect the upper house of the Union legislature. It would represent the interests of the Member States like the *Bundesrat* in Germany represents the *Länder*. In this case, the Council's present executive powers would be exercised by the Commission and probably the control of this body by the new two-tier legislature would be strengthened. This would consolidate the inchoate parliamentary system that now already exists. Some have suggested that the President of the Commission should be directly elected in these circumstances. This makes little sense as there is an inherent contradiction in the direct election of an executive

---

163   *Contra* M. Donnelly and E. Ritchie in "The College of Commissioners and their Cabinets" in G. Edwards and D. Spence (eds.), *The European Commission* (1994) at page 34.

that is responsible to and can be dismissed by Parliament.[164] A more sensible suggestion is to pick the members of the Commission from the MEPs, which would give them democratic legitimacy within a workable system. Certainly, important changes in the way the Commission is appointed and supervised would be a pre-condition to adopting this solution.[165]

The other possibility is for the Council to renounce its legislative powers and to retain its present executive powers. It could not be responsible to Parliament as its present make-up precludes this possibility. However, this would be possible if the new Council were constituted as a permanent body. This solution would create a powerful independent executive and would shift the Union towards a presidential system, particularly if the President of the Council were directly elected. It is not, however, a particularly desirable solution. It would preserve the present confusion unless Parliament, which acts on occasion with the Council in the executive area, were to be constituted as a purely legislative organ. Even if this happened, the problem of the relationship with the other executive organ, the Commission, would need to be re-worked. It is probable that the Commission would end up as the executor of the Council's policies,[166] which would strengthen the intergovernmental principle in the governance of the Union. If the Commission remained responsible to Parliament while the Council was not, this arrangement could prove unworkable.

What is most likely is that the European Union will continue in its present mode. Indeed it is condemned to do so until a distinction is made between Union acts that are executive and those that are legislative in nature. The advantage of the status quo for the Member States is that it preserves their influence in the decision-making processes through the intermediary of the Council. For, however much one may argue that it is a Union institution, the Council is nonetheless a throwback to the intergovernmental impulses that formed the original EEC Treaty. This is not, however, a reasonable solution for a Union that now has a federal-like jurisdiction over many aspects of national life,[167] and which demands to be governed more like a state than an intergovernmental organization.

---

164   In Israel, the Prime Minister is directly elected but is responsible to the Knesset. This leads to the situation experienced by Mr. Barak, who, despite his direct election, could not remain in office because he lost the confidence of the Knesset.

165   As D. Rometsch and W. Wessels put it in "The Commission and the Council of Ministers," in G. Edwards and D. Spence (eds.), *The European Commission* (1994) at page 207, the Commission at present simply lacks the necessary political prestige and legitimacy as well as procedural control to aspire to the position of a government.

166   *Ibid* at page 207.

167   G. Edwards and D. Spence go further in "The Commission in Perspective," in G. Edwards and D. Spence (eds.), *The European Commission* (1994), when they claim at page 17 that "no area of concern of the traditional nation-state now escapes some kind of involvement at a European level."

VI.6 The Protection of Fundamental Rights in the European Union

VI.6.1 Introduction

For an entity that is so pre-occupied with fundamental rights, it is surprising that the founding Treaties of the European Union contained no reference to them. It is true that they prohibited discrimination on grounds of nationality,[168] but this was necessary in order to establish the common market. Even the provision requiring equal pay for equal work in the case of female and male workers[169] owed more to a desire to prevent distortions in the conditions of competition within the common market than a passion for gender equality. It was in fact left to the Court of Justice to develop a concept of fundamental rights that would apply to the Union's legal system.[170] This did not satisfy the Commission or many human rights activists, who argued that what was needed was the accession of the European Communities to the European Convention on Human Rights and Fundamental Freedoms.[171] In their view, this would have given the Community a clear and written code against which to measure its actions.[172] Moreover, if the Union accepted the right of individual petition, complainants would be able to bring the Union bodies before the European Commission of Human Rights once they had exhausted their judicial remedies within the Union.

No move was made at this stage towards accession. Instead, the Member States incorporated into the TEU the jurisprudence of the Court of Justice,[173] which the European Parliament, the Council and the Commission had already pledged themselves to respect.[174] Eventually, accession to the European Convention was envisaged, but the Court of Justice held that the Community did not have the

---

168 Article 7 of the original EEC Treaty—now Article 12 (ECT).

169 Article 119 of the original EEC Treaty—now Article 141 (ECT). The Treaty of Amsterdam added the words "or work of equal value."

170 Most of the cases deal with the Community as they were decided before the TEU. However, I have used the word "Union" as they also now apply to activities within the TEU as well.

171 The Commission's view is found in E.C. Bulletin (1979), Supp. 2. See also A.Z. Drzemczewski, "Fundamental Rights and the European Communities," (1977), 2 The Human Rights Review 80.

172 I have always been surprised by the attachment people place on written codes of fundamental rights. Some of the worst tyrannies have enshrined fundamental rights in their constitutions. Closer to home, slavery was banned under the common law of Great Britain while it still flourished in the United States despite the fundamental rights guaranteed by the American constitution. In fact, as the minority opinion of the German Constitutional Court in the Internationale Handelsgesellschaft case points out "the assertion that only a codification offers adequate certainty of law does not bear examination"—[1974] CMLR 540 at 563.

173 Article 6(2) (TEU).

174 Joint Declaration by the European Parliament, the Council and the Commission on Fundamental Rights, OJ C 103/77.

power to make rules on human rights and hence it could not enter into international agreements in this area.[175] As a result of this rebuff, the Treaty of Amsterdam strengthened and added to the human rights provisions in the Treaties. It also cleared the way for accession by the Union to the European Convention by conferring on the Council the power to adopt measures in the area of fundamental rights.[176] This has not yet happened. Instead the European Parliament, the Council and the Commission have drawn up a Charter of Fundamental Rights which they are pledged to respect.[177]

VI.6.2 The Case Law of the Court of Justice

The issue of fundamental rights first came before the Court in *Stauder*,[178] where the beneficiary of a Community scheme for selling butter more cheaply to people of limited means objected to having to reveal his name and address to the retailer. He claimed that the requirement of nominative identification violated his rights under the German constitution. The Court recognized for the first time that the protection of fundamental rights was a principle of Union law and that respect for them was a condition of the lawfulness of Union acts.[179] On the facts of the case, however, it found that no fundamental right had been violated.

The Court's language in *Stauder* is very general; it does not elucidate the scope of the protection to be afforded to fundamental rights under Union law. The Court was more forthcoming a year later in *Internationale Handelsgesellschaft*[180] when it was faced with a reference from a Frankfurt court concerning two Community regulations that seemed to violate the right to pursue trade activities, which was enshrined in Article 12 of the German constitution. The action was brought by a German exporter who had had to forfeit over 17,000 marks for failing, through no fault of his own, to make full use of a Community license to export maize groats. This considerable sum of money had been deducted from the exporter's original deposit pursuant to a Council regulation. In its reply to the reference, the Court categorically rejected any recourse to national constitutional law and set up in place of such national guarantees a Union concept of fundamental rights that had as its source the constitutional principles common to the Member States. It then proceeded to hold that the regulation in question did not violate this Union concept of fundamental rights.

---

175 *Opinion 2/94*, [1996] ECR I-1759 at 1787-1788.

176 Article 13 (ECT).

177 OJ C364/00. This charter is discussed *infra* in Section VI.6.4.

178 *Stauder v. City of Ulm, Sozialamt*, 29/69, [1969] ECR 419.

179 *See* also *Opinion 4/94*, [1996] ECR I-1759 at 1789.

180 *Internationale Handelsgesellschaft mbH v. Einfuhr- und Vorratsstelle für Getreide und Futtermittel*, 11/70. [1970] ECR 1125.

This decision of the Court of Justice led to an open rift with the German judiciary. The Frankfurt court flatly refused to follow a Union concept of fundamental rights that legitimized legislation that, in its view, was in conflict with the German constitution. It referred the matter to the German Constitutional Court, which, while upholding the regulation, took the position that German constitutional guarantees would continue to apply as long as the Union had not developed an adequate alternative.

Despite the furore that it caused, the view of the German Constitutional Court was not without merit, for the concept of fundamental rights that had hitherto been enunciated by the Court of Justice was still very vague. Some tangible and reassuring evidence of the Court's genuine concern for individual rights was clearly in order, and such evidence was in fact provided two weeks prior to the decision of the German Constitutional Court. In *Nold*,[181] which concerned a reference on the validity of a Community decision that had the effect of depriving a German merchant of much of his business, the Court spelled out the central position and basis of the Union concept of fundamental rights:

> As this Court has already held, fundamental rights form an integral part of the general principles of law which it enforces. In assuring the protection of such rights, this Court is required to base itself on the constitutional traditions common to the Member States and therefore could not allow measures which are incompatible with the fundamental rights recognized and guaranteed by the constitutions of such states. The international treaties on the protection of human rights in which the Member States have co-operated or to which they have adhered can also supply indications which may be taken into account within the framework of Community law.

A year later, the Court applied these principles in *Rutili*.[182] Faced with a French decree restricting where an Italian national could reside in France, it held that the decree was contrary to Union law because it violated the European Convention on Human Rights. The case is interesting for two other reasons. Firstly, the Court was dealing here with a national law rather than a Union measure. The point made was that national laws in an area where the Union has jurisdiction are also subject to the Union concept of fundamental rights.[183] Secondly, it indicates that, despite the broad language of *Nold*, the Court of Justice is concerned above all with the European Convention. The other international treaties on human rights, such as the UN Covenants on Economic, Social and Cultural Rights and on Civil and Political Freedoms, do not figure in its jurisprudence.

The best example of the Court's use of its sources for the concept of fundamental rights is *Hauer*,[184] where it was asked to give a preliminary ruling on the

---

181 *J. Nold, Kohlen- und Baustaffgroßhandlung v. Commission*, 4/73, [1974] ECR 491.

182 *Rutili v. Minister of the Interior*, 36/75, [1975] ECR 1219.

183 *See* also *Ellinki Radiophonia Tileorassi AE (ERT) v. Dimotiki Etaira Pliroforissis et al*, C-260/89, [1991] ECR 2925 at 2964.

184 *Liselotte Hauer v. Land Rheinland-Pfalz*, 44/79, [1979] ECR 3727.

validity of a Community regulation that was used as the basis for denying a German wine-grower the authorization to plant vines on land suitable for wine-growing. Once again there was an infringement of German constitutional guarantees—in this case the right to property—and the Court began its considerations by re-affirming its objection to the use of national constitutional norms for judging the validity of Union law. Then, applying the *Nold* principles, it went on to consider the property rights accorded by Article 1 of the First Protocol to the European Convention[185] and noted that the Article permits a derogation from these rights when a state wishes "to enforce such laws as it deems necessary to control the use of property in accordance with the general interest. . . ." Finally, the Court reviewed the constitutional traditions of the Member States and noted that, in the context of this exception, restrictions similar to those contained in the Community regulation were generally accepted. It therefore concluded that the regulation did not violate fundamental rights.

Throughout the cases we have discussed above, it is clear that the Court does not regard fundamental rights as absolute. In *Schräder*, it spelled out the parameters for restricting them "They may be restricted," said the Court, "provided that the restrictions in fact correspond to objectives of general interest pursued by the Community and that they do not constitute, with regard to the objectives pursued, a disproportionate and intolerable interference which infringes upon the very substance of the rights guaranteed."[186]

VI.6.3 The Treaties

VI.6.3.a The TEU

Fundamental rights are covered primarily by the TEU, which enshrines the jurisprudence of the Court of Justice. Article 6(2) obliges the Union to respect fundamental rights as guaranteed by the European Convention and as they flow from the constitutional traditions common to the Member States. This concept of fundamental rights is a general principle of Union law. It is interesting to note that the TEU does not mention any other international agreements on human rights, which also accords with the Court's approach. It does, however, define the common constitutional principles of the Member States. These are liberty, democracy, respect for human rights and fundamental freedoms and the rule of

---

185   This Article reads as follows:

> Every natural or legal person is entitled to the peaceful enjoyment of his possessions. No-one shall be deprived of his possessions except in the public interest and subject to the conditions provided for by law and by the general principles of international law.

> The preceding provisions shall not, however, in any way impair the right of a State to enforce such laws as it deems necessary to control the use of property in accordance with the general interest or to secure the payment of taxes or other contributions or penalties.

186   *Hermann Schräder HS Kraffutter GmbH & Co. KG* v *Hauptzollamt Gronau*, 265/87, [1989] ECR 2237 at 2268.

law. The Union is founded on these rights and must respect them. The Article is not a model of draftsmanship, but its meaning is clear.

Article 6 is not empty rhetoric as the fundamental rights that it enshrines can be enforced against both the Member States and the bodies of the Union. The Court of Justice sees to the respect of these rights by the latter through its powers of judicial control. It also enforces them against national laws within the areas of Union jurisdiction through preliminary rulings. Otherwise, the Council looks after the Member States.[187] Meeting in the composition of heads of state or government, it has the power to suspend certain of the rights of a Member State under the TEU where it determines the existence of a serious and persistent breach by that state of the fundamental rights set out in Article 6. Sanctions may include suspension of voting rights in the Council. Similar action can be taken under the EC Treaty on the basis of a finding of breach under the provisions of the TEU.[188] In both cases, the obligations of the Member State in breach continue to be binding. The Treaty of Nice goes further and gives the Council the power to determine that there is a risk of a breach. In this case, it will not be able to impose any sanctions but it can make appropriate recommendations to the Member State in question.[189] As yet, however, the suggestion that it should be possible to eject a Member State from the European Union has not been taken up.[190]

VI.6.3.b The EC Treaty

The EC Treaty contains some very precise provisions on fundamental rights. The narrow discrimination clause of the original treaty is now expanded to include discrimination based on nationality, sex, racial or ethnic origin, religion or belief, disability, age or sexual orientation.[191] Somewhat oddly, however, these other types of discrimination are not prohibited outright as is discrimination on grounds of nationality. Instead the Council is given the power to take measures

---

187   Article 7 (TEU).

188   Article 309 (ECT).

189   It is to be hoped that this new power, if it ever comes into effect, will not be abused. This is to be feared after the unedifying fiasco of the Union's sanctions against Austria, whose electors in a perfectly free election had made inevitable the entry into the Austrian government of a party whose leader had made some ill-judged remarks in praise of Hitler's labor policies. The fact that the most strident cries against the new fascist danger came from France, whose government contained representatives of a Communist Party that has never repudiated the murderous soviet regime that financed and controlled it for years, showed up the sanctions for a sanctimonious hypocrisy. After it became clear that the whole hullabaloo was complete nonsense and that the new Austrian government posed absolutely no threat of a fascist resurgence, the Union had to beat a humiliating retreat, orchestrated by the same French President who had so eagerly worked to have the sanctions imposed in the first place.

190   This suggestion is made in P.S.R.F. Mathijsen, *A Guide to European Union* Law (6th ed., 1995) at pages 6-7.

191   Article 13 (ECT).

to combat them. As mentioned above, this new power may mean that the Union could accede to the European Convention.

The provisions on gender equality are now quite far-reaching. The Community itself is obliged to eliminate inequalities and to promote equality between the sexes in all its activities.[192] Member States must still ensure the application of the principle of equal pay for equal work or work of equal value,[193] but this provision is now complemented by the Council's obligation to adopt measures with respect to equal opportunities and equal treatment of men and women in matters of employment and occupation. This includes the principle of equal pay for equal work. Community acts protecting individuals with respect to the processing of personal data have bound the bodies of the Community as from January 1, 1999.[194] Some of the rights of citizenship discussed in Section II.3.2.g could also be considered to come under the rubric of fundamental rights.

VI.6.4 Other Acts

In 1977, the European Parliament, Council and Commission drew up a joint declaration reiterating the Court's concept of fundamental rights and pledging themselves to respect them.[195] This declaration is now defunct as the TEU has enshrined the Court's jurisprudence and requires the Union to respect it. However, it was perhaps too much to expect that the Union would content itself with that without drawing up at least some sort of code that sets out every conceivable right that one can think of and some that one would not normally think of.[196] Thus, a Charter of Fundamental Rights of the European Union[197] was signed at Nice on December 7, 2000 by the European Parliament, the Council and the Commission. It sets out a whole array of rights, some of which are already enshrined in the Treaties. It is divided into six sections: dignity, freedoms, equality, solidarity, citizens' rights and justice. Due to intense pressure from the British government, it was decided not to make the Charter binding and it was adopted, somewhat pompously, as a Solemn Proclamation. The three institutions that signed it, however, have pledged to respect its provisions.

---

192 Article 3(2) (ECT).

193 Article 141(1) (ECT).

194 Article 286(1) (ECT).

195 OJ C103/77.

196 Citizens of Europe must be enormously relieved to know that they now have a right under Article 29 of the Charter to free placement services.

197 OJ C 364/01.

ment of federalism. The second is the territorial (or national) fragment, or a

CHAPTER VII

THE NATURE OF THE EUROPEAN UNION[1]

VII.1 Introduction

Although the European Union has not yet evolved a coherent system of government, whether parliamentary or presidential, it has federal aspects. Its institutions are separate from the Member States making up the Union. It exercises through them jurisdiction over an array of areas of human activity that pre-empts the legislative authority of the Member States and generates law that directly affects their subjects and takes precedence over national law. There is a supreme court of sorts that upholds these prerogatives through its exclusive right to pronounce on the interpretation, validity and legality of Union law. Despite these federal aspects, there is general agreement, however, that the European Union is not a federation.[2]

Federal states may not be uniform, but they have two basic characteristics, namely autonomy at both the federal and state[3] levels of government within their respective areas of jurisdiction and an overall national cohesion.[4] The first characteristic, which is self-explanatory, has been termed the "functional" element of federalism.[5] The second is the "territorial" or "political" element, and it

---

1   This chapter is based on an earlier article of mine, which appeared in (1994), 32 *Archiv des Völkerrechts* 24.

2   The prevailing view is best summed up by T.C. Hartley in "Federalism, Courts and Legal Systems: The Emerging Constitution of the European Community," (1986), 34 *American Journal of Comparative Law* 229, when he writes at 299 that the Union "is not a federation, though it may one day become one."

3   The component parts of a federation go by many names, e.g. states, provinces, lands. For the sake of simplicity, I will use the term "states."

4   *See* P. Pescatore in his foreword to T. Sandalow and E. Stein (eds.), *Courts and Free Markets* (1982); P. Hay, *Federalism and Supranational Organizations. Patterns for New Legal Structures* (1966) at page 98; E Stein, "On Divided-Power Systems: Adventures in Comparative Law," (1993), 1 *Legal Issues of European Integration* 27 at 28.

5   For a discussion of the terms "functional" and "territorial" federalism, *see* G. Schwarzenberger, "Federalism and Supranationalism in the European Communities," (1963), 16 *Current Legal Problems* 17 at 19-20.

requires that the freedoms of the states, which can be quite considerable, nevertheless be contained within an internal and external unity or identity.

The European Union possesses neither basic federal characteristic. It lacks the cohesion of a nation-state and is not autonomous within its area of jurisdiction. For this latter reason, it is incorrect to call it even a functional federation as some scholars have done.[6] However, there is no doubt that the Treaty on European Union (TEU)[7] reinforced the federal vocation of the Union, and the Treaty of Amsterdam[8] takes the process one step further. What this chapter attempts to do is to ascertain just how federal the European Union has become.

VII.2 The Autonomy of the European Union

VII.2.1 Sovereignty and Autonomy in Federations

Sovereignty is relation to federations is a vexed question. For those who maintain that sovereignty is indivisible, the issue is whether it resides in the federation or the states. The classical view is that sovereignty resides in the federation but is exercised in certain matters by the states.[9] For the increasing number of scholars who see sovereignty as a bundle of powers that can be divided between the federation and its states,[10] the nature of this division must be established. There is general agreement that the internal division follows the allocation of competences in the constitution.[11] On the other hand, external sovereignty is still seen as indivisible and the preserve of the federation,[12] but this view has been challenged.[13]

While it behoves us to make passing reference to this important issue, there is no need to pursue it here for we are concerned with the evolution of the European Union towards a federal state in which sovereignty may reside completely, partially or not at all. In order to analyse this development and the contributions made by the TEU and the Treaty of Amsterdam, we need to concentrate on the concrete features of a federation rather than the abstract political theory behind it. This is why we approach federalism in terms of autonomy rather than sovereignty, although clearly the two terms are related.

---

6   *See* Hay (fn. 4) at page 78; Schwarzenberger (fn. 5) at 20.

7   [1992] 1 C.M.L.R. 573.

8   OJ C340/97.

9   J. Hurd, *The Theory of Our National Existence* (1881) at page 123.

10   *See* Hay (fn. 4) at page 79.

11   *Ibid* at page 70.

12   *See* W. Gunst, *Der Begriff der Souveränität im modernen Völkerrecht* (1953) at page 63. K.P.E. Lasok and D. Lasok, *Law and Institutions of the European Union* (7th ed., 2001) at pages 29-31.

13   *See* Hay (fn. 4) at pages 71-72.

VII.2.2 Independence of the Union Institutions

Autonomy for the center in a federation must be based on independence in the appointment and decision-making processes of its legislative, executive and judicial institutions. The criterion for the European Union is freedom from control by the Member States, but it is still far from being achieved.

The major institutions of Union involved in the adoption of executive and legislative acts are the Council, the Commission and the European Parliament. The European Parliament is, of course completely autonomous. Its members are directly elected by universal suffrage and it is master in its own house. The problem is that Parliament only has an equal say with the Council under the Co-Decision Procedure and a veto under the Assent Procedure. Many matters are decided under other procedures where its influence is less. The Council represents the Member States and can hardly be considered an autonomous Union body. However, the increase in qualified majority voting brought about by the TEU and the Treaty of Amsterdam at least improves its functional autonomy as it acts independently of individual Member States in this situation.

The Commission is solely an executive body. The EC Treaty requires it to act independently of the Member States, but it cannot be considered completely autonomous because of the method of its appointment. There has, however, been some progress here. Prior to the TEU and the Treaty of Amsterdam, the Commission was appointed by the Member States without any formal involvement of the Union institutions although it was customary for the new Commission to receive a vote confidence from the European Parliament. Now, Parliament has to approve the Member States' nominee for President of the Commission before they proceed to nominate the other Commissioners, which they must now do by common accord with the nominee for President. The final step in the process is the approval by Parliament of the entire Commission. This reform goes some way towards securing the autonomy of the Union in the appointment of the Commission. However, it is still the Member States that nominate the President, and they play the dominant role in nominating the other Commissioners as well. This preserves for them an important influence over the composition of the Commission. In true federations, the regions play no role at all in the appointment of the central government. The head of the federal government is either elected or appointed by the head of state and in turn chooses the other members of the executive.

The Treaty of Amsterdam also reinforces the position of the President of the Commission. The fact that the President is approved by Parliament prior to the appointment of the other Commissioners and must approve their nominations gives the post greater authority within the Commission and vis-à-vis the Member States. It should also militate against the practice of filling the Commission with political hacks and loyal servants of Member State governments. Both factors must inevitably enhance the functional autonomy of the Commission.

The judicial branch of the European Union is constituted by the Court of Justice. In federations, the center has an important role in appointing the judges of constitutional and supreme courts[14] whereas the appointment of the judges of the Court of Justice is done exclusively by the Member States. This would suggest that the Court is not autonomous, at least in its manner of appointment. However, if we look at the experience of Canada and the United States, it is possible to argue that, just as federal appointment does not necessarily lead to dependence on the federation, so appointment by the Member States is not incompatible with independence from them.[15] In other words, in the case of the judicial branch, functional autonomy may be what counts, and on this score the record of the Court of Justice in creating and upholding the Union legal order speaks for itself. Nevertheless, a better arrangement would still be for the European Parliament at least to approve appointments to the Court of Justice.

VII.2.3 Plenary Authority for the European Union within its Jurisdiction

VII.2.3.a Introduction

A federation exercises plenary authority by virtue of the intrinsic quality of its acts and its irrevocable and exclusive rights in the areas of jurisdiction that it is assigned.[16] Within the European Union, the center continues to lack such authority despite some improvements effected by the TEU and Treaty of Amsterdam.

VII.2.3.b Quality of Union Acts

A federation is able to impose its will on its subjects directly and without interference from the states.[17] It laws and decisions are directly applicable throughout the federation and they both take priority over state laws and pre-empt them in those areas of jurisdiction that are occupied by the federation.[18]

These conditions are met in part within the European Union. Although the EC Treaty bestows direct applicability only on Union regulations, the Court of Justice has extended this concept to other Union acts, Treaty provisions and inter-

---

14 *See* Articles 99 (Belgian Constitution), 92-96 (German Constitution) and II, Section 2 and III, Section 1 (United States Constitution); Section 96 of the Constitution Act, 1867 (Canada).

15 T.C. Hartley, *The Foundations of European Community Law* (4th ed., 1998) takes this view at page 54.

16 *See* K. Lanaerts, "Constitutionalism and the Many Faces of Federalism," (1990), 38 *American Journal of Comparative Law* 205 at 263.

17 T. Sandalow and E. Stein, "On the Two Systems: An Overview," in T. Sandalow and E. Stein (eds.), *Courts and Free Markets* (1982) assert at 15 that "the existence of direct relations between individuals and central institutions in indeed generally taken to be a defining characteristic of a federal system."

18 *See* Articles 31, 37, 70, 71, and 72 of the German Constitution.

national agreements concluded by the Union. The Court has also found that Treaty provisions and Union acts are capable of creating rights for individuals that must be directly enforced by the courts. It has also established the doctrine of the supremacy of Union law. However, the Court's jurisprudence stops short of creating federal law. Not all Union acts are directly applicable and direct rights cannot always be enforced against private parties.[19]

VII.2.3.c Irrevocability of Jurisdiction

In a federation, a re-allocation of jurisdiction is always possible within the context of a constitutional revision. However, such a revision invariably requires the consent of both the federation and the states.[20] Irrevocability is thus a relative term and means in reality that the federal jurisdiction is not subject to unilateral revocation by the states.

Despite its elaboration of the concept of an autonomous Union legal order, the Court of Justice has never denied that the competences of the Union can be revoked. This must be done, however, by way of the amendment procedure that is set out in Article 48 of the TEU. The problem is that this procedure is controlled by the Member States and does not require the consent of any Union institution, not even the European Parliament.[21] This means that the Union is prey to the unilateral reduction or revocation of its powers by the Member States. Indeed, the TEU may be considered to have effected such a unilateral reduction by virtue of the subsidiarity provisions that it introduced.[22]

VII.2.3.d Exclusivity of Jurisdiction

In a federation, there is no encroachment on federal prerogatives by the states. This does not mean that there are not areas of shared jurisdiction as in the European Union; it means that the states are not involved in the exercise of federal powers. At the very most, there may be some state input into legislation and even a right of veto over enactments that affect state interests. The *Bundesrat* has such a role within the German federation.[23]

In the European Union, this exclusivity of jurisdiction does not exist. The Council, which is composed of delegates from the Member States, has largely dominated the legislative process and wields considerable executive powers. The

---

19   *See* the discussions *supra* in Sections IV.2.6, IV.3.2.6.a and IV.3.2.6.b.

20   *See* Article V (United States Constitution); Sections 38-43 of the Constitution Act, 1867 (Canada). Under Articles 131 and 79(2) of the Belgian and German Constitutions, respectively, constitutional revisions require the approval of the federal parliament alone. However, in both countries, the upper chamber represents the regions and it must agree to the changes.

21   The revision procedure is discussed in more detail *infra* in Section VII.2.4.c.

22   Subsidiarity is discussed *supra* in Section IV.1.3.c.

23   *See* Articles 74a, 81, 91a, 105-109 and 115a (German Constitution). *See* also D. Kommers, *The Constitutional Jurisprudence of the Federal Republic of Germany* (1989) at page 107.

latter were increased by the TEU and now extend to the common foreign and security policy (CFSP), police and judicial cooperation in criminal matters (PJC)[24] and economic and monetary union (EMU). The Treaty of Amsterdam, however, transfers many matters that were originally in CHJA to the EC Treaty, and they may eventually be subject to the Co-Decision Procedure.

Certainly, the TEU and the Treaty of Amsterdam make inroads into the Council's dominant position in the decision-making process of the Union. The TEU introduced the Co-Decision Procedure, which gave a much greater say to Parliament in the adoption of Union acts, both legislative and executive, as well as a final veto if the Council insisted on adopting an act against Parliament's wishes. However, this veto required an absolute majority of MEPs. Under the changes made by the Treaty of Amsterdam, the Council loses its right to adopt an act unilaterally. If there is disagreement between Parliament and the Council on the final text, this must be resolved by the adoption of a joint text that both institutions approve. Parliament and the Council are thus equal under Co-Decision, which may not establish exclusivity of jurisdiction for the Union but at least frees it from the control of the Member States exercised through the Council. The Treaty of Amsterdam also extends the scope of the Co-Decision Procedure. Nevertheless, there are still many matters that are decided under other procedures where the Council is dominant.

The exclusivity of the European Union within its areas of jurisdiction is also undermined by the direct involvement of the Member States. They wield executive power, as for example when they appoint senior officials of the Union or initiate acts, as well as legislative power when they adopt conventions pursuant to the Treaties. The Member States are also required to ratify any provision permitting the Union to raise revenue,[25] thus depriving it of an autonomous taxing power. This is a crucial restriction, and it circumscribes the parameters of Union action all the more as the EC Treaty requires the Union's revenue and expenditure to be in balance. This precludes the Union from financing additional expenditures by borrowing. Parliament has always wanted to give the Union control over its own sources of revenue and to repeal the prohibition on borrowing, but this has not been done.

More generally, the Union's exclusivity of jurisdiction is impaired by the role of the European Council in setting overall policy directions for the Union. The President of the Commission in the European Council ensures that the Union viewpoint is heard but it hardly changes this body into an autonomous Union institution.

---

24 This area of jurisdiction was called cooperation in the fields of justice and home affairs (CHJA) in the TEU. It was revised and renamed by the Treaty of Amsterdam.

25 Article 269 (ECT).

Paradoxically, the TEU increases the role of both the Member States and the European Council. The latter acquires specific powers with the CFSP as well as official sanction to provide the necessary impetus for the development of the Union and to define its political guidelines. The Member States acquire a right of initiative in PJC, although, since the Treaty of Amsterdam, this no longer happens to the exclusion of the Commission.

VII.2.4 The Constitutional Relationship between the Union and the Member States ✓ No constitution type

VII.2.4.a The Constitutional Basis of the European Union

In a federation, the relationship between the center and the states is determined by an organic law and enforced by judicial procedure. The hallmarks of this constitutional relationship are federal loyalty, mutual control over the constitution and independent federal and state legal orders. The autonomy of both the federation and the states is secured by the operation of law.

The European Union, by contrast, is based on international treaties, but this does not necessarily mean that they cannot form the basis of a constitutional relationship between the European Union and its Member States.[26] After all, Great Britain originated in an international agreement between sovereign states.[27] Moreover, like national constitutions, the Union Treaties confer legislative, executive and judicial sovereign rights on institutions that are separate from the signatory states and also create obligations and rights within the national legal orders of these states. Certainly, a number of eminent scholars openly refer to the Treaties as the constitution of the Union.[28] This is also the approach of the Court of Justice, which has stated categorically that "the EEC Treaty, albeit concluded in the form of an international agreement, nonetheless constitutes the constitution of a Community based on the rule of law."[29] However, it is a constitution that establishes a relationship between the European Union and its Member States that falls short of federalism.

---

[26] See Hartley (fn. 2) at 229 at 231; W. Rudolf, "Federal States" in R. Bernhardt (ed), Encylopedia of Public Intenational Law (1983), vol. 10, 165 at 165.

[27] The Act of Union (1706) (6 Ann, c.11) between England and Scotland. Although at the time the two countries had shared a common monarch for over a century (as well as the years of republican rule from 1649-1660), they were nonetheless two independent countries.

[28] See K. Lanaerts (fn. 16) at 210; R. Bindschedler, "International Organizations. General Aspects" in R. Bernhardt (ed), Encyclopedia of Public International Law (1983) vol. 5, 119 at 121; E Stein (fn. 4) at 28; Hartley (fn. 15) at page 85. P.S.R.F. Mathijsen in A Guide to European Union, (6th ed., 1995) at page 148 is the most categorical:

> The Treaties therefore present many analogies with national constitutions. It can therefore be said that, although they started out as international treaties, these texts have become the "Constitution of the European Union."

[29] Opinion 1/91, [1992] 1 CMLR 245 at 269.

VII.2.4.b Federal Loyalty in the European Union

The EC Treaty contains a general obligation of loyalty as well specific provisions in the same vein.[30] The TEU requires loyalty with respect to the CFSP but, regrettably, lacks a general provision. Nevertheless, the obligations of the Member States towards the Union go beyond the normal international obligation of *pacta sunt servanda* and resemble the concept of federal loyalty. They form the basis of the Court's rejection of the idea that the Member States have reserved powers that they can invoke against the Union.[31] Unlike the signatories of other international treaties, the Member States cannot take action within their areas of jurisdiction that conflicts with Union law.[32] The concept of federal loyalty also underpins the Court's manner of interpreting the Treaties in favor of the Union and against national sovereignty. The doctrines of supremacy of Union law and its direct effect are examples of this approach. We may conclude, then, on this issue that the European Union is close to federalism. All that is needed to complete the picture is a general provision on federal loyalty in the TEU that applies to all the Union's activities.

VII.2.4.c Revision of the Treaties

In a federation, the revision of the relationship between the federation and the states is a matter for mutual agreement.[33] This raises two issues with respect to the European Union. The first is that, if the Treaties are considered to be regular international agreements, would it be possible for the Member States to amend them unilaterally by simply agreeing among themselves on a new treaty? This is in fact what they did when they fused the Community institutions.[34] Most scholars[35] take the view that this is no longer possible and the Court of Justice has definitively ruled against such a possibility.[36] Yet, the issue will not be completely

---

30   This topic is discussed *supra* in Section II.3.8.

31   *Commission* v. *France*, 6 & 11/69, [1969] ECR 523 at 540. As Lenaerts (fn. 16) puts it at 220: "there is simply no nucleus of sovereignty that the Member States can invoke, as such, against the Community."

32   In *Commission* v. *France*, 6 & 11/69, [1969] ECR 523 at 540, the Court stated that "the exercise of reserved powers cannot therefore permit the unilateral adoption of measures prohibited by the Treaty."

33   R. Lane, "Federalism in the International Community", in R. Bernhardt (ed), *Encyclopedia of Public International Law* (1983) vol. 10, 178 at 178-179.

34   Treaty establishing a Single Council and a Single Commission of the European Communities, OJ 152/67.

35   *See* Kapteyn and Verloren van Themaat, *Introduction to the Law of the European Communities* (3rd edition by L.W. Gormley, 1998) at page 81; J. Usher, *European Community Law and National Law: The Irreversible Transfer?* (1981); J. Lodge, D. Freestone and J. Davidson, "Some Problems on the Draft Treaty on European Union," (1984), *European Law Review* 387 at 393-394.

36   *Commission* v. *France*, 7/71, [1971] ECR 1003 at 1018.

settled until the Treaties are replaced with a constitution derived from a form of constituent assembly.

Even if the Treaties are considered to be constitutional documents that can be amended only according to the procedure they set down for the purpose, the Union still violates the federal requirement that such amendments be a matter for mutual consent between the Union and the Member States. Constitutional revisions are drawn up and ratified by the Member States alone.[37] The Commission may play an important part in elaborating the changes, but there is no Union veto. Parliament has to give its assent to a couple of administrative amendments to the EC Treaty,[38] but this hardly creates a federal relationship between the Union and its Member States in this crucial area. This will not be achieved until, at the very least, Parliament's assent is required for general amendments to the Treaties.

VII.2.4.d An Independent Union Legal Order

Despite the Court's elaboration of the concept of an autonomous Union legal order,[39] its independence is far from being completely assured. Contrary to the views expressed by some scholars,[40] this is not because Union law is largely administered and enforced by national authorities and national courts. Both these phenomena are found in federal states.[41] There must, however, be courts at the federal level to ensure the uniform interpretation and application of federal law and to protect it against state encroachments.[42] Moreover, they must be able to exercise this jurisdiction independently of the state courts. In the European Union, this has not yet been achieved.

The Court of Justice is given exclusive jurisdiction over the interpretation and application of Union law, which should secure uniformity. It also reviews the validity of Union laws, and it has protected the exclusivity of this jurisdiction by denying national courts the right to declare a Union law invalid.[43] However, as Justice Wendell Holmes pointed out in a much quoted passage,[44] the autonomy of a federal order depends above all on the federal courts' ability to invalidate

---

37   Article 48 (TEU).

38   *See* the discussion *supra* in Section II.3.3.f.

39   This issue is discussed *supra* in Section IV.6.

40   *See* J. Bridge, "Procedural Aspects of the Enforcement of European Community Law through the Legal Systems of the Member States," (1984), 9 *European Law Review* 28 at 38; F. Mancini and D. Keeling, "From CILFIT to ERT: the Constitutional Challenge Facint the European Court," 11 *Yearbook of European Law* 1 at 1.

41   *See* Articles 83-85 of the German Constitution. *See* also Hartley (fn. 2) at 231; Rudolf (fn. 26) at 165; Lenaerts (fn. 16) at 263.

42   *See* Hartley (fn. 2) at 231; Lenaerts (fn. 16) at 263.

43   *Foto-Frost v. Hauptzollamt Lübeck-Ost*, 314/85, [1987] 3 ECR 4199 at 4231.

44   "Law and the Court" in *Collected Legal Papers* (1957) at pages 295-296.

state laws that encroach upon or are incompatible with federal laws. The Court of Justice has no such mandate, although it has taken jurisdiction through subterfuge. Precluded from pronouncing on the validity of the actual national provision at issue, the Court considers instead the validity of an identical *hypothetical* national provision.[45]

Theoretically, therefore, the Court of Justice does seem to fulfil the dual role of a federal supreme court. However, its effectiveness is undermined by procedural inadequacies. In the first place, it cannot review, even surreptitiously, the validity of national laws under Article 230 of the EC Treaty, which is a straightforward constitutional reference that is open to the Community institutions, the European Central Bank (ECB) and natural and legal persons. This can only be done by way of a preliminary ruling under Article 234, which occurs only upon a reference from a national court. This creates a very narrow scope for the Court's role as protector of Union law against national encroachments.

The second procedural problem is that the national courts, when making their reference under Article 234, do so as equals of the Court of Justice. This equal relationship has two unfortunate consequences. In the first place, the ruling of the Court is not substituted for that of the national court, which can refuse to follow it. Secondly, the Court cannot even be sure to adjudicate the matter as it is up to the national court to make the reference. A national court of last instance is supposedly obliged to do so, but they can avoid doing so by alleging that the issue has already been adjudicated satisfactorily by the Court (*acte éclairé*) or that the answer is self-evident *(acte clair).*[46] In the *CILFIT* case,[47] the Court of Justice sought to circumscribe the use of these devices, particularly the *acte clair*, which is more open to abuse. In order to evoke this principle, a national court must be "convinced that the matter is equally obvious to the courts of the other Member States and to the Court of Justice."[48] However, if a national court acts unreasonably, the Court is powerless.

This ability of national courts to defy or ignore the Court of Justice means that the Union legal order is not at present self-enforcing. In the final analysis, the Union has to rely on the traditional international remedy of bringing a Member State before the Court of Justice for the failure of its courts to respect their obligation to refer. Such an action, which the Commission in any case has shown itself reluctant to bring, does not rescind the wrong decision of the national court

---

45   *See NV Algemene Transport- en Expedite Onderneming Van Gend en Loos v. Nederlandse Adminstratie der Belastingen,* 26/62, [1963] ECR 1; *Cowan v. Trésor public,* 186/87, [1989] ECR 195.

46   Two examples of suspect refusals to refer are *Minister of the Interior v. Daniel Cohn-Bendit,* [1980] 1 C.M.L.R. 543 (French *Conseil d'Etat*) and *Re Value-Added Tax Directives* [1982] 1 C.M.L.R. 527 (German *Bundesfinanzhof*).

47   *Srl CILFIT et al v. Ministry of Health,* 283/81, [1982] ECR 3415. *See* also H. Rasmussen, "The European Court's Acte Clair Strategy in CILFIT," (1984), 9 *European Law Review* 242.

48   *Srl CILFIT et al v. Ministry of Health,* 283/81, [1982] ECR 3415 at 3430.

and is wholly inadequate in a federal system. The suggestion that the ability now to fine Member States for infringements of the Treaty somehow makes up for this shortcoming cannot be taken seriously.[49] All this does is to make the traditional remedy more effective; it does nothing to secure the autonomy of the Union legal order.

Federal law has to apply uniformly and be protected automatically by virtue of the federal legal order. In the European Union, this requires giving the parties before national courts as well as the national courts themselves the right to make a reference for a preliminary ruling. It also requires that the Court's ruling be substituted for that of the national court. In other words, the Court of Justice must become an appellate court with jurisdiction to rule on the validity of national laws if it is to fulfil the duties incumbent on a federal supreme court.

VII.3 The Cohesion of the European Union

VII.3.1 The Basis of the Cohesion

The most effective basis for the cohesion that is necessary to sustain a nation state is a sense of national identity emanating from a collective consciousness rooted in common myths and symbols.[50] In the European Union, there is no identity that transcends the Member States.[51] There may be the beginning of a European consciousness,[52] but there are no common myths or symbols. Even the shared cultural and religious traditions are but obscurely perceived as such by significant sectors of the European populace. The Union is charged with trying to change this by developing "a European dimension in education"[53] and by "bringing the common cultural heritage to the fore."[54] However, it is doubtful that the European Union will achieve cohesion on the basis of a European identity within the foreseeable future.

---

49   U. Everling, "Reflections on the Structure of the European Union", (1992), 29 *Common Market Law Review* 1053 at 1073.

50   M. Forsyth, *The Theory and Practice of Confederation* (1981) at page 14 describes the citizens of a national state as a "single collection of individuals that has become conscious of its identity." *See* also A. Smith, "National Identity and the Ideal of European Unity", (1992) 68 *International Affairs* 55 at 73. K Doehring, "State Sovereignty" in R. Bernhardt (ed), *Encyclopedia of Public International Law* (1983) vol. 10, 422 at 424 prefers to talk in terms of national loyalty, but the underlying concept is the same.

51   *See* Smith (fn. 50) at 68-83; E. Stein, "Foreign Policy at Maastricht: 'Non in commotione Dominis'," (1992) 29 *Common Market Law Review* 663 at 667.

52   This is Everling's view in (fn. 49) at 1074.

53   Article 126(2) (ECT).

54   Article 128(1) (ECT).

However, national cohesion can also be based on the functional unity of the state. There may exist a sufficiently important degree of commonality to provide a sense of political unity even in the absence of a shared identity.[55] Indeed, this is the only possibility in two particular situations, namely where regional identities are strong enough to eclipse the national identity as a focus of loyalty (Belgium, Basque region of Spain) and where sovereign states come together to form a new nation (Great Britain, Canada, United States). The European Union, as a federation, would be both a new nation and one where regional identities remain the primary focus of loyalty. Its cohesion will therefore have to be based on functional unity.

The issue is what degree of commonality within the European Union is necessary to create and sustain a sense of political unity. Unfortunately, there is no uniform model of federalism to use as a guide. Nor are the theoretical bases that are usually advanced to explain the division of power in a federal state particularly helpful. The concept of federal power as the minimum incursion on state power compatible with national unity[56] is inappropriate for the European Union. A greater degree of commonality is needed in a diffuse community than in a compact state like Belgium, where the regional groups interact on a daily basis.[57] The Union's competences should not, therefore, be restricted to where the scale or effects of the action necessitate its involvement. Subsidiarity is all well and good, but the EC Treaty is wise to restrict it to areas of concurrent and ancillary jurisdiction.[58] It should not be used as the criterion for a division of power in the Union.[59]

In the final analysis, we can only speculate on the degree of commonality that is required for the European Union to achieve a sense of political unity, although there are certain minimum requirements that are met by most federations. These are a commonality of essential rights and purpose and unity on the international scene with respect to matters that affect the federation as a whole. Progress has been made on both fronts in the European Union without, however, fully establishing a functional unity.

---

55   *See* Hay (fn. 4) at 92.

56   *See* Lane (fn. 33) at 178.

57   The European Parliament certainly takes this view—*see* its Resolution of July 11, 1990 on the guidelines for a draft constitution for the European Union (OJ C231/90) at page 91. *See* also Everling (fn. 49) at 1067-1069.

58   Article 5 (ECT); Protocol on the application of the principles of subsidiarity and proportionality, which is attached to the EC Treaty.

59   This is suggested by V. Constantinesco, "Who's Afraid of Subsidiarity?", (1991) 11 *Yearbook of European Law* 33 at 52.

VII.3.2 The Internal Cohesion of the European Union

VII.3.2.a Commonality of Rights

The essential common rights that citizens of a federal state possess may be summarized as the ability to move freely throughout the country and to live and work anywhere with equal access to social benefits, education and civic rights and protected by the same fundamental rights.[60] These essential rights, which may be subject to reasonable and objective restrictions, such as a period of residence or acceptable qualifications in the case of work,[61] are guaranteed by a common citizenship that also serves as a concrete symbol of a shared adherence.[62]

Prior to the TEU, the European Community, as it then was, had already made significant progress in this area. Nationals of Member States were able to move freely throughout the Community as tourists or service-providers or in order to look for or pursue a livelihood. The mutual recognition of qualifications, which still causes problems in some federal states,[63] was largely resolved by Community legislation. Nationals of Member States residing in another Member State enjoyed the same social and educational rights as citizens of the host state and were protected at Community level by a common code of fundamental rights elaborated by the Court of Justice and endorsed by the Council, Commission and European Parliament.[64]

Nevertheless, all this falls short of the commonality required for a federal state. Above all, there was no common citizenship. This was introduced by the TEU and extended in scope by the Treaty of Amsterdam.[65] The most important rights that it confers on European citizens are the right to enter and reside in any Member State and the right to vote and stand as a candidate anywhere in the Union in municipal and European elections.

Union citizenship is not, however, a true federal citizenship. This is not because it exists alongside national citizenships, which is common in federations,[66] but

---

60   *See* Sections 1-15 of the Constitution Act, 1982 (Canada); Articles 1-19 and 101-140 (German Constituton). *See* also *Edwards v. California*, 314 US 160 (1941), where the United States Supreme Court declared at 183: "[I]t is a privilege of citizenship of the United States, protected from state abridgement, to enter into any state of the Union, either for temporary sojourn or for the establishment of permanent residence there."

61   *See* Section 6(3) of the Constitution Act, 1982 (Canada); Articles 11(2) and 12(1) (German Constitution).

62   *See* Rudolf (fn. 26) at 168, C. Closa, "The Concept of Citizenship in the Treaty on European Union," (1992) 29 *Common Market Law Review* 1137.

63   With respect to the United States, *see* Sandalow and Stein (fn. 4) at page 40.

64   Joint Declaration on fundamental rights (OJ C 103/77).

65   Union citizenship is discussed *supra* in Section II.3.2.g.

66   *See e.g.* Article 74(8) (German Constitution); 14th Amendment, Section 1 (United States Constitution). *See* also Rudolf (fn. 26) at 168.

because it is the nationality of a Member State that gives the right to Union citizenship. In a true federation citizenship is bestowed by the center and may give a right to state citizenship once local residency requirements are met.[67] Union citizenship is in fact an incidence of national citizenship. As a result, Union citizens have no intrinsic rights.[68] The rights that come with Union citizenship are expressly accorded rather than flowing automatically from the citizenship. As such, they are limited in scope and subject to curtailment. Conditions may be placed on the right of free movement[69] and derogations are permitted from the provisions on civic rights.[70] Moreover, Union citizens remain aliens in Member States other than their own. They have no right to take part in the national political life of the host state[71] or to accede to posts in the public service or occupations involving the exercise of official authority.

Both the TEU and the Treaty of Amsterdam have strengthened the Treaty provisions on fundamental rights, and recently the Council, Commission and European Parliament adopted a charter of fundamental rights.[72] However, we must not confuse the issue of human rights with that of federalism. It is nowadays an important element of the commonality of rights, but it is not a prerequisite for federal statehood that fundamental rights be protected by the federation.[73] In Canada, this was not achieved until 1982, but no-one would deny that Canada was a federal state from its inception in 1867.

VII.3.2.b Common Internal Purpose

The competences that are assigned to the center may differ from federation to federation,[74] but they must be sufficient for the federal authorities to ensure that the nation functions internally with a common economic and political purpose.[75]

---

67 *See* 14th Amendment, Section 1 of the United States Constitution, which provides that "all persons born or naturalized in the United States . . . are citizens of the United States and of the State wherein they reside." *See* also Articles 4 and 5 (Belgian Constitution); Closa (fn. 62) at 1140-1141 and Sandalow and Stein (fn. 4) at page 38. In Canada, there is no concept of provincial citizenship.

68 It also means that the Member States rather than the European Union regulate the acquisition and loss of Union citizenship, but this is an issue of jurisdiction, not of commonality of rights.

69 Article 18(1) (ECT).

70 Article 19 (ECT).

71 Closa (fn. 62) at 1139 calls this right "the defining and primordial element of citizenship." *See* also Section 3 of the Constitution Act, 1982 (Canada) and Article 33 (German Constitution).

72 The topic of the protection of fundamental rights in the European Union is discussed *supra* in Section VI.6.

73 Hartley (fn. 2) makes the same point at 243.

74 *Compare* Articles 73 and 74 (German Constitution), Article I, Section 8 (United States Constitution) and Sections 91 and 92 of the Constitution Act, 1867 (Canada).

75 *See* Article 72(2) of the German Constitution, which refers to "the maintenance of legal or economic unity" within the Federal Republic.

On the economic side, this common purpose is substantially present in the European Union. The common market has now been largely achieved and EMU has fused it into a single economic unit for the twelve Member States participating in its third stage.[76] The common monetary policy provides for the Union to control the money supply, set interest rates and credit policy and take charge of exchange-rate policy and the management of national foreign currency reserves. National currencies will give way to a single currency, the euro, in 2002. Economic policy may remain formally a national responsibility, but the Member States within EMU are severely restricted in their freedom of action.[77] The objectives of national economic policy, such as full employment, low inflation, economic growth and a positive balance of payments, are subject to guidelines set by the Union. The choice of economic instruments is also controlled. National governments no longer have jurisdiction over monetary measures and they must follow the Union's rules on budget deficits. In addition, they no longer enjoy credit facilities at national central banks or privileged access to financial institutions. Even with respect to fiscal policy, there is an ever-increasing need to harmonize at least indirect taxes, not only because of the Union harmonization measures but also due to market pressures. The result of all this is a high level of cohesion in national economic policies that resemble more and more a common economic policy.

On the political side, there has been less progress. The Union still lacks its own coercive means to secure the protection of its citizens and the enforcement of Union law.[78] However, the Union has now set up a European Police Office (Europol) and the Treaty of Amsterdam tightens up the provisions in the TEU on creating within Europe an area of freedom, security and justice.[79] This is to be achieved by common action designed to combat and prevent crime, terrorism, trafficking in persons, offences against children and the drug and arms trade. The Union can even take measures to harmonize the criminal law of the Member States.

Another very important contribution to creating a common political purpose in the European Union is the integrative policies pursued by the Union.[80] They go beyond mere economics and aim at creating a common home. Article 2 of the

---

76   The entry of the other three Member States (Denmark, Sweden and the United Kingdom) is, *pace* British public opinion, a matter of time.

77   *See* P. Verloren van Themaat, "Some Preliminary Observations on the Intergovernmental Conferences: The Relations between the Concepts of a Common Market, a Monetary Union, an Economic Union, a Political Union and Sovereignty," (1991), 28 *Common Market Law Review* 291 at 300-301.

78   *See* H. Steinberger, "Sovereignty," in R. Bernhardt (ed), *Encyclopedia of Public International Law* (1983) vol. 10, 408 at 409; Doehring (fn. 50) at425. *See* also Articles 35, 37 and 73(1) (German Constitution).

79   Articles 29-31 (TEU).

80   This type of policy-making is discussed *supra* in Section II.3.2.a.

EC Treaty includes among the objectives of the Union the promotion of a high level of employment and of social protection, equality between men and women, a high level of protection and improvement of the quality of the environment, the raising of the standard of living and quality of life and economic and social cohesion and solidarity among Member States. The policies of the Union reflect these ambitious objectives.

It is possible, therefore, to discern quite distinctly a common internal purpose within the European Union that is stronger in the economic sphere but not limited to it. Whether this is matched by a similar external cohesion is the subject of our next discussion. *not complete*

VII.3.3 The External Cohesion of the European Union

Whether or not the states in a federation enjoy international legal personality,[81] they are nevertheless invariably represented by the federation in foreign matters that affect the whole federation.[82] This is both the most effective way to advance the common interest and also a prerequisite for the external unity of the federation. The states may well have an international competence, but it is restricted to matters that come within their internal jurisdiction and affect them alone.[83] In addition, they usually need the approval of the federal government before they can enter into agreement with foreign states.

External cohesion thus requires the European Union to exercise exclusive jurisdiction over political, military and commercial relations with third countries as well as over the entry, residence and expulsion of foreign nationals. These are matters that in federal states do not normally fall within the jurisdiction of the states.[84] The Union should also have an external competence in internal areas that come within its jurisdiction and for those areas under national jurisdiction where the Union interest requires a common international approach.

The European Union has a wide international competence.[85] It is in charge of commercial relations with third countries except for some aspects of services and intellectual property. It has specific international competence for certain other matters, such as research and development, the environment, develop-

---

81 *See* a discussion of this controversial issue in Hay (fn. 4) at 18-26; Lane (fn. 33) at 180; Doehring (fn. 50) at 424-426; Rudolf (fn. 26) at 169-170.

82 G.C. Lewis in *Remarks on the Use and Abuse of Some Political Terms* (1898) states at page 97 that "a federal state is one, all parts of which are represented, for international purposes, by one government". *See also* Rudolf (fn. 26) at 168-169 and the United States Supreme Court in *United States* v. *Curtiss-Wright Export Corporation*, 299 US 304 (1936).

83 Articles 68(3) (Belgian Constitution); 32(3) (German Constitution); I, Section 10 (United States Constitution).

84 *See* Articles 68(1) (Belgian Constitution); 32(1) and 73(3),(10) (German Constitution); I, Sections 8 and 9 (United States Constitution).

85 This competence is discussed *supra* in Sections II.3.2.f, II.3.3.a and II.3.3.c.

ment cooperation, monetary matters and PJC. More importantly, the Court of Justice has given it a general international competence over all areas where it exercises jurisdiction internally pursuant to the EC Treaty. This jurisdiction is not, however, necessarily exclusive, particularly where expenditures by the Member States are at issue. The Union has no international competence just because an issue requires a common approach that is best provided by the Union. On the other hand, asylum, external border controls, immigration and other rules affecting foreign nationals have been brought by the Treaty of Amsterdam within the jurisdiction of the Union.

On the political and military side, there is the CFSP and the new European security and defense policy (CESDP).[86] However, the CFSP only operates when the Union takes over a matter; otherwise the Member States conduct their own foreign policies. The CESDP is limited at present to humanitarian and rescue tasks, but the formation of the European Union Military Committee and the Military Staff of the European Union[87] seems to herald the dawn of a genuine European defense policy. The events of September 11, 2001 will doubtless give impetus to this development.

There is, therefore, a certain external cohesion to the European Union, but there are serious shortcomings. Foreign and military affairs are still to a very great extent under the control of the Member States. In the Afghanistan operation, for example, the British are largely acting on their own, both politically and militarily, despite a show of European Union solidarity. The provisions on foreign nationals have not yet led to a common Union policy in this area, although the war against terrorism is pushing the Member States along this path. Even in commercial matters, there has been some backsliding on the exclusiveness of the Union's jurisdiction with the result that the Member States still exert significant influence. Yet, the Union is certainly present internationally and even when they pursue national policies, Member States have to take increasing notice of this fact.

VII.4 Conclusion: Evaluation and Prospects

VII.4.1 Evaluation

There is no doubt that the European Union now resembles a federal state more than an international trade grouping. There are, however, important issues that must be resolved with respect to both autonomy and cohesion before we can talks with confidence of a European federation.

---

86   These policies are discussed *supra* in Section II.3.3.a.

87   The EUMC is discussed *supra* in Section III.4.4., and the Military Staff is established by Council Decision 01/80 (OJ L27/01).

There cannot be full autonomy for the Union as long as the Member States retain a role in the appointment of the Commission.[88] The dominant position of the Council must be eliminated, probably by making it the upper house of a legislature that includes an equally powerful lower house, the European Parliament. In this way, it can play the same role in the European Union as the *Bundesrat* in the German Federal Republic. This change would necessitate transferring the Council's executive powers to the Commission, which, in turn, would demand a closer supervision by Parliament of the latter's activities and ideally a requirement that the members of the Commission be chosen from among MEPs. The appointment of judges of the Union's courts should have to be approved by Parliament. The role of the Member States and the European Council must be reviewed and at least brought under the ultimate control of Parliament. The present uncertainty over the constitutional status of the Treaties needs to be resolved by the creation of a genuine European constitution that can be amended only by the mutual deliberation and agreement of the Member States and the Union. Above all, amendments must be subject to Parliament's assent. Finally, the Court of Justice has to be given an appellate jurisdiction over the national courts in addition to the present reference procedure, which should nonetheless be kept. In this way, both the parties and the courts can bring issues before the Court of Justice, which would then be able to pronounce on the validity of both national and Union laws and substitute its ruling for that of the national court.

As far as cohesion is concerned, a federation requires a federal citizenship to which all the usual rights of citizenship attach by virtue of that very citizenship. It can still be restricted to those who hold the citizenship of a Member State as long as it is not at the same time reduced to a mere incidence thereof. The European Union already enjoys a substantial degree of common internal purpose but it sorely lacks the coercive force needed to enforce Union law and objectives. The internal cohesion must also be complemented by a more comprehensive external cohesion. The Union's international competences must include services

---

88 The changes in the appointment of the Commission are the most far-reaching in the Treaty of Nice. The Member States no longer nominate and appoint the President and other Commissioners; it is done instead by the Council. This may not seem particularly significant when one considers that the Council is made up of representatives of the governments of the Member States and, in the case of nominating the President, acts in the composition of heads of state or government. Moreover, the Council acts in accordance with proposals made by each Member State. Nevertheless, the changes represent a clear move towards federalism. The power to appoint the Commission is taken away from the Member States and given to a Union institution that one day could come to constitute the upper house of the Union legislature. We could thus arrive at a constitutional situation where the Commission is appointed by the upper house and confirmed by the lower house of the legislature. This is an unusual but not unacceptable practice for a federation.

and intellectual property,[89] and it must evolve a genuine common foreign and defense policy rather than the patchwork that exists presently.

VII.4.2 Prospects: A Personal View

As to whether the European Union will realize its federal vocation or indeed whether this is desirable is a matter for speculation and personal preference. As to the latter, the author shares the distaste of many British people for the idea of a European federation, preferring to hunker down in a centuries-old loyalty to the Crown. But euroskepticism is a dead end. Europe has simply gone too far down the path of integration, and the United Kingdom with it, to turn back now. We are saddled with the European Union whether we like it or not.

As to speculation, the real question for this writer is just how large the European Union can become before it is too cumbersome to function as a federation. Just how many official language can one nation accommodate? How many cultures? The European Union smothers these issues with the verbiage of human rights, but they could come to haunt it. There is also the financial side of the issue. The Union had great difficulty absorbing Greece, Spain and Portugal, and one wonders how it will afford the cost of absorbing the present list of candidates. The Treaty of Nice provides no answer. In any case, its institutional reforms are a shoddy compromise. In the context of an enlarged Union, I suspect that the mechanism of closer cooperation could well be the instrument that keeps the process of integration going.

But let us end on an optimistic note. European integration has constantly confounded the skeptics and the faint of heart. Few would have predicted a few years ago that the single currency would have been successfully introduced. Few earlier would have wagered too extravagant an amount on the completion of the internal market. In 1958, only incurable romantics could have envisaged the European Union as it exists today. It may well be that, despite all obstacles, the European federation is quite simply an idea whose time has come.

---

89 The Treaty of Nice extends the external commercial competence of the Union to services and intellectual property. However, jurisdiction over trade in cultural, audiovisual, educational, social and health services is still shared by the Union and the Member States.